MW00353988

FRAGILE CONNECTIONS

Memoirs *of* Mental Illness *for* Pastoral Care Professionals

DONALD CAPPS

CHALICE PRESS

ST. LOUIS, MISSOURI

© Copyright 2005 by Donald Capps

All rights reserved. For permission to reuse content, please contact Copyright Clearance Center, 222 Rosewood Drive, Danvers, MA 01923, (978) 750-8400, www.thenewcopyright.com.

Bible quotations, unless otherwise noted, are from the *New Revised Standard Version Bible,* copyright 1989, Division of Christian Education of the National Council of the Churches of Christ in the United States of America. Used by permission. All rights reserved. Quotations marked KJV are from the *King James Version.*

Excerpts in chapter 1 from OUT OF THE DEPTHS by Anton T. Boisen, copyright © 1960 by Anton T. Boisen, renewed 1988 by Morton C. Bradley, Jr. Reprinted by permission of HarperCollins Publishers Inc.

Excerpts in chapter 2 from DARKNESS VISIBLE by William Styron, copyright © 1990 by William Styron. Used by permission of Random House, Inc.

Excerpts in chapter 3 from AN UNQUIET MIND by Kay Redfield Jamison, copyright 1995 by Kay Redfield Jamison. Used by permission of Alfred A. Knopf, a division of Random House, Inc.

Excerpts in chapter 4 from SOULS ARE MADE OF ENDURANCE: SURVIVING MENTAL ILLNESS IN THE FAMILY by Stewart D. Govig, copyright 1994 by Stewart D. Govig. Used by permission of Westminster John Knox Press.

Excerpts in chapter 5 from THE STORY OF MY FATHER: A MEMOIR BY SUE MILLER, copyright 2003 by Sue Miller. Used by permission of Alfred A. Knopf, a division of Random House, Inc. World rights except UK. Used by permission of Bloomsbury Press. UK rights.

Excerpts marked DSM-IV reprinted with permission from the DIAGNOSTIC AND STATISTICAL MANUAL OF MENTAL DISORDERS, copyright 2000, American Psychiatric Association.

Excerpts from John Donne's "Love's Growth" on page 254 are from THE COMPLETE ENGLISH POEMS, edited by A. J. Smith (New York: Penguin Books, 1996). Reprinted with permission of Penguin Group (UK) Ltd.

Cover design: Elizabeth Wright/ Interior design: Hui-Chu Wang

Visit Chalice Press on the World Wide Web at www.chalicepress.com

10 9 8 7 6 5 4 3 2 1   05 06 07 08 09 10

Library of Congress Cataloging-in-Publication Data

Capps, Donald.

Fragile connections : memoirs of mental illness for pastoral care professionals / Donald Capps.

p. cm.

Includes bibliographical references.

ISBN-10: 0-827223-31-5

ISBN-13: 978-0-827223-31-8

(pbk. : alk. paper)

1. Church work with the mentally ill. 2. Mental illness--United States--Case studies. I. Title.

BV4461.C27 2005

259'.42—dc22   2005016121

Printed in the United States of America

What's madness but nobility of soul at odds with circumstance?

THEODORE ROETHKE

To the memory of the Reverend Ansel Bourne

CONTENTS

ACKNOWLEDGMENTS

I want to thank the production staff at Chalice Press, especially Trent Butler, Sarah Tasic, and copy editor Eleanor Beach, for the work that they have done, behind the scenes, to transform my manuscript into an attractive book. Joan Blyth typed the manuscript with her customary dedication, skill, and good humor. Nathan Carlin, Eugene Degitz, and Shawn Zanicky provided tips and assistance with regard to sources and resources.

In an earlier version of these acknowledgments, I had made special mention of Stewart Govig, one of the authors of the memoirs presented here, for responding to my queries about his son's illness with openness and grace and providing me with photographs of the Govig family that I have been able to share with my classes. Stewart died of a massive heart attack on April 10, 2005, at the age of 78.

In an e-mail message to Stewart's friends, Rev. Philip Nesvig of Tacoma, Washington, noted that the heart attack occurred after Stewart had picked up his son John at his group home and the two to them were returning to the Govig home. Stewart was driving when the heart attack occurred, but John managed to control the car to prevent further damage, then ran home to inform his mother. Alice drove to the scene and found a good Samaritan administering CPR, but there were no signs of life, and the medics could not save her husband. Rev. Nesvig concluded his e-mail message with this word of benediction: "Blessed be his memory in our midst."

That Stewart and his son John were together at the end, and that John acted as he did in such a difficult circumstance, is congruent with the relationship of father and son portrayed in *Souls Are Made of Endurance,* and a profound testimony to the fact that love creates connections that would be unthinkable without it.

INTRODUCTION

Throughout my teaching career, I have assigned autobiographies in my classes and have encouraged students to engage in the introspective or self-reflective processes in which many, though certainly not all, autobiographers engage. When I decided a decade or so ago to teach a course on mental illness, I knew that the course would focus on autobiographies or personal memoirs. In fact, it was my own reading of autobiographies by mentally ill persons and family members of mentally ill persons that inspired me to teach a course on mental illnesses. As I read these personal accounts, it dawned on me that the subject of mental illness had fallen by the wayside in seminary curricula in pastoral care. Present generations of seminary students were not being taught much about mental illness unless they had done a unit or two of clinical pastoral education in a mental health facility or similar setting.

Studies of Mental Illness

E. Fuller Torrey and Judy Miller provide compelling evidence in *The Invisible Plague* (2001) that serious mental illness has been increasing over the past two hundred years. Although reliable statistics have been difficult to come by since the 1950s (when the national program of deinstitutionalization of the mentally ill began), we have every reason to assume that this trend has continued.

This increase in mental illness is not reflected, however, in the major pastoral care journals. While excellent books on the subject of mental illness are available for ministers (Ciarrocchi 1993) and pastoral counselors (Collins and Culbertson 2003), the very fact that the authors assume that their readers will not have much if any background knowledge of the subject is illustrative of the problem. Mental illness gets very little attention in the seminary context.

For someone like myself who became attracted to the pastoral care field in large part because it was concerned with mental illness, it now seems almost unforgivable that I neglected the subject in several decades of teaching and did not offer a course on it until I reached my mid-fifties. This book, then, is long overdue.

1

The present volume builds on the strengths of the books by Joseph W. Ciarrocchi, and Gregory B. Collins and Thomas L. Culbertson. The purpose of their books is not to turn ministers into amateur psychiatrists but to give them the basic knowledge they need to understand the mentally ill persons with whom they come into contact.

Ciarrocchi's book is especially strong in its presentation of the various mental disorders. In addition to chapters on pastoral care and abnormal psychology, theories of abnormal behavior (with brief presentations and evaluations of biological, psychoanalytic, learning, humanistic, and cognitive theories), and pastoral assessment, it provides individual chapters on anxiety disorders, mood disorders, addictive disorders, schizophrenia, sexual problems, and personality disorders. Each of these chapters identifies the general disorder and its various subtypes by noting their signs and symptoms, explains their etiology (what is believed to be their cause or causes), and describes current forms of treatment. Each chapter then concludes with a discussion of how the disorder, or its various subtypes, might be understood and, where appropriate, addressed from a pastoral care perspective.

The book by Collins and Culbertson begins with a chapter on the history of psychiatry and modern psychiatric treatment. This chapter is designed to disabuse readers of a simplistic bias against psychiatry based on representations of psychiatrists in films and other popular media. The succeeding chapters cover the same mental illnesses as the Ciarrocchi text (though without a separate chapter on sexual problems). The strength of this book is that it focuses on the person who is suffering from one of these disorders. This focus is evident from the chapter titles: "The Depressed Person," "The Anxious Person," "The Chemically Dependent Person," "The Person Experiencing Loss of Contact with Reality," and "The Person with a Personality Disorder."

Each chapter has several case examples. These chapters give less attention to current forms of treatment for these disorders and more attention to the role that the pastoral counselor might play as a member of the health team. They emphasize recognizing the signs that a person is becoming mentally or emotionally ill, taking appropriate actions (crisis intervention), and providing counseling when the person is in the recovery phase. This text was written primarily for pastoral counselors, but many of its recommendations for pastoral counselors are appropriate for ministers in other contexts (including congregational ministry). Its emphasis on what pastoral counselors should *not* attempt to do is relevant, perhaps even more so, to ministers who do not have specialized pastoral counseling training or experience.

One of the strengths of the Collins and Culbertson book is that it provides case examples. These are summaries (ranging from 200–600 words) of cases of persons who have manifested the signs and symptoms of a mental or emotional illness. Each case summary contains references to the changing life conditions that precipitated the crisis and to the reactions of family members to the altered behavior of the person. Typically, a family member or friend would become concerned and urge voluntary seeking of professional help, arrange for the person to see a professional (a psychotherapist, psychiatrist, etc.), or take the person to a local hospital. These cases enable the reader to recognize the signs and symptoms of the disorder, to make an assessment of its severity, and to reflect on what one would do by way of crisis intervention or what one would advise a concerned family member to do.

Because the cases focus on the incipient illness, they are more useful for reflecting on crisis intervention than on how the person might regain health. The Ciarrocchi book is perhaps more helpful in the latter regard because it discusses the various forms of treatment currently in use. These, however, are treatments that were carried out by trained professionals and are, for the most part, beyond the skill or legitimate practice of even a trained pastoral counselor.

The "Memoirs" Approach

Like the Ciarrocchi and the Collins and Culbertson books, this volume has individual chapters devoted to specific types of mental illness, and it employs the "case example" approach that is especially prominent in the Collins and Culbertson book. Where it differs from both works is that it focuses on "memoirs" written either by the person with the mental illness or by a family member of a person so afflicted. The particular value of these memoirs is that they provide a richer *context* than a "case example" provides for appreciating the devastating effects of mental illness on the afflicted persons and their families.

The Context of Mental Illness

Essentially five issues comprise the "context" of mental illness:

1. the *characteristics* of the mental illness
2. its *causes*
3. its *course*
4. its *consequences*
5. its *curability*

Because book-length memoirs offer a much fuller narrative than a case example of 200–600 words provides, these memoirs are valuable for illuminating all five "c's" and especially for providing insight into the causes of the illness, its course over time, and its long-term consequences for both the afflicted individual and for loved ones.

Causes

While determining the causes of mental illness is extremely difficult in most cases, family members of the mentally ill often seek answers to the questions of what caused their loved one to become ill. Sometimes this results in self-blame. A full-length narrative can be helpful in discriminating between factors that may, in fact, have played a role in the development of the illness and those that are more doubtful or unlikely causes.

Course

These narratives may also shed light on the environmental factors that have moderated the devastating effects of the illness, enabling the mentally ill person to live a more productive life than would otherwise be the case. Mental illnesses typically follow a rather erratic course. While the illness may not appear until one is in late adolescence, middle or late adulthood, it is often possible, in retrospect, to discover signs of the incipient illness in childhood or in an earlier period of adulthood.

Once the illness has become recognizable and efforts to treat it have been initiated, periods of improvement typically alternate with phases of recidivism so that the course of recovery is rarely, if ever, progressively smooth. Relapses are also common. Nor is complete recovery the typical outcome. In fact, some mental illnesses (such as dementia) do not conclude in recovery; instead, they eventually end in death. The narratives that will be presented and discussed here provide a much fuller account of the course of the illness than does a case example, which typically focuses on the weeks or months immediately preceding the crisis.

Consequences

The consequences of the illness, both for the one afflicted and for family members and friends, are also presented in richer detail in a full-length narrative. A brief case example can make allusions to a family member's distress when the illness begins to become apparent, and it can also report on the more immediate consequences of the illness for the afflicted person (loss of employment, termination of educational pursuits, strained or even severed interpersonal relationships).

But the case example is less effective in presenting long term consequences of the illness for the afflicted person and for family members, who are faced with the fact that one of their loved ones is seriously ill and may well be permanently disabled. The consequences of the illness are also likely to change over an extended period, and family members are especially likely to identify several stages or phases in their experience of living with the mental illness of a loved one.

Also, while many if not most of the consequences of a mental illness are negative—otherwise, it would not be considered an illness—some positive aspects may be identified in an extended narrative. The one who has suffered from a mental illness and survived to tell about it and the family member who has reflected deeply on the mental illness of a loved one are very likely to see the illness as having provided certain benefits, such as lessons for living or for understanding the meaning and purpose of human life.

The Meaning of Mental Illness

Another way in which this book builds on the strength of the books by Ciarrocchi and Collins and Culbertson is that, whereas their books emphasize what ministers can do for mentally ill persons and their families, this book focuses on what the mentally ill and their families have to teach ministers about mental illness. The authors of these memoirs have struggled deeply with the meaning of mental illness and the light that it sheds on human existence itself.

In effect, they are contemporary Jobs. Ministers—especially those who have not experienced mental illness in their immediate families—have much to learn from these writers. Glib theological talk is the first casualty of reading such memoirs, but what takes its place is not cynicism or ultimate despair but deep and penetrating insights into the question of whether life is worth living and, if it is, what are the experiences that make it so.

Jesus and Mental Illness

A few years ago, I wrote a book about Jesus (Capps 2000) that includes a chapter on Jesus' role as "village healer." As I read books by biblical experts on his role as healer, I was struck by the fact that they did not focus much, if at all, on the question of why the persons healed by Jesus were suffering from these particular illnesses and not others? Why blindness? Why paralysis? Why leprosy? Why demon possession?

As I began to ask myself this question, I came to realize that these were illnesses that were physical (organic) in nature, but each was psychological as well. I concluded that Jesus was able to heal these individuals because he understood the fact that their physical illness had a psychological basis, and, more specifically, he addressed the personal and social anxieties that underlay the physical symptomatology. In effect, he persuaded those who suffered from these illnesses that they did not need the protections or secondary benefits that these illnesses provided. In doing so, he "disabled" the anxiety that had so disabled them.

I suggested, therefore, that Jesus was a kind of village psychiatrist. To address the inevitable objection that this view of Jesus diminishes his healing powers, I noted that exactly the opposite is the case, for mental or emotional illnesses are often more resistant to treatment than purely physical illnesses. Also, the sufferers, their families, and the community are more likely to interpret these illnesses in moral and religious terms.

While I do not discuss Jesus' role as a village psychiatrist in *this* book, I would encourage readers to think of the healing stories in the gospels as case examples of the mental and emotional illnesses that were especially common in Jesus' day. These same illnesses are present among the mentally ill in our day, but much evidence suggests, as Torrey and Miller contend, that a greater percentage of persons are suffering today from what Collins and Culbertson call "loss of contact with reality." For this reason, the personal stories that I have selected for this book reflect these types of mental illness.

Curing a Disease/Healing an Illness

A distinction employed in medical anthropology between the curing of a disease and healing of an illness is especially relevant to a book–like this one–that focuses on personal memoirs. In the scientific paradigm of modern medicine, *diseases* are abnormalities in the structure and function of body organs and systems. In this book, the abnormalities are in the neurological system with a particular locus in the brain, the organ that controls the functioning of the neurological system. While the word "disease" may seem to be more appropriate in relation to other organic abnormalities–liver, lungs, heart–it applies equally well to the brain. (Other words, like disorder or dysfunction, are, however, useful and are frequently employed in the psychiatric literature.)

Illnesses, then, are disvalued changes in states of being and in social function. They are the personal and social effects and consequences of the fact that one has a disease. Physicians diagnose and treat diseases; patients suffer illnesses. The personal stories related in this book concern individuals who have a disease (or, if you will, disorder or dysfunction) of the brain. There are abnormalities in the structure or functioning of their brains. This is a fundamental assumption of this book and one that, in my view, does not require any special defense or argumentation. The primary emphasis of the book, however, is on the illness side of the issue, on how and in what ways patients experience the disease in their everyday life–on how they suffer, how they cope, and how their loved ones also suffer and cope.

The Structure and Approach of This Book

This means that the individual chapters in this book are necessarily weighted toward the personal accounts themselves. The bulk of each chapter provides a verbatim account of what the sufferer or the sufferer's loved one has written. These accounts include descriptions–often very vivid ones–of what they have experienced and continue to experience. They also include interpretations, their efforts to understand these experiences and either to make sense of them or declare that they are without sense or meaning. The concluding section of each chapter involves my own reflections on what the sufferer or sufferer's loved one has written.

It is only fair that I alert the reader to the fact that I think the psychoanalytic approach to understanding mental *illness* has a great deal of validity. I think of my reflections, then, as "meta-interpretations," which make sense to me and, at the very least, should encourage readers to engage in similar sorts of "meta-interpretation" according to whatever conceptual models seem appropriate to them. In some instances, I also make use of writings that focus on the *disease* issue itself, especially in cases where I feel that these may help to illumine specific points made by the original author.

The five chapters that follow present a mere handful of cases of mental illness. Aware of the vast number of types of mental illness, I make no claim whatsoever that these cases are representative of the whole spectrum of mental illness, or even that these particular cases are typical of the mental illnesses that *are* covered in this book. In fact, these cases allow us to make a rather different observation, namely, that each instance of mental illness reflects the unique personality of the person who is afflicted with it. Thus, these personal accounts illustrate the point that mental illness is highly subject to personal variability. This is one reason why mental illnesses are difficult to treat and why their course and consequences for sufferers and loved ones are difficult to predict in advance.

Three of these five accounts were written by the one who suffered from the mental illness, while two are the work of a devoted family member of the mentally ill person. Four of the five mentally ill persons are male, and this means that the book is disproportionately focused on men's personal struggles with mental illness. This, however, reflects the fact that over the past several years I have been writing about male melancholiacs (Capps 1997, 2002). In my most recent book, I focused on the two cases of hospitalized men—Douglas O'Duffy and Daniel Miller—presented by Ana-Marie Rizzuto in her study, *The Birth of the Living God* (1979).

On the other hand, this book *does* reflect one of the more general truisms about mental illnesses that involve "loss of contact with reality." Different illnesses appear at different times in the life cycle. Psychoses in the form of schizophrenia and manic-depressive illness (or bipolar disorder) tend to have their onset in early to late young adulthood, while simple depression occurs at all ages, and dementia tends to occur among the elderly.

No assumptions should be made, however, about the fact that the two cases of schizophrenia are male, the case of manic-depressive illness is female, the case of a major depressive episode is male, and the case of dementia of the Alzheimer's type is male. Attempts to establish gender ratios for the various mental illnesses reflected in this book are confounded by the fact that some studies have been hospital-based and others community-based, and that gender is, in general, less predictive than family history of mental illness. In any case, I would again emphasize that this book is designed to make the point that mental illness is deeply and profoundly *personal,* both for the sufferers, who experience it in their own unique ways, and for the loved ones who write about it.

The title—"fragile connections"—is borrowed from Rose Styron's reflections on the mental illness of her husband, novelist William Styron. She speaks of "nurturing the fragile connections" that exist between the sufferer and the sufferer's loved one (R. Styron 2001, 137). The phrase also applies, however, to the "fragile connections" between and within the various components of the brain, which mental illness severs, leaving the sufferer the victim of internal disconnections that then produce the external disconnections between the sufferer and others. The quotation that appears in the frontispiece is from Theodore Roethke's poem "In a Dark Time" (1975, 231). Roethke, an English literature professor who was afflicted with manic-depressive illness (see Jamison 1993), suffered his first mental breakdown in 1936 and lost his teaching position at Michigan State University because of it. Ten years later, he was about to be fired by Bennington College when he suffered a second mental attack, this one more terrifying than the first because he was given electric shock treatments (Blessing 1974, 57). He was teaching at the University of Washington when I was introduced to his poetry as an undergraduate student at Lewis and Clark College in Portland, Oregon, in 1959–1960. I learned at the time that he was in and out of mental hospitals in the Seattle area, and this fact kindled my interest in his poetry. This book is dedicated to the memory of the Reverend Ansel Bourne, a nineteenth-century American minister whose name is unlikely to be mentioned in church history courses. For readers who cannot wait to find out who he was and why I have dedicated this book to him, the answer may be found in the epilogue. But as with mystery books, so with this volume, the last few pages are better understood and appreciated if one has taken the trouble to read the earlier ones first.

1

THE AWFUL WILDERNESS OF THE INSANE

▓ ANTON BOISEN

I have chosen to begin this book with Anton Boisen because he was one of the first chaplains in a psychiatric hospital and the instigator of clinical pastoral education in theological seminaries. What makes his story compelling, however, is that he himself suffered from mental illness. His hospitalization inspired the idea of providing seminary students the opportunity to learn about mental illness through direct exposure to hospitalized patients. Boisen wrote his memoir, *Out of the Depths: An Autobiographical Study of Mental Disorder and Religious Experience* (1960), when he was in his early eighties.

Boisen's Context

Ironically, he was writing about his struggle with mental illness in the first decade of an ambitious program of deinstitutionalization of the mentally ill. As E. Fuller Torrey and Judy Miller point out in their recent study of the rise of mental illness from 1750 to the present, 68 percent of American psychiatrists worked in mental hospitals in 1940, but by 1957 this figure had fallen to 17 percent (2001, 298). The number of mentally ill hospitalized patients totaled 558,922 in 1955. If the public mental hospitals that existed in 1955 had not been closed, Torrey and Miller estimate that, allowing for the increase in population, the census of public mental hospitals would be approximately 932,000 today. Moreover, because serious mental illnesses (psychotic disorders like schizophrenia and manic-depressive illness) steadily increased from the mid-1800s through the mid-1900s, it is very likely that this figure would be even higher. The problem, in their view, is that we have no clear idea as to the number of seriously mental ill persons in the United States today because the vast majority of these persons are being seen, if at all, on an out-patient basis.

Boisen's Diagnosis

Boisen was first hospitalized in 1920 at the age of forty-four. He was initially sent to Boston Psychopathic Hospital and then transferred to Westboro State Hospital a week later. The official diagnosis was schizophrenia of the catatonic type.

Criteria for Schizophrenia

The diagnostic criteria for schizophrenia established by the American Psychiatric Association and presented in *The Diagnostic and Statistical Manual (DSM-IV* 1994) include the following characteristic symptoms (two or more of the following, each present for a significant portion of time during a one–month period, or less if successfully treated):

1. delusions
2. hallucinations
3. disorganized speech (for example, frequent derailment or incoherence)
4. grossly disorganized or catatonic behavior
5. negative symptoms, that is, affective flattening, alogia, or avolition. (Affective flattening is especially common and is characterized by the person's face appearing immobile and unresponsive, with poor eye contact and reduced body language. Alogia or poverty of speech is manifested by brief, laconic, empty replies. Avolition is characterized by an inability to initiate and persist in goal-directed activities.)

Only one of these symptoms is required if the delusions are bizarre or the hallucinations consist of a voice keeping up a running commentary on the person's behavior or thoughts, or two or more voices conversing with one another. There must also be social/occupational dysfunction (such as work, interpersonal relations, or self-care that is markedly below previous levels) and signs of the disturbance must persist for at least six months, including one month of symptoms that meet the above criteria (*DSM-IV*, 285).

Criteria for Catatonic Schizophrenia

Schizophrenia has several identifiable subtypes. The *DSM-IV* identifies the following: paranoid, disorganized, catatonic, undifferentiated, and residual. The diagnostic criteria for the catatonic type of schizophrenia are the presence of at least two of the following:

1. motoric immobility as evidenced by catalepsy or stupor
2. excessive motor activity that is apparently purposeless and not influenced by external stimuli
3. extreme negativism (an apparently motiveless resistance to all instructions or maintenance of a rigid posture against attempts to be moved) or mutism
4. pecularities of voluntary movement as evidenced by posturing (voluntary assumption of inappropriate or bizarre postures, stereotyped movements, prominent mannerisms, or prominent grimacing; and echolalia or echopraxis (parroting the words or imitating the behavior of others). (*DSM-IV*, 289)

The Diagnostic Question

The accuracy of the diagnosis of schizophrenia, catatonic type, for Boisen has been questioned. In a recent article, Curtis W. Hart (2001) notes that even though Boisen himself accepted the diagnosis, there has been an ongoing debate as to whether he suffered from a mood disorder, that is, was manic-depressive or, in today's nomenclature, had bipolar disorder. Hart cites an article by Carol North and William M. Clements (1981) that suggests he most likely suffered from bipolar affective disorder. They based this judgment on the grounds that Boisen's own description of his symptoms in *Out of the Depths* indicates that he met the "elevated mood" category for this diagnosis. (The diagnostic criteria for bipolar disorder will be presented in chapter 3 .)

Difficulty of Diagnosis

Significantly, the *DSM-IV* notes that a diagnostic distinction between psychotic disorders such as schizophrenia and mood disorders such as bipolar disorder may be difficult. This is because they share a number of presenting symptoms, such as grandiose and persecutory delusions, irritability, agitation, and catatonic symptoms, especially early in their course. The most useful way to distinguish the psychotic disorders from bipolar (a mood) disorder is that, in the former, the periods of psychotic symptoms occur in the absence of prominent mood symptoms.

The psychotic symptoms that Kay Redfield Jamison experienced (as described in chapter 3) provide a valuable reference point, as no one has seriously questioned the fact that she suffers from manic-depressive (or bipolar) disorder. Other helpful considerations include family history, as well as previous course or episodes, and the accompanying symptoms.

While Hart believes that North and Clement's "use of quotations from the autobiography may strike some as forced, an effort to confirm a point of view," he considers their argument "worthy of attention and serious debate" (2001, 427). Of particular note is the fact that North and Clements do not challenge the accuracy of Boisen's account of his own condition. They do challenge "the accuracy of his diagnosis *as it is understood in contemporary psychiatry* and applied retrospectively to the clinical condition detailed by Boisen in his autobiography" (quoted in Hart 2001, 427, italics in original). Hart proposes a resolution to the debate about Boisen's diagnosis based on a book by a German psychiatrist, Karl Ludwig Kahlbaum, *Catatonia or Tension Anxiety,* originally published in 1874 and not translated into English until 1973. Kahlbaum believed that symptoms of catatonia could be viewed as the onset of thought disorders (that is, schizophrenia), mood disorders (that is, manic-depressive or bipolar disorder), or certain organic illnesses.

In light of Kahlbaum's view that catatonia may be identified with either a thought or a mood disorder, Hart concludes that perhaps both sides of the prolonged debate about Boisen's diagnosis "have a significant piece of the truth" (2001, 428). Thus, as far as diagnostic categories are concerned, "Boisen was not bipolar and schizophrenic at the same time but demonstrated aspects of both in his thought, affect, and behavior. These aspects of illness overlapped at some points and remained distinct at others" (428). He adds: "Fittingly, it is Boisen himself who emerges as possessing the most holistic and arresting grasp of the diagnostic question. He acknowledged both components of thought and mood disorders in the patients whose rapid onset of illness he describes in his [other] writings. And his autobiography identifies thoughts, feelings, and behaviors that can be interpreted along both lines" (428).

The Appropriate Subtype?

What Hart does not directly address, however, is the question whether the original diagnosis of schizophrenia identified the appropriate subtype. As manic-depressive illness (or bipolar disorder) typically includes delusions, and delusions are not a necessary feature of catatonic type of schizophrenia, the very fact that Boisen relates instances of delusional thinking in his autobiography helps to explain why, for example, North and Clements would be dissatisfied with the original diagnosis. If, however, he had been diagnosed as schizophrenic, paranoid type, this dissatisfaction might not have emerged, as the major criterion for the paranoid type of schizophrenia is a "preoccupation with one or more delusions or frequent auditory hallucinations" (*DSM-IV,* 287). As we will see, while Boisen seems not to have experienced auditory hallucinations, he did experience visual ones, and he was given to delusional thinking.

Thus, it is altogether possible that the catatonic features were of such prominence when he was admitted to Boston Psychopathic Hospital that the admitting psychiatrist did not recognize the features more clearly related to paranoia. This would be congruent with Kahlbaum's view that catatonic symptoms are prevalent at the onset of thought disorders. In any event, I believe that a diagnosis of paranoid schizophrenia would have been appropriate. I am somewhat surprised that this was not the diagnosis ascribed to Boisen when he arrived a week later at Westboro State Hospital, for as Boisen noted in a statement about his hospitalization at Westboro written two years later:

> My first memory is that of Dr. Gale filling out the admission blank, and of one particular remark he made. I had asked that I might be taken to a certain friend whom I trusted, because I did not want to talk to doctors whom I did not know. Dr. Gale said, "That is clear proof that he belongs here." (1960, 87)

In other words, Dr. Gale seems to have taken this statement to suggest that Boisen was suffering from persecutory delusions. Boisen's account of the ideas with which he was obsessed over the next several days indicates quite clearly that he was beset with both persecutory and grandiose delusions.

Criteria for Paranoid Schizophrenia

This is how the *DSM-IV* describes the paranoid type of schizophrenia:

> The essential feature of the Paranoid Type of Schizophrenia is the presence of prominent delusions of auditory hallucinations in the context of a relative preservation of cognitive functioning and affect. Symptoms characteristic of the Disorganized and Catatonic Types (e.g., disorganized speech, flat or inappropriate affect, catatonic or disorganized behavior) are not prominent. Delusions are typically persecutory or grandiose, or both, but delusions with other themes (e.g., jealousy, religiosity, or somatization) may also occur. The delusions may be multiple, but are usually organized around a coherent theme. Hallucinations are also typically related to the content of the delusional theme. (*DSM-IV*, 287)

Associated features include anxiety, anger, aloofness, and argumentativeness. The individual may have a superior and patronizing manner and either a stilted, formal quality or extreme intensity in interpersonal interactions. The persecutory themes may predispose the individual to suicidal behavior. When combined with anger, the persecutory and grandiose delusions may predispose the person to violence. There is little or no impairment on neuropsychological or other cognitive testing. The onset tends to be later in life than the other types of schizophrenia, and some evidence suggests that the prognosis for the paranoid type is considerably better than for the other types of schizophrenia, especially with regard to occupational functioning and capacity for independent living (*DSM-IV*, 287). As we will see, Boisen's delusions were organized around a coherent theme, what he referred to as "the family-of-four."

Although various opinions on the diagnostic question are possible, I will take the view that he suffered from paranoid schizophrenia. What is beyond debate is that Boisen was a very sick man when his mother arranged to have a physician examine him. This subsequently led to the appearance of six policemen who picked him up and took him to Boston Psychopathic Hospital. How did he get this way? This is a question for which Boisen seems to have sought an answer, and his memoir, *Out of the Depths,* reflects his awareness of the fact that, in the case of severe mental illness, the answers are neither simple nor clear-cut.

Instinctual Cravings

Boisen covers the first twenty-five years of his life in two chapters, one titled "Ancestry and Social Background," the other "Early Years."

Ancestry and Social Background

His mother's family was of English background. His maternal great-grandfather was a Reformed Presbyterian pastor and later professor of Latin and Greek at the University of Pennsylvania. His maternal grandfather taught mathematics at Indiana University in Bloomington. Boisen's father immigrated from Germany to the United States to gain a doctorate. He remained in the United States and began teaching modern languages at Indiana University. Boisen's mother, one of the first women to enroll at Indiana University, married her teacher of modern languages. Boisen was the first of their two children. He was born in 1876. His sister was born in 1879.

Boisen's father resigned his position at Indiana University in 1879 because he objected to the dismissal of a colleague. He was appointed to a vacancy at Williams College in Williamstown, Massachusetts.

The Early Years: Sexual Episodes

While the Boisens were living in Williamstown, Anton, now age four, was circumcised. He explains the doctor's medical rationale for this procedure, then offers his own explanation:

> Quite spontaneously, it seemed, there had developed a sex-organ excitation which seemed beyond the normal. I can recall my parents' anxious concern and the consultation with the

doctor. He was sure it was due to local irritation, and the operation was performed. As a matter of fact, the trouble lay in a more than average interest in matters eliminative and sexual. I may add that I do not remember ever overhearing or seeing anything in the behavior either of adults or of other children which might explain it. Since it was thus primarily psychical, the treatment failed to correct it. (1960, 24)

As evidence that the treatment failed to correct it, Boisen goes on to tell about an episode that happened the following summer when the Boisens were staying at the home of his maternal grandparents in Bloomington, Indiana. He relates that

this [sexual] interest led to some mutual explorations with a boy cousin about a year younger. We were promptly caught and my mouth was washed out with soap and water. This treatment seems to have put an end to the trend for the time being. The horror on my mother's face and her volunteered promise that she would not tell my father are impressions which still remain. (25)

Readers have offered a variety of interpretations of this passage. Some think it points to an early—perhaps genetically-based—homosexual orientation. Others speculate that the manner in which he was punished implies that their mutual explorations involved oral sex. I think it is impossible to know just what happened that day and what it might mean with regard to his sexual orientation. With this and the circumcision stories, Boisen intended to convey the fact that sexual conflicts were to play an important role in his life and, more particularly, in his mental illness.

Boisen's father's appointment at Williams College proved to be temporary, and for the next two years he taught modern languages in the Boston public school system. Then he was invited to join the faculty at Lawrenceville School near Princeton, New Jersey, a prep school for boys. He taught there for two years. Boisen notes that in receiving this appointment his father "felt that he had found just the right opening" (26).

During the time that the Boisens were living in Lawrenceville, an episode occurred that, like the sexual explorations with his boy cousin, has bearing on his sexual conflicts. At Lawrenceville School, each master had his own family of boys. His father was assigned to the boys in Davis House, and this is where the Boisen family lived. His father, who had a deep interest in nature, continued efforts begun in Massachusetts to acquaint his son with trees and plants.

THE DOLL AND DRESS INCIDENT

He also took him to the school gymnasium to teach him certain simple exercises. One day Anton went with his father and several of the Davis House boys on a hike. They were to search for trailing arbutus, his father's favorite flower, which was reported to be growing nearby. His father promised him a silver dollar for the first leaf he found of the trailing arbutus. It was a very long hike, some ten or twelve miles.

While Anton "came through without the dollar," he had "enough energy left to demand inclusion" in a drive his father was taking to Trenton, some four miles south of Lawrenceville. When his father refused, Anton "set up a loud wail," to which his father responded by putting his son in a dress and giving him a doll to play with. Boisen explains:

> This he did somewhat playfully, saying that boys of seven who could go on long hikes were too big to cry. My recollection is that I at once stopped crying and the dress was promptly removed. I caught his spirit, and felt that he was perhaps proud of the fact that I had gone through with the hike. (26)

He does not comment further on his father's action that day. By prefacing his account of the experience with how his father would take him frequently to the gymnasium, Boisen suggests, perhaps, that his father continued to worry about his son's sexual development. While his father presumably never learned about his mutual exploration with his cousin, he *was* involved in the circumcision decision. Therefore, we can reasonably assume that he wanted to insure that his son would develop into a manly, not effeminate, boy. For his own part, Boisen's own anxieties seem to have focused more on making his father proud of him.

HIS FATHER'S DEATH

In the very next paragraph, however, he recounts his father's early and sudden death. He writes: "My father always worked under tension, very high tension, and he had both the strengths and the weaknesses which go with such a temperament. In any case, at the age of thirty-eight he burned himself out, dying of heart failure on January 16, 1884" (27). Boisen was only seven years old when his father died, "but his memory, reinforced by my mother's picture of him and that of others who knew him, has remained a potent force in my life, one which for me has been associated with my idea of God" (27). As we will see, his father figured prominently in his delusional system during his first major psychotic episode.

Boisen's mother returned to Bloomington with her two young children, and they took up residence in her parents' home. She took a position in the Bloomington public schools as a teacher of drawing. Boisen notes that this was "the beginning of a very trying period" for his grandparents. A new president had taken over at the University and wanted a faculty of young specialists. Boisen's grandfather "was the outstanding representative of the old order that had to go" (29). He had hoped to round out fifty years of service but was instead forced to retire after forty-nine. To make matters worse, his son, Anton's uncle, who had stepped into the position of assistant in chemistry without having obtained his doctorate, was also relieved of his office.

ANTON'S ACCIDENT

Meanwhile, Anton's own schooling had been delayed due to his transfer from Lawrenceville. A freak accident shortly before his eighth birthday caused a further delay and cost him the permanent loss of his left eye. He describes the accident as follows:

> I can remember quite well how it happened. At dinner that day the conversation had turned to the reaction of winking. My grandfather spoke of its protective function, and I left the table, curious about it all, and went to the front yard. There I began to swing on a gate underneath a large pear tree full of ripening pears. Two boys came along and demanded some pears. I refused. Thereupon one of them aimed a toy gun at me, one of the type that carried a rubber contraption on a wooden stock. Half curiously, half defiantly, I resolved not to wink. He banged away, and I was struck by an iron nail directly in the pupil of the eye. The eyelid was not touched. (30–31)

Accompanied by his grandmother, he visited a distinguished oculist in Cincinnati, but the doctor was unable to save the eye. Boisen minimizes the effects of the loss: "Its loss may have had an adverse effect upon my skill on the ballfield and the tennis court, but I have not been aware of the difference" (32). Nor does he mention the physical pain or the psychical trauma involved. He seems resolved not to feel sorry for himself, even for the young boy who stood his ground some seventy-five years earlier.

High School Years

Continuing his narrative of his early years, he notes that he did reasonably well in academics but had difficulties in his social relations owing to shyness and a tendency to be distrustful of himself. In high school, he had a "special chum," the son of a college professor, with whom he spent "a good bit of time" (36). They made expeditions together out into the country in search of butterflies or hickory nuts or whatever the season offered, and they went together to baseball and football games. They also experimented in woodworking. He does not "recall that we discussed girls or sex matters except incidentally" (37).

He regularly attended the Presbyterian church to which the family belonged. While he experienced "great distress of mind" when reading "a verse of scripture or some pious sentiment" of the Christian Endeavor Society, which he had joined, "There were at no time any intellectual difficulties. The faith of my fathers was, for me, at one with the authority of science" (39). He notes that his grandfather was probably on the conservative side in the warfare between science and religion that waged so furiously during the later nineteenth century—though he knows that he accepted the scientific account of the age of the earth. His father, however, "had not been able to accept Bloomington's brand of Presbyterianism. Later on he had joined the Congregational church. On that occasion he wrote out a statement of belief which shows that he was a thoroughgoing liberal" (39). As his mother had also accepted the liberal position early in her life, his "own problems were therefore not theological. They had to do with my inner adjustment" (39). Later, we will see how he suffered his first major psychotic episode in the midst of an effort to write out a statement of his beliefs. This, it seems, was an attempt to replicate his father's example. If so, it also revealed the convergence of theological problems and his inner adjustments.

Onset of Mental Illness

Boisen's problems, which led eventually to serious mental illness, seem, by his own account, to have begun in 1896, when he was a twenty-year-old junior at Indiana University. His grandfather's death in his sophomore year, followed by the death of his uncle, "removed the last of the significant men in the family." This left him "feeling the pressure of a situation" to which he felt unequal. Apparently of the pressure he felt was pressure to assume the role of the family's male leader. His "sense of inadequacy" was exacerbated when his sister entered college in 1896, for her social success reminded him of his own social deficiencies. Noting that he attended social affairs from a sense of duty and not because he found any satisfaction in them, he goes on to confess:

> It is only with difficulty that I am able to recall the steps in the development of the inner conflict which has given me so much trouble. I seldom discussed the subject of sex with other boys, not even with my most intimate friends, and I had little dealing with girls. But all the while I was extremely sensitive on the subject, and the entire realm of sex was for me at once fascinating and terrifying. (43)

The "essence of the difficulty" lay in the fact that "these sexual interests could neither be controlled nor acknowledged for fear of condemnation. Because of the presence of instinctual cravings which to me were forbidden, I felt isolated from my fellows." This, he feels, "is the explanation of the grave social maladjustments of this period—the shyness, the self-consciousness, the anxiety" (43). He worried, especially, that he would get caught (as had happened, we recall, when he and his cousin engaged in mutual sexual exploration when he was four). He notes, "I was never any good at bluffing. When I did wrong, I always got caught" (43).

Form of Anton's Cravings

If his "instinctual cravings" were sexual, what form did they take? He indicates that he "did not permit myself to read the ordinary obscene stuff or to look at the vulgar cards which the boys sometimes passed around" (43–44). Instead,

> What I did was to turn to certain parts of the Bible, to certain plays of Shakespeare, and to certain articles in the encyclopedias, deceiving myself with the idea that I was seeking after knowledge. Such temptations were increased when, as a specialist in languages, I was free to browse around in the departmental library. Certain French novels had an influence upon me which was far from wholesome, not necessarily because these books were "bad," but because they dealt frankly with emotionally charged problems. They added fuel to fire that was already more than I could control. (44)

He relates how once he attempted to burn out the caterpillars in a walnut tree in their orchard, using a long pole capped on the end with rags soaked in kerosene. When he finished, he lay the pole down on the ground. Later, he returned, inspected the pole, and leaned it up against the woodhouse. He went to his room and buried himself in Tolstoy's *Anna Karenina*: "This was for me in that period of my life the kind of reading which was equivalent to playing with fire, but I permitted myself to read it, especially in vacations, because it was something which men of culture ought to be acquainted with" (44).

He still recalls the feeling that had come over him from the reading, "a sort of vertigo," when he suddenly heard the cry of "fire!" The woodhouse was on fire, caused by the pole that he had leaned against it. The city fire department put out the fire with only moderate loss—much of the woodhouse was destroyed but the fire did not reach the house—but the episode was, to him, symbolic of his "personal situation" (44–45). This happened, he recalls, in the vacation preceding his senior year.

University Graduation and Crossing the Line

Boisen graduated in 1897 at the age of twenty, the youngest in his class. He hoped to secure a teaching position at the high school level. Because no position materialized, he enrolled in the graduate school at

Indiana University and became deeply interested in his studies. He took special interest in reading William James's *The Principles of Psychology* under the guidance of Dr. William Lowe Bryan, professor of philosophy and psychology (*Out of the Depths* is dedicated to Bryan's memory.) He also attended a Bible class taught by Dr. Bryan at the United Presbyterian Church. All was going well until Christmas vacation:

> Then came a fall from grace. I read a novel of Zola's, one of the kind I could not assimilate, and I crossed the line I had determined not to cross. As a result I felt stripped of self-respect and burdened with a heavy sense of failure and guilt. It was in this mood that I entered the new quarter of study. (46)

In a footnote, he explains the statement about crossing the line he had determined not to cross: "The 'transgression' referred to was that of a psychically induced orgasm. Concerning my problem, I may say that it had to do chiefly with erotic fantasy derived for the most part from reading. Actual orgasm was not frequent; and when it did occur, it resulted usually from psychic stimulation. The fantasies were always of the opposite sex" (46). He seems concerned to challenge the inference that his primary problem was that of masturbation, which, at the time, was thought by many medical doctors to be the primary cause of insanity in young men (see, for example, Skultans 1975). He also seems concerned to lay to rest any suspicion of homosexual feelings, which his earlier account of his sexual explorations with a boy cousin seems to some readers to invite.

The "inner tension" he felt as the winter quarter began was intensified by the class's reading of James's chapters on "Habit" and "Will," neither of which brought him "any comfort" (46).[1] Then, Colonel Francis Parker, one of the recognized educational leaders of the country and an old friend of Boisen's father, came to the University to lecture. "He made some pointed remarks about abuse of the imagination" (46). Following the lecture, Boisen and his mother went up to speak with Parker, and Parker remarked that Boisen's father was the greatest teacher he had ever known: "Here, then, was the touching of a sore spot [Boisen's "abuse of the imagination"] by a man who represented my father. It intensified the idealistic component and at the same time made me aware of my shortcomings" (46).

Then, toward spring, he received a letter from his great-uncle in Philadelphia, his grandfather's brother and the pastor of the old Wylie Memorial Church. He inquired about Anton's "spiritual condition." This letter came at the very time he "had made an alarming discovery." As he turned the pages of his Greek dictionary, "obscene words leaped out of its pages and hit me in the eye; and so they would leap out of other dictionaries also. It was obvious that something was seriously wrong"

(46–47). It is worth noting that he describes the obscene words as "hitting" him in the eye, as though he was reexperiencing the trauma of the iron nail puncturing the pupil of his other eye on the day he had resolved not to wink or blink.

A Great Burden Lifted

On Easter morning, a beautiful day, he felt there was "no sunshine there for me, and no beauty—nothing but black despair" (47). He retired to his room after taking a turn in his mother's garden "and threw myself on my knees with an agonized call for help. And help came! Something seemed to say to me almost in words, 'Don't be afraid to tell'" (47). With this it seemed as though a great burden had been taken away, and he felt "very happy." Later that day he had a talk with his mother, and she understood. Then he went to speak with Dr. Bryan. He is unable to recall much of this conversation, but one thing stands out clearly: "He told me that it would always be necessary to fight for control of the instincts and that I must look to Christ for help, and to some good woman" (47).

Following that Easter Sunday, he underwent a major change. He found that he was unable to do his routine classwork. Only what was related to his dominant interests held his attention. His mind "was in a tumult, surging with all sorts of ideas, ideas which came from many sources, vivid memories from out of the past, especially from the period of childhood, and others which seemed to come from no previous experience of my own" (47). There were even "ideas of having lived before and of being more important than I had ever dreamed. But I was hopeful, happy, confident" (47). These "ideas"—especially those of having lived before and of being more important than he had ever dreamed— suggest that he was at least mildly psychotic. While his feelings of happiness and confidence may seem to suggest that this was a hypomanic episode characteristic of a mood disorder, I think that the delusional character of these ideas argues, instead, for the view that this experience was an incipiently schizophrenic one.

In any event, Boisen has his own explanation of what had happened that Easter morning in 1898 and during the year that followed:

My development had been checked by the presence of instinctual claims which could be neither controlled nor acknowledged for fear of condemnation. The prompting, "Do not be afraid to tell," brought relief by socializing the difficulty, and it did so on the level of what for me was abiding and universal. I was now at one with the internalized fellowship of the best, the fellowship which is represented by the idea of God. I felt now like a new being. There was new hope and new confidence, and the painful shyness which so long had troubled me seemed to have disappeared. At least, I felt a freedom in my association with others which I had not felt before; I found new interest in my work, and increased effectiveness. (48–49)

He began teaching French at Indiana University. For the first time in his life he "found myself enjoying friendly relationships with young women," attributing this change to "the release from the diffidence of the earlier years, also to the fact that my sister was now at the height of her popularity in college" (49). He traded, it seems, on her reputation and was perhaps best able to relate to *her* young women friends as her devoted brother.

THE ENEMY REGAINS CONTROL

The change, however, did not last. His memory is now hazy on the course of events, but the fact is that he became "less watchful, and the old enemy got hold of me again" (50). Because, in teaching French, he was constantly confronted with the "unassimilated sex problem," a change in occupation seemed called for. He decided to give up his career as a teacher of languages and to embark on a new course, that of forestry.

While this decision appears to have been sudden and without much foundation, he contends that it had its explanation "in interests of longstanding," especially in the fact that he had succeeded in cultivating the trailing arbutus, his father's favorite wildflower, and also with the related fact that forestry "grew out of loyalty to my father's memory which had become one with my religion" (51). No doubt he also felt that his problems involving sexual stimulation from books might be allayed by a more physically vigorous lifestyle, and it was reasonable to believe that a career in forestry would provide this.

The Good Woman

His decision to become a forester is recounted in the final paragraph of his second chapter ("The Early Years"). The very next chapter, however, is titled, "The Call to Ministry." This chapter introduces the biblical theme of the Exodus. The first half is titled, "Borders of the Promised Land," and the second half is headed, "Years of Wandering."

Borders of the Promised Land

In the first half, he tells about meeting Alice Batchelder, a twenty-two-year-old woman who had come to Indiana University to become the secretary to the Young Christian Women's Association. She was introduced to the student body at convocation and gave a short address. Boisen no longer recalls what she said, but he "fell in love with her then and there" (52). This was, he admits, "a one-sided affair, a love that swept me off my feet" (52). While he and Alice never married, she was to be the love of his life. In the epilogue titled, "The Guiding Hand," he concludes that it was for her sake that he undertook his "venture into the unexplored." He notes that "her compassion on me, her wisdom, her courage, and her unswerving fidelity have made possible the measure of success achieved. And my love for her has been linked with all that is best and holiest in this life of mine" (210).

During the single year they were both at Indiana University, he took her out driving several times. On one of these occasions, he confessed to her his love and asked at least for her friendship. Her response "was not the one I hoped for," and she felt it best that their relationship should cease immediately. This was to be the general pattern of their relationship for the thirty-three years between their initial meeting in 1902 to Alice's death from cancer in 1935.

At the end of the year, she became the state secretary of the YWCA in Missouri, and he went off to Maryland to begin his career in forestry, entering Yale Forestry School in the fall of 1903. His "wayward erotic ideation" was proving difficult to control. He continued to place his hopes in Alice, who seems to have been for him the "good woman" that Dr. Bryan had advised him to find, and who, along with Christ, would help him in the "fight for control of the instincts" (47).

He promised himself, however, that if he could "keep the record clear" for three months, he would then write to her at the end of that time period. He did this and wrote to tell her that he continued to think of her. There was no response: "This was a severe blow and I did not know what to do. I recognized that she meant what she had said. Was it fair either to her or to myself to keep on hoping?" (53).

THE BIBLICAL ANSWER

One evening as he was wrestling with the question of what to do, he resorted in his desperation to an act of "rank superstition." He took his Bible and opened it at random. The first time he tried this, his eyes fell upon the words, "Ask and ye shall receive" (Mt. 7:7). The next evening he tried the same thing and the words were these: "Therefore we ought to give the more earnest heed to the things that were heard, lest haply we drift away from them. For if the word spoken through angels proved steadfast and every transgression received a just recompense of reward, how shall we escape if we neglect so great salvation" (Heb. 2:1–3a, as these quotations differ from the original biblical texts, and the specific citations are not given, Boisen appears to be relying on his memory of these verses). Admitting that this passage was less clear, nevertheless, he "saw an answer to the question on my mind," and, in any case, "the thought of her more and more took possession of me" (53).

After completing his first year at Yale's School of Forestry, he was assigned to make a working plan for a five-thousand acre tract in southwestern New Hampshire. He requested this assignment because it took him to Alice's home state. On one occasion in the late fall of 1904, he stopped off at Portsmouth, hoping to see her. It so happened that she was home, but, calling unannounced, he met with "a very chilly reception" (54). He was heartbroken, and, "with a mind tense with despair," he went on to Washington, where the Forestry School men were to meet with the American Forestry Association.

While there, he attended church services. One morning the sermon on the migration of Abraham focused on the difference between following a certain course out of arbitrary desire and doing so in obedience to God's will: "Because of the tense and suggestible state of mind I was in that morning this sermon could hardly have failed to have a profound effect. I took it as a message to me. It was followed by several sleepless nights" (54).

This tenseness did not subside with his return to New Haven. Toward Easter, seven years from the time of his first dramatic Easter morning, he had another powerful experience. One evening while reading Ralph Waldo Emerson's essay on the "Oversoul," a passage arrested his attention. Emerson had written about how one may run to "seek your friend" and of the need to accept what happens: "If you do not find him, will you not acquiesce that it is best you should not find him?" (Emerson 1983, 398). These words, again, seemed to apply to his situation. They "helped to induce an attitude of resignation and trust, and thus brought peace to my troubled mind" (55).

As he lay half awake, half asleep, that night, something seemed to say to him just as on that earlier Easter morning, "Write and tell her all about it." He sat down and wrote Alice a letter telling her of the moral struggle he was having and of his reason for studying forestry. After he wrote the letter, however, he began to question it and took up his Bible. After saying a prayer, he once again opened it at random.

John 19:27 leaped out to him, "Then said he to the disciple, 'Behold thy mother!'" (Boisen's version). He was deeply moved by this, for "regardless of its origin, this 'message' pointed to what I was really seeking in Alice. I realized that my love for her was really a desperate cry for salvation and an appeal to a beloved person stronger than myself" (55). It is perhaps noteworthy that he makes no explicit reference here to the word "mother" and does not say, for example, that he was seeking in Alice what he despaired of receiving from his own mother. On the other hand, the verse makes an association not dissimilar to the one he made earlier between the religious meaning of his father and his inner struggles.

THE CALL TO MINISTRY

In any event, he sent the letter off to Alice. Shortly after he did so, the idea surged into his mind, "You have found the hills where the flowers grow. It must be your task to show the way to them" (55–56). He adds, "This for me was the call to ministry." In effect, his previous belief that he was destined for a career in forestry had been a literal interpretation of something more deeply metaphorical. He continues:

> I had never before dreamed of such a step, for I had never seen in myself the qualifications requisite for that calling. I felt that I had no gift of expression, either in speech or in writing; neither did I have the personal qualities which a minister ought to have. But the idea seemed to carry authority because of the way it came. (56)

Furthermore, "It also made sense," for even as he had been led to discover new "haunts" of the flower his father loved out of his devotion to his father's memory, "so now through that same devotion I had tapped anew the eternal sources of religious faith and renewal. It would also permit me to claim a place as a fellow worker with Alice" (56).

Even so, he questioned. The next morning he attended worship services at Battell Chapel on the Yale campus, and the theme of the sermon was the call to ministry: "It seemed to be a message for me, and it set my doubts at rest. I then wrote two more letters to Alice, telling her of my decision, and voicing the hope that we might be able to serve together" (56). Three days later he received her reply. She indicated that his letters had caused her great distress, and she asked him not to write to her again or to think of her any further.

On receiving this response, he felt dashed to pieces: "It was as if I had been trying to fly and had been brought crashing down. I gave way to a reaction of weakness and despair" (57). In a footnote, he explains that "the reaction referred to here was physiologically that of emission without erection. It occurred three times in rapid succession," and "left me now with a horrible sense of failure and guilt.... Psychologically, it was the collapse of faith, which left me at the mercy of ideas of despair and self-pity" (57).

When the school year came to an end, he entered the Forest Service and fulfilled three successive assignments over a two-year period, all the while continuing to think of Alice and meditating on the call to ministry that he believed he had received. During a sojourn in Washington, D. C. between assignments, he attended a Sunday evening service at First Congregational Church. The sermon, "Broken Vessel," concluded with a statement that he felt was directed at himself. The preacher said that if there was someone listening to his words "who has had a great vision of God's purpose for him and who has been unfaithful to that vision, I call upon him to arise and give himself into the hands of the Great Potter in order that he may be made again another vessel as it seemeth good unto the Potter" (58).

This sermon, he recalls, "had the effect of driving me nearly psychotic" (58). While he cannot remember what followed, he does know that he wrote to Alice, informing her of his steady purpose of entering the ministry but also of his great perplexity due to his failure "to stand the test two years before" (58). This time, she consented to see him, owing, he guesses, to the fact that she had recently been informed that her request for foreign service in the YWCA had been rejected due to her rather fragile health. When they met in Philadelphia in the winter of 1908 (he was then thirty-two years old), she offered a prayer for him and assured him that God's promises always come true.

He made plans to enter Union Theological Seminary in New York in the fall, receiving his mother's full consent to this change of course and her financial support as well. He wrote Alice to inform her of his plans. Because he was concerned that what he took to be her promise of a commitment to him was given more out of pity than of love, he told her that he would "never accept from her anything that she could not give freely" (58–59). She replied that he must have misunderstood, that she had in fact made no promises. Her first answer to what seems to have been a proposal of marriage was final and unchangeable.

This threw him into "an abnormal condition" which he can "recall only hazily" (59). He saw himself, as it were,

> in the thick of a great fight. I had been entrusted with a responsibility on which everything depended, but I had fallen and could not rise. Then I saw her, and it seemed that she had appeared and reappeared through the centuries. And always across her path stood a poor wretch whose claim of need could not be denied, one who for her was a heavy cross. She was therefore always lonely and sad. Then it came to me that even though I had fallen, even though I was a broken vessel, I might give her to someone else. (59)

Something about all this was at least quasi-delusional, a combination, it seems, of persecutory feelings on the one hand and a certain grandiosity on the other, for what right had he to give Alice to another man?

A Terrible Darkness

Another man, one of his fellow foresters, "seemed pointed out," so he went to him and asked him to accept this task. The other man seemed to understand and, to Boisen himself, it seemed as though the struggle was over and the fight had been won. He felt happy. Then, however, came a "terrible darkness." He was "horrified at the breach of conventionality" of which he had been guilty, the fact that he had "given" Alice to another man.

He thought that he "must surely be insane," and yet "this prompting had seemed to carry authority just like that of the Easter experience in 1898 and that of the call to the ministry in 1905" (59). In this state of turmoil he "felt impelled" to begin a Bible class at the boardinghouse where he and other Forest Service men were taking their meals. This action "went awfully against the grain for me, but I had to do it, so it seemed" (59). In retrospect, it is evident that he was "in this period at least near-psychotic, and that such behavior today would surely land me in St. Elizabeths," the federal mental hospital in Washington, D. C. However, in those days, "some of my friends, deeply troubled though they were, stood by me" (59). These near-psychotic ideas and behaviors occurred a full twelve years before the major psychotic episode that *did* land him in a psychiatric hospital.

THE HAPPY YEARS

He entered Union Theological Seminary in the fall of 1908. This began "three of the happiest years of my life" (60). Alice agreed to correspond with him, and he was well received by his classmates. Looking back on his first two years at Union, however, he feels that he could have made better use of the privilege of writing Alice. Specifically, he "did not respond affirmatively to her suggestion that we correspond in French" (which is not surprising given his earlier experiences of being sexually stimulated by his reading of French novels). Nor did he "devote to my letters the time and thought needed to make them really worthwhile" (62). On the other hand, his academic work was going well, and "the old battle for self-control seemed to be in hand" (62). Around Christmastime in 1910, he and Alice had several meetings. One day she informed him that there was no other man in her life and that "she had decided to give her heart a chance" (63).

He looked forward to spring, when they would meet again, this time in New Hampshire. But as the date approached, she vetoed his plans for the meeting and proposed a counterplan, also announcing that a woman friend of hers would be accompanying her. This letter "hurt." He "gave way to the same reaction of weakness that had followed the 'call' of New Haven in 1905" (63). As a result, he went to New Hampshire with a "wrong" attitude.

MISSED OPPORTUNITY?

In retrospect, he believes that he misinterpreted Alice's intentions, as he is "reasonably sure that she was ready to give the answer I hoped for more than anything else in the world" (63–64). He bases this surmise, in part, on the fact that at one point her friend left, by agreement, he believes, and remarked as she did so that Alice looked like a bride with all the flowers she had collected on their walk together:

Clearly it was time for me to speak, and I longed to do so and felt a deep tenderness come over me. But I was not ready, and the words would not come. All that I did was to take her picture–twelve exposures! Then the friend returned, and the precious chance was gone. I felt utterly miserable. How to account for it I do not know. (64)

He complicated matters further by "inadvertently" purchasing his return ticket to Boston, where his sister lived, instead of to Lowell, where Alice lived. He "can still see the flash in Alice's eyes as she inquired whether she had heard correctly" (64). While he corrected his error and returned with Alice to Lowell, she would not allow him to accompany her any further:

Looking back, I am sure she interpreted my ineptness as due to resentment on my part. I felt at the time as though an evil spirit had taken possession of me, but that spirit was not one of resentment. I was just feeling terribly uncomfortable, and I wanted to get off by myself. (64)

Brokenhearted, he phoned Alice later that day and she consented to see him the following day: "But nothing I was able to say could repair the damage. She gave her answer. Our friendship had brought happiness to neither of us, and she was sure that it was not God's will that it should continue" (64).

He returned to Seminary and made repeated efforts to secure permission to see her again, but she refused. Years later he learned that she had lost her position in Lowell: "In view of her splendid efficiency and of the fact that she left Lowell only a few months after the tragedy" of their ill-fated meeting in New Hampshire, he "cannot but wonder if her vocational setback must not be charged to my account" (65).

WHAT MIGHT HAVE BEEN

Boisen concludes the first section of the call to ministry chapter with a reflection on what difference it would have made in his life if he could have gone through the years with Alice:

She was, as I saw her, a charming, highly gifted, level-headed woman with deep feelings and a high temper, which she kept under strict control. The key to her character I find in her statement to me that she had "decided to give her heart a chance." She had a New England conscience. She could always be counted on to do what she thought was right and to follow a consistent course regardless of her feelings...Of one thing I am sure. Any household of hers would have been well-ordered. (65)

Even allowing for the more formal times in which Boisen lived, contemporary readers of this testimony find it to be rather lacking in feeling itself, leading, as we will see later, one interpreter of Boisen's memoir to suggest that he was in love with the "idea" of Alice Batchelder.

Years of Wandering

The second half of the chapter on the call to ministry focuses on his activities following graduation from seminary in 1911. This section introduces his younger classmate, Fred Eastman, in whom he found "a friend to whose understanding and loyalty I am forever indebted" (65). Both enlisted in rural church work in response to an appeal from the director of the Presbyterian Board of Home Missions. Their initial work involved making surveys of church attendance in rural areas of Missouri, Tennessee, Kentucky, and Maryland.

Alice entered the picture again around Christmastime, 1911, giving her consent to correspond again. In the spring when he announced his intention of taking a church, she wrote a long letter in which she spoke of her skill in keeping house and making doughnuts. This he interpreted as an "opening" and "replied accordingly." He received, however, a "stinging letter" in response, stating that she had never loved him and that her original answer was irrevocable.

RENEWED DESPAIR

Once more, he "gave way to the reaction of weakness and despair" that had followed earlier rebuffs. Nonetheless, he proceeded with his plans to become a minister, going to Ames, Iowa, to become the Congregational college pastor at Iowa State University. His state of mind, however, was not conducive to "successful work," and his "usefulness was over by the end of the first year," which is to say that he was asked to resign (69).

In the early summer of 1913, he returned to his ancestral home in Bloomington for his grandmother's funeral services and remained throughout the summer. At summer's end, his sister, who had married in 1900, returned to her home in Arlington, Massachusetts, taking their mother, who was in her mid-seventies, with her. In the fall, Boisen took a small rural church in Wabaunsee, Kansas, but left after two years, feeling that it had been a complete failure. He took another church, this time in North Anson, Maine, and stayed for two years. This time, he felt he had succeeded: "The church held its own, and I was not thrown out" (71). Moreover, "Since 1912 there had been no recurrence of that physical reaction of weakness" (72).

When World War I began, he applied for a position with the Overseas Young Men's Christian Association and was sent to France in

September, 1917. He was first assigned to a machine-gun battalion, then to an artillery regiment. He returned to the United States in July, 1919, and was immediately offered the position of director of the North Dakota Rural Survey project under the auspices of the Interchurch World Movement.

Once in North Dakota, it occurred to him "that I had been incredibly blind and stupid in my dealings with Alice," so he began to write her regularly, "giving much time and thought to the letters and trying to make them interesting and helpful to us both" (75). He wrote a long account of his experiences with the Army, worked out an illustrated lecture on the country church, wrote out several sermons, and tried to formulate a confession of faith: "These productions, as I read them over now, still seem worthwhile. They should have helped to allay any fears for my sanity which she may have had" (75).

This is his first explicit reference to the likelihood that Alice's seeming vacillation in response to his overtures was due, in part at least, to questions in her mind about his mental stability. In any case, she replied that they could always be friends "provided it was clearly understood that it was and could be nothing more" (75). He replied that he would rather have "just her friendship" than "the love of any other woman in the world" (75).

His work with the Interchurch World Movement came to an end the following summer through no fault of his own. As he was awaiting a new church assignment, Alice agreed to see him in person if he would not be daunted by the presence of two other women with whom she shared an apartment in Chicago's West Side. He met her for the first time in nine years, and he "found her all that I had dreamed, with only the changes a man would wish to see in the woman he loved" (76). She would not, however, allow a second visit.

The Psychotic Episode

The fourth chapter of Boisen's memoir, "A Little-Known Country," is an account of the events that led up to his hospitalization, of the hospitalization itself, and of his release, which enabled him to take up further theological studies at Episcopal Theological Seminary in Cambridge, Massachusetts. He was forty-four to forty-five years old during this period in his life.

Into the Depths

The first section of this chapter, "Into the Depths," begins with a brief account of his difficulties in securing a church assignment: "Churches were not too plentiful, especially for a man whose record as a pastor had been no better than mine" (77). While waiting for something to develop, he found temporary employment at the Interchurch World Movement offices in New York and spent six weeks with his friend, Fred Eastman, and his family on Long Island.

In October he went to stay with his sister in Arlington, Massachusetts, with whom his mother was also living. While there, he began work on a statement of his religious experience and then a statement of his religious belief. Nine years earlier, the Brooklyn Presbytery had required him to write two such statements. Because he was now "entering upon a new period" in his life and career, it seemed fitting that he should try to reexamine his religious experience and reformulate his message. All went well for three or four days. He completed the religious experience statement and began working on the statement of belief. On Wednesday, October 6, 1920, however, "some strange ideas came surging into my mind, ideas of doom, ideas of my own unsuspected importance. With them began the frank psychosis, as shown in the documents which follow" (79).

STATEMENT OF BELIEF

The statement of belief that follows consists of seven paragraphs, six of which begin with the phrase, "I believe..." The first paragraph concerns his belief "in the Love which came to my rescue on that Easter morning years ago," the Love that has "pitied my weakness and borne with my failures and forgiven my sins," and which has "lighted my way through the dark nights of despair and has guided me through the awful wilderness of the insane, where the going is difficult and very dangerous" (79).

The second paragraph centers on his belief in the revelation of God in the life and teaching of Jesus of Nazareth. It emphasizes Jesus' "patience with our shortcomings, his compassion upon our infirmities, his unfaltering faith in men, even in his enemies." It goes on to observe that Jesus' method of dealing with his enemies was "not through force, but through the power of love, culminating in his death upon the cross, where he died, the just for the unjust, the perfect for the imperfect, the strong for the weak" (79).

Boisen indicates that his transition into "the abnormal state" begins to become evident in this last sentence of the second paragraph. He recalls that the writing of this statement of belief "began without evidence of undue excitation beyond what may have been explicit in the plan itself, but about the end of the second paragraph a change occurs" (81). He

can remember distinctly how it came to me as I was sitting at my desk there in my sister's home on October 6, 1920, trying to determine what to say and pondering over what I had included in my ordination statement of nine years before. Suddenly there came surging into my mind with tremendous power this idea about the voluntary sacrifice of the weak for the sake of the strong. Along with this came a curious scheme which I copied down mechanically and kept repeating over and over again, as if learning a lesson. (81)

Where this scheme came from he "cannot imagine. I can remember nothing in my previous reading which would even remotely suggest it. It was indeed precisely this fact which so impressed me. Besides, the impact was terrific, and I felt myself caught up, as it were, into another world" (81–82). (The scheme, diagrammed, consists of a frame with four sections; the two top sections are designated "Strong" and "Perfect," the two lower sections are termed "Weak" and "Imperfect.")

The statement of belief continues in the third paragraph with the observation that for nineteen centuries the strong have been giving themselves for the weak and the perfect for the imperfect, and this has resulted in "a crossing process" (79). The divine "has been coming into the world disguised in ugliness, crippled by disease, shackled by sin, and impotent with weakness" (80).

The fourth paragraph states his belief that "the weak and the imperfect should no longer accept this sacrifice." "They should be willing to give their lives, the imperfect for the perfect and the weak for the strong," so that "the divine may be freed from its prison house of infirmity and be able to come into the world in health and in disguise" (80).

The fifth paragraph continues this theme by noting that "a better race" would come about were the weak and the imperfect to refuse "to accept their claim of pity and of need," a renunciation that would enable the divine "to overcome the world" (80).

The sixth paragraph expresses his belief "that the family should consist of four and not of two" (80). Here he seems to qualify the theme in previous paragraphs of the strong and perfect no longer sacrificing themselves for the weak and imperfect. He notes that in the joy of seeing and sharing in the happiness of those they love, they will find "compensation for the sacrifices which some will always have to make" (80). He also alludes to the guardian angels, who, with the strong and the perfect, make up the family-of-four. He suggests that they, "no longer in the darkness of the tomb, but in the light of life, may select for those they love the true mate and the true friend" (80).

Alluding to the diagram, he notes that whereas some of his ideas in this statement of belief receded over time, "the idea about the voluntary sacrifice of the weak for the strong and of the family-of-four remained constant, not only in this but in subsequent episodes" (82). This is what it seemed to mean:

It seemed that there were other men in the same position as myself. Their only hope of salvation lay in their love for some good woman, and in that fact lay hardship and suffering for the woman, and a real loss to society, since it would be only the finer-type of woman who would be moved by such an appeal. There ought to be a way out, and the family-of-four scheme seemed to provide the answer. The essence of this idea was that of producing a thoroughbred type of character by setting the best types free from the appeal of those whose love was based on need. This was to be done by letting them choose mates, each for the other. (82–83)

How this was to be accomplished was by no means clear, but the basic principle was that "the true lover must be willing to give his place to another and that all self-seeking must be ruled out" (83).

In effect, he was articulating in this statement of belief the earlier "abnormal condition" he had experienced in Washington, D. C., some fourteen years earlier. At that time he asked a fellow forester to accept his offer of his own beloved Alice: "This statement of Belief therefore demanded of me that I should give up the hope that had dominated my life for seventeen long years." At this point, he became clearly psychotic: "Everything then began to whirl. It seemed that the world was coming to an end" (83). Earth, a tiny organism in the vast universe, "was hurrying on at a rapidly accelerating speed toward some impending change" (83). After all these millions of years, humanity was just beginning to draw upon the earth's stored up resources, and already they were approaching exhaustion: "Some sort of change was due. Only a few of the tiny atoms we call 'men' were to be saved. I was not to be one of these. I might, however, be of help to others" (83).

CLEARLY PSYCHOTIC

Clearly, some "strange ideas" had come surging into his mind, "ideas of doom" but also "ideas of my own unsuspected importance" (79). The delusional quality of these ideas warrants his own conclusion that by the time he had completed his statement of belief he had become psychotic.

His excitement at the time was evidenced by the fact that the letter he immediately wrote to Fred Eastman to accompany the two statements was almost illegible due to "an improperly adjusted [typewriter] ribbon which I was too excited to fix" (84). In his letter to Fred, he acknowledges that he has been having "some strange ideas these last two weeks" and that "you may think that I am insane, for these problems with which I have been concerned lie beyond the usual. But some of them may be 'important'" (84). He goes on to describe his "family-of-four" plan which would do away with crossbreeding (strong mated with weak, perfect with imperfect). If such crossbreeding were eliminated, the current system, which produces "spiritual averages," would instead produce clearly delineated positives and negatives.

His own situation illustrates the problems with the current system. His father was a "strong-strong-imperfect" and this meant that his father's son was destined to be a "weak-weak-imperfect." This son of a strong father was therefore also destined to seek the love of a strong and presumably perfect woman. This, he now sees, has been a fundamental mistake, though one that is understandable and perhaps inevitable given the prevailing mating system and the cycle of generations. Sadly, "That man whose love is really nothing but a despairing call for help has little chance of finding that help in our present system of mating" (84).

He goes on to say in the letter that, despite appearances, his case "is not one of ordinary insanity" (84–85). After all, he "has not been bothered recently with troublesome thoughts, and the motive which has sustained me throughout this affair is not desire but the conviction that I was really acting in obedience to a divine command" (85). He had thought that the command "was to go forward, but it seems not. It is rather to get out of the way," and "it is time for me to give up" (85).

On the other hand, he feels "that there has been some definite purpose in this journey of mine," this purpose being "to give my place to some other man" (85). By doing this, there will be "a chance for my father and for what he could do in the world" (85). The implication here is that, by relinquishing his claim on Alice, another man, one of the strong type, will mate with Alice, and Boisen's father's legacy will be continued through their progeny. Strength will produce strength, and this will have been possible because the weak man, whose love for this "good woman" was based on need, will forgo his claim on her.

TAKEN AWAY

While the idea of the family-of-four that Boisen articulates in his letter to Eastman has a certain logic, Boisen found himself both "excited and bewildered." The ideas that were surging into his mind "were more and more foreign to my usual modes of thought" (86). For several days he said nothing to the family, then finally broke his silence and "began to share my fears" (86). As he did so, another source of terror arose, as it came to him "that there were other forces, hostile forces of which I had not dreamed before" (86). He felt that malevolent forces had been eavesdropping on his revelations to family members and that "the words which I had spoken would bring about my undoing, and defeat the causes with which I was concerned" (86). On Saturday afternoon, three days after he had written his statement of belief, he had a "sickening sensation," one that he could not account for, and "went down at once to see Mother and told her that something awful had happened. I did not know what it was, but I thought I had been 'betrayed'" (86). Then he went into the next room and found a man sitting there whom he did not recognize. The doctor whom his mother had summoned said nothing at the time, but later that evening six policemen entered his room and one of them announced that he had better come quietly or there would be trouble. He went quietly.

The Hospitalization

Boisen wrote an account of his hospitalization two and a half years later. It focuses on the week he spent at Boston Psychopathic Hospital before being transferred to Westboro State Hospital. This account, which he includes in his memoirs, begins by noting that even though it was only a week, "it seemed like thousands of years" (87). Throughout the entire period he was in "a violent delirium," often pounding on the door of his room and singing. How much of the time he was unconscious he does not know or recall, but he can remember "quite distinctly what was going on in my head as well as my actual behavior" (87).

As indicated earlier, his first memory was of Dr. Gale filling out the admission forms. The following morning he was lying on his bed in Ward 2 and overheard a nurse say that he was there on a homicidal and suicidal charge, which she considered a mistake, as he did not look in the least violent. She suggested his transfer to Ward 4. This overheard comment struck him "like a thunderbolt," as he knew that he had not the slightest thought of injuring anyone and, while he had held the idea of taking his own life for "a short time," he had "immediately rejected it" (88).

Viewing the World's End

The false charge, however, seemed "clear evidence that evil forces were at work" (and this suspicion was also evidence, in my view, that he was most likely suffering from paranoid schizophrenia). He was transferred to Ward 4 and invited by another patient to play checkers with him, but he could not continue the game because he was "too much absorbed in my own thoughts, particularly those regarding the approaching end of the world" (88).

By nightfall his head "was all in a whirl. It seemed to be the Day of Judgment, and all humanity came streaming in from four different directions," arriving in "a common center" (88). There, everyone was brought before the judgment seat, but each person judged himself. There were certain passwords; and they made certain choices, with each person having three choices. The first was a difficult "right the first time affair," the second involved an element of sacrifice and meant that one would become a woman and not a man, and the third was only an apparent chance that sent one at once to the lower regions (89). He had the impression that his consciousness had gone to a lower level, that something in the process had been short-circuited.

That night, as he lay in bed, the idea came surging into his head: "You are in the wrong place in this comfortable ward. You ought to be downstairs" (89). When he requested permission to go to the other ward, the attendant, seeming to miss the irony of his response, told him to go back to bed" or "we will have to take you to Ward 2." Boisen began to make a disturbance, calling out at the top of his lungs the first and craziest thing that came into his head, which happened to be, "I've got to go insane in order to get married."

New Worlds Forming

As a result, he was transferred back to Ward 2. Now, however, he began to feel himself joined with "some superhuman source of strength" and felt "new life pulsing" all through him (89). It seemed, too, that many new worlds were forming, with music, rhythms, and beauty everywhere. A choir of angels kept hovering over the hospital, and he heard something about a little lamb being born in the room just above his own. When he made inquiries about the little lamb the next day, another patient, apparently mocking him, said that a lamb had in fact entered his room the night before. This not only confirmed Boisen's belief but also led him to accept his fellow patient as "the embodiment of a very exalted personage" who had assumed the form of this rather loathsome-looking man (90).

It was a case, in other words, of the problem that he had identified in his statement of belief, that the strong and the perfect are in the world in the disguise of the weak and imperfect. He continued to worry about the little lamb and kept inquiring about it until, at last, the idea came to him that the doctors had immediately killed it and preserved it in alcohol because of its scientific interest.

Later in the day a psychiatrist visited him and said he had been informed that Boisen "had some important ideas about saving people." The doctor asked if he would be willing to talk about them. But he replied that he would rather not, and the doctor left. The next night he was visited not by angels but by a whole lot of witches. He felt the presence of detectives out to locate the exact place where he was. By stuffing his blanket in the ventilator shaft, he felt he had not only succeeded in checking the invasion of black cats but also had found "some sort of process of regeneration which could be used to save other people" (91).

He was instructed to feel the back of his neck. There he would find "a sign of my new mission" (91). The next day when a psychiatrist asked him why he had stufffed his blanket into the ventilator shaft, he felt the "evil gleam" in the doctor's eye and made some remark about the sign on his neck. The doctor "laughed a peculiar laugh and said he'd better put some iodine on it" (91). But Boisen broke away and told him to be careful: "He seemed to be frightened, though I had no thought of touching him" (91).

Cold-pack Treatment

An examination by the staff took place that day, during which he was asked about his ideas of the "family-of-four" and his "delusions of grandeur." The examination resulted in his being placed in a cold-pack. At the time, he felt this treatment was due to his admission that he was "a very exalted personage" and that the staff either wanted to exploit him in some horrible way or hoped to disabuse him of his ideas of grandeur. He recalls hoping that they might succeed in the latter purpose because these ideas were agonizing, but the only thing that happened was that the cold-pack caused him to lose consciousness (92).

The following morning, he felt he was in some labyrinthine tunnel deep in the recesses of the earth. A little later he came upon a horse blanket in which some peculiar white linen fabric was wrapped. Then he came upon some sacred relics, which were connected with the search for the Holy Grail "and represented the profoundest spiritual struggle of the centuries" (93). Then he heard the most beautiful voice he had ever heard and realized that it was the celebration of the Last Supper. In the morning, he refused to eat the food he was provided because he suspected it was drugged. He heard voices repeating the phrase, "little lamb, little lamb," over and over again in a singsong fashion that sounded insincere. He thought he recognized in the priest who was conducting this ritual an attendant whom he tried to befriend despite his suspicion that the food he was bringing him was drugged (93).

At this point, he could no longer distinguish day from night and felt he was "an old stallion who had remained behind at the time of the flood in order to help his friends escape and had been forgotten by them" (93–94). Boisen recalls that he became wilder and wilder during this phase of his psychosis, singing, shouting, and pounding on the door of his room with his fists and elbows. This led to his being placed in a cold-pack once more.

Then he experienced himself in the Moon (Boisen's capitalization). The Moon, he perceived, was the abode of departed spirits who were at the mercy of the medical men. These medical men would spirit them away and bury them alive in a cell in the Moon, "while in the meantime some designing person, a sort of double, would take their place in this world" (94). He discerned that the medical men "were frankly and openly concerned with the problem of reproduction and of sex," and he found this "appalling" (94). What happened when one arrived on the Moon was that one's gender was likely to change, and what the doctors wanted to know was whether one was a man or a woman.

When they examined Boisen, he heard them say in great surprise, "He is a perfect neutral" (94). This meant that they could not consign him to either side "and thus they had no power over me," and in this "lay my hope of safety" (94). Another source of salvation was the injunction, "tell the exact truth" instead of depending on tokens and passwords as others did. It was very important to be on one's guard as the doctors would chop off heads and send the bodies down an invisible chute to the lower regions (95).

At some point, he succeeded in climbing into the Sun, but through some clumsiness he destroyed the balance of things. As a result, thousands of his friends and relatives lost their lives. He was engaged in the effort of restoring the balance, which also involved keeping his room from tipping up and sending everything down to the lower regions, when several men, accompanied by a psychiatrist, entered his room and told him to put on his clothes. He perceived this as a plot to undo him, so he resisted. They had come to take him to Westboro State Hospital. He concludes the account of his week at Boston Psychopathic Hospital on this ironic note: "I had therefore the honor of being transported to Westboro in a strait jacket" (95).

Figuring Out What Happened

At Westboro State Hospital, he remained acutely disturbed for about two weeks. Then, as though waking from a nightmare, he "snapped out of it" (95). He was placed in the convalescent ward, and over the next several weeks he tried "to figure out what had happened to me" (95). In the months that followed, he wrote several letters that reflect these efforts. As the length of his hospitalization was fifteen months (he was released at the end of January in 1922), he had ample time to engage in this self-study; as he put it in a letter to Fred Eastman, he would "try to analyze my own case" (97).

A letter to Fred in late November, six weeks after his transfer to Westboro, contains his initial efforts to understand what had happened. He suggests that what precipitated his psychosis was "a sort of autohypnosis" (98). He recalls a discussion in one of Professor George A. Coe's seminars at Union Theological Seminary on the various methods of inducing the hypnotic condition. Coe had been a student of William James, whose *Principles of Psychology* Boisen had read in a course taught by William Lowe Bryan at Indiana University; James was very interested in the powers of hypnosis to reveal the subconscious mind.

Psychosis and Autohypnosis

Boisen notes that what was brought out in this discussion was that the key to hypnosis lay in the narrowing of attention to a single object or idea. One of his classmates had gone home and fixed his attention on an electric light bulb. The experiment succeeded. He fell into a trance, but he injured his eyes. This illustration seems significant in view of the permanent eye injury that Boisen himself suffered when he tried not to wink as the other boy aimed and fired his toy gun. In any event, as the classmate's experiment was a form of autohypnosis, so, in Boisen's view, was his own psychosis, though in his case it was not an object but an idea that was the focus of his attention. He does not identify the idea here, but it was undoubtedly the "family-of-four" idea that had figured so prominently in his statement of belief.

Why, though, would such autohypnosis result in psychosis? Boisen believes the psychosis was due to his assumption, a false one, that "an idea carried authority because of the way in which it came," that is, via what was, in effect, a trance state (98). He does not make a connection between this observation and his earlier experiences of seeing obscene words leaping off the pages of his Greek dictionary, or of his eye lighting on specific Bible verses when he opened the Bible at random. All these cases bear a certain similarity in that he seems to be the passive recipient of an intervention by an external agent. This, too, is not unlike the episode in which he lost the use of his left eye.

Ideas of Grandeur Analyzed

In the letter to Eastman, however, he admits to being "especially puzzled regarding the origin and significance of my ideas of grandeur. How is it possible that I could ever fancy myself in such exalted roles as I did in the insane period?" (98). He proposes two related explanations. First, if you have given "everything you have for a certain end and you then feel yourself called upon to give that thing up, it is equivalent to giving up your life" (98). Second, when you give up everything that makes life worthwhile, you do not care about anything else (wealth, power, honor) and therefore you "feel no enormity in the ideas of grandeur, much as you may later be horrified by them. They are felt rather as a burden which is wholly unwanted" (99). Thus, the ideas of grandeur, such as the idea that one has a special mission to save thousands and thousands of people, derive from the fact that one has renounced everything, including life itself. Such renunciation qualifies one to become the savior of others.

As for the ideas that came to him during his psychosis, beginning in the middle of the second paragraph of his statement of belief, he will not "attempt an explanation." But he insists that "periods of crisis are fertile in suggestions, some of which may stand the test of experience and some may not" (99). Their authority at the time, however, derived from the fact that "they were so absolutely different from anything I had thought of or heard of before, and because they came surging into my mind with such a rush" (99).

Later in the letter, Boisen provides an explanation for why his delusions persisted as long as they did. It had to do with the appearance of the Moon. Each time the Moon appeared, it was centered in a cross of light. At the time, he viewed this as proof that he was right in ascribing "great importance" to what was happening to him: "The cross stands for suffering. Therefore the Moon knows, and the Moon is suffering on my account" (102).

But one night as he lay awake on the sleeping porch "speculating on this dire portent," he made a discovery: "When I changed my position to a certain spot, the cross no longer appeared. The explanation was simple. From that particular spot I was looking at the Moon through a hole in the wire screening!" (101). This discovery, plus the fact that his sister and Fred Eastman visited him the following day, was "a big help toward recovery." After that he "improved rapidly and within a week I was transferred to the convalescent ward" (101). It is worthy of note that the hallucination in this case was a visual, not an auditory one, thus more readily amenable to his own efforts to challenge its authority. Of course, the fact that the hallucination was visual points back to the trauma of the loss of his eye in childhood.

Curing the Abnormality

He concludes the letter to Eastman with this comment on why he has taken the trouble to provide a "long and wearisome and fragmentary account of a very unpleasant experience" (101). The reason for engaging in this exercise is that it reflects "a very important principle," which is that "the cure has lain in the faithful carrying through of the delusion itself" (101). If, in other words, the abnormality is in the mind, then the only way that a cure may be effected is if this abnormality is subjected to a thoroughgoing analysis. The only one in a position to make such an analysis is the one who knows the content and features of these abnormal thoughts.

Because the staff at Westboro focused on physical restraint rather than the mental processes, he believes that the treatments he received there were of little value. Moreover, it is his impression that most of the doctors view religion as a superstition "which is responsible for many of the ills they have to treat." They are, therefore, poorly fitted to deal with religious problems: "If they succeed in their aims, the patient is shorn of the faith in which lives his hope of cure" (102). He recognized from the outset "the abnormal character of my own experiences" and the fact that they "would be classed by physicians as insanity," but he believes that "this experience, painful though it is, may be an adventure of which use can be made" (102). He now shudders to think that he could have been hospitalized in Washington when he was with the Forestry Service, in which case "it would probably have been fatal" (102). Why? Because he would not then have had the capacity to engage in the analysis of the experience that he has presented here.

Reading Freud

In a subsequent letter to Eastman two weeks later, Boisen acknowledges Fred's gift of Sigmund Freud's *Introductory Lectures* (first published in English translation in 1920). He alludes to his excitement in discovering that "Freud's conclusions are so strikingly in line with those which I had already formed that it makes me believe in myself a little bit once more" (Boisen 1960, 103). Freud, he has discovered, contends that "the cure is to be found not in the suppression of the symptoms but in the solution of the conflict." This, Boisen notes, "is just what I tried to say in my last letter" (103). He goes on to note Freud's view that in practically every case of successful treatment in which the sex instinct is involved, the patient's affections are transferred to the physician. Then the transference is redirected, sublimated, or eliminated when the right time comes, and this marks the completion of the cure.

Interpreting the Family-of-four Idea

Boisen believes that his "family-of-four" idea was an attempt to express this principle. His idea recognizes that there are those, like himself, for whom "the hope of salvation is involved with sexual love." It also asserts that those in whom the needy ones pin their hopes of salvation (the Alice Batchelders of this world) have no obligation to respond: "It seemed to me that the finest men and the finest women are precisely the ones most likely to respond to the appeal of weakness and of need. Such a response has had blaming attached to it, but it has also meant sacrifice which should not have to be made" (104).

The "family-of-four" idea provided the rationale for "the destruction or sublimation of the transference relationship" and thus "the completion of a process which has been going on for many years." In a footnote to this statement, Boisen adds, "I remember clearly what I meant here. The 'physician' in my case would be Alice" (104). He directs the reader to the page where he related his opening the Bible at random and hitting upon John 19:27—"Then said he to his disciple, 'Behold thy mother!'"—and where he interpreted this to mean that his love for Alice "was really a desperate cry for salvation and an appeal to a beloved person stronger than myself" (55).

If Alice was his "physician," the one onto whom he "transferred" his affections (affections that she, in denying their direct satisfaction, causes to be destroyed or sublimated onto another object), the John 19:27 text suggests that the original object of his affections would have been his mother. In fact, there is a sort of "crossing process" in this verse in John, as Jesus hands his mother over to his faithful friend, the disciple John. This was Jesus' ultimate sacrifice before he breathed his last.

If Boisen saw Fred Eastman as the equivalent of Jesus' disciple John, he does not say so, but this would fit with his asking Fred, in the letter he wrote immediately after composing his statement of belief, to "go and see her [Alice] and lay the case before her. You have been a perfect friend. Therefore I dare to ask this of you. My thought would be a quiet ceremony, a little time together. Then I would eliminate myself. I could not ask such a thing for myself, but only for my father" (85). Thus, we may perhaps conclude that, for Boisen, the underlying problem was his desire to be the object of his mother's love, a desire that was transferred onto Alice.

Affections: Destroyed or Redirected?

If so, were the affections bestowed on Alice to be destroyed altogether, or were they to be sublimated and redirected toward some other object or objective? Writing in 1920, and only recently introduced to Freud's writings, Boisen would not have been expected to know about Freud's case of Daniel Schreber (Freud 1993; first published in German in 1911). Schreber had been hospitalized at the age of forty-two after having a devastating psychotic episode. He had a second episode nine years later. Freud points out that while Schreber's delusions appear to be entirely pathological—after all, they are extremely bizarre—their appearance signals, in fact, "an attempt at recovery." The delusions are a projection of what had been repressed, so that "what was abolished internally returns" from the unconscious region to which it has been assigned (142).

In addition, Freud provides an explanation of what happens to the "sex instinct" in psychosis: It is transferred from the other to oneself. This very transfer explains the megalomania (or ideas of grandeur) that are a feature of the psychotic delusion. In fact, the psychosis begins when the individual relinquishes his claim on the person he loves, as Boisen does in the case of Alice, by "giving" her to "another man." In Freud's view, however, the sexual desires that were directed toward the other person—in this case, Alice—must go somewhere. In the psychosis itself, they are self-directed (141). Developmentally, megalomania is of "an infantile nature" and is "sacrificed to social conditions" as development proceeds (141). It returns in psychosis, however, and does so precisely at that point where one abandons any claims on another, as happens in Boisen's case.

More Psychotic Episodes

Of course, megalomania is not a cure. As Boisen recognized, the very ideas of grandeur that seem appropriate and valid in the psychotic episode may be viewed with horror when one wakes up from this terrible nightmare. The cure in his own case lay ultimately in the redirection of the sexual instincts in the form of a creative enterprise, a redirection implied in his view that this personal experience "may be an adventure of which use can be made" (Boisen 1960, 102).

We recall that he began work on his statements of religious experience and belief when he was waiting for a call and was becoming increasingly frustrated that none seemed forthcoming. The fact that he was unmarried made him, at this age, less desirable than other men. But the aftermath of this "adventure" was the offer of the position of chaplain at Worcester State Hospital. As my concern here has been to focus on the experiences and events that led up to his psychotic break and the psychosis itself, I will not discuss his account of his life following his release from Westboro State Hospital in 1922. But this account of his plunge into mental illness would not be complete if note were not taken of the fact that he continued to write to Alice. At one point he even proposed that she might "share in the new task which I saw opening before me," a proposal that elicited a "sharp and decisive" no (153).

Also, a letter written less than three months following his release from Westboro contains a paragraph that is especially interesting in light of the suggestion above that he had transferred to Alice his desire to be the object of his mother's unconditional love. He tells Alice that he had gathered flowers from the place in New Hampshire where they had their ill-fated rendevous eleven years earlier and had wanted to send them to her. But he decided to "send them to Mother instead–who will get them fresh in the morning" (146).

The Second Episode

Also imbedded in this chapter on his adventure in theological education is an account of his second psychotic episode, one that did not lead to the prolonged hospitalization of his earlier episode, but one that he also believes lacked the empowering significance of the previous one. This episode occurred in November, 1930, just after his mother died. We should therefore assume that he was in a vulnerable emotional state at the time due to the loss of his mother, of whom he writes in tribute:

> My indebtedness to Mother cannot be measured. She lived for her children and made every sacrifice in order that they might have their chance to develop. Perhaps her most important characteristic was her faith in us. She was even too careful to leave us free to choose for ourselves. There was thus no word of reproach when I failed to make the grade after graduation in 1897. She acceded at once to my change of profession in 1903, and again in 1908. And finally in 1922, it was her faith in me that made possible the new undertaking. Not only did she back me financially to the limit of

her resources, but in the dark days at Westboro she always stood by me, and her beautifully written letters brought their all-important message of comfort and faith. (168)

The Other Woman

On the very next page, he begins his account of his second "acute psychotic episode" (169). While he lacks the full data he had for the previous episode almost exactly ten years earlier, "the causative factors are fairly clear." "There were complications in my relationship with Alice. The shadow of another, younger woman lay between us. It was a gracious shadow, sanctioned, seemingly, by the idea of the family-of-four, which had been so strangely insistent during the psychotic episodes" (169). This woman knew about Alice, and Alice knew about her, and there "was no disloyalty to either one" (169). He had even discussed the situation with Alice, and, as always, found her "wise and helpful. But it was hard to see the way, and I was greatly troubled. The climax came as a delayed reaction following a meeting of the three of us, held at my suggestion, when the finding of the right solution became for me an urgent problem" (169).

He does not identify this other woman by name, but references to Helen Dunbar at this point in the narrative indicate that it was she. He had met Helen in 1925 at Union Theological Seminary where he had gone to recruit students for his fledgling educational program at Worcester State Hospital. He had stopped by Union on his return from a trip to Chicago, during which Alice had refused to see him, a refusal that for some unexplained reason "was for me a particularly significant one" (154). Dunbar worked at Worcester during the summer of 1925 and in the spring of 1927. She was now a Yale Medical School student and wanted to study the symbolism of schizophrenic patients. In January, 1930, a council for the clinical training of theological students was formed. Boisen was appointed secretary, and Dunbar was appointed medical director.

This was the situation that prevailed at the time his mother died. He was again seeing Alice, and he was working closely with Helen. His "family-of-four" concept seemed to "sanction" his relationship with "the younger woman," but how it did so was apparently unclear, even or especially to Boisen himself. The psychotic episode followed, as did the previous one, "a period of intensified absorption and prayer" (169). He was working on a version of the hymnal for the patients at Worcester State Hospital. He had initially developed the hymnal in 1925, the year he met Helen. It was published in 1926 under the title, *Lift Up Your Hearts: A Service-book for Use in Hospitals* (Boisen 1926). As he worked on the revision of the hymnal, he began to experience "a period of uncontrollable sobbing. It seemed that something which ought to have been was not to be. I had failed, and the world was in danger. In great distress of mind I started forth in my car" (169).

Renewed Hospitalization

He first looked up Philip Guiles, who was the field secretary of the new council, and turned over to him the responsibility for the project. Then he drove to his sister's house, then to a cousin's home in Exeter, New Hampshire, then back to Boston, where he took a train to New York. He returned to Boston and called on Dr. Richard Cabot, president and treasurer of the new council. On this occasion, he identified with his father and inquired about himself in the third person. Cabot arranged for his hospitalization.

In his delusional state, he experienced himself as a very important person whose failure was chiefly responsible for the fact that the world, which was supposed to become a brilliant star, was to be a Milky Way instead. His disturbed state cleared up in three weeks, and "So far as I can determine, I was none the worse for it. In fact, it solved the problem which had occasioned it. The two women both stood by me, but they could not ignore the seriousness of the disturbance, and my attempt to interpret the family-of-four idea in accordance with my own wishes was definitely ended" (170).

Where this episode differed from the earlier one is that it served no real constructive purpose, but merely "saved me from a situation which should not have arisen" (170). Furthermore, Cabot decreed that Boisen was to have nothing further to do with the program of instruction to which the council was dedicated, and Guiles agreed. Only the support of Helen Dunbar made it possible for him to continue, but, shortly thereafter, he left Worcester and took a chaplaincy position at Elgin State Hospital in Illinois.

The Third Episode

This move enabled him to see Alice on a fairly regular basis until, in April, 1935, he received a note from her indicating that she was going to have an operation and would not receive callers. He learned shortly thereafter that she was suffering from a terminal cancer, and she died four months later. Between the time he received her note and her death, he suffered a third psychotic episode. At the time of her death, he was in a hospital in Baltimore, where members of his clinical training group had arranged for him to stay (177). In this episode, he again had the idea that the earth became only a Milky Way instead of a brilliant star. He also recalls "identifying myself with my father, and feeling that he was getting old and would be unable to carry on much longer" (177).

The Question of Causality

A question that naturally arises from Boisen's account of his mental illness is that of causality. The cause of mental illness is one of the five c's (along with characteristics, course, consequences, and cure) that warrant the attention of students of mental illness. One value of a two-hundred-page memoir like *Out of the Depths* is that it challenges any attempt to answer this question in a simplistic way. In the final chapter of the book, titled "Observations and Reflections," Boisen comes closest to his own answer to this question when he suggests that the "basis of the conflict" was "the sexual hypersensitivity which caused me so much agony in the adolescent period" (198). He thought of himself at that time in his life as having "a diseased mind." Because he thought so, this raises for him the question whether he "exaggerated the trouble" and "worked myself up into a morbid condition over something which was not so bad after all" (198). Was his sense of guilt, in Henry Emerson Fosdick's phrase, a "needless and harmful intruder"? (Fosdick 1943, 150). Was a "measure of intelligent common sense about a small prohibitory detail" all that he really needed? (Boisen 1960, 198).

Boisen's Explanation

He would like to believe this, but cannot. The fact of the matter is that he was "fighting a losing battle on a crucially important front" in the years preceding his decision to study forestry. He was "a really sick person" in need of something "more thoroughgoing than intelligent common sense" (198–99). In his own view, the "present-day tendency to seek the solution of a troublesome sex drive by lowering the conscience threshold and looking upon sex as a natural desire to be lightly satisfied" is "a serious mistake" (199).

From a purely biological standpoint, "the sex drive has to do with the perpetuation and improvement of the race." Therefore, despite the fact that the control of the sex drive "gives rise to difficult problems," the solution "is surely not to be found in easy self-indulgence, at least for those who are concerned with the realization of the personal and social potentialities that ought to be" (199). As such a person, he has "no regret for the anxiety and distress of mind which I suffered in those early years, but only for my stupidity and failure to learn the elements of self-discipline" (199). His own explanation for his psychosis, then, focuses on his failure to exercise adequate self-control over—and in light of—his "sexual hypersensitivity."

Psychotic Episodes as Problem–solving Experiences

Later in this relatively brief concluding chapter, however, he puts forward a somewhat different explanation for his psychotic episodes: "severe though they were, they have been for me problem-solving experiences." In this sense, "They have left me not worse but better" (202). While it may seem a bit odd to suggest that psychosis is a way for a person to extricate himself from an intolerable social situation, Boisen provides quite a lot of evidentiary support for this assessment. As noted earlier, his first illness coincided with a period in his life when he was unemployed. Also, the psychotic episode of November, 1930, seems to have extracted him from an untenable situation involving two women, and he even refers to his psychotic breakdown in 1935 following his discovery that Alice was dying as "another problem-solving experience" (177).

This view of his psychotic episodes as a form of problem solving has support in Erik Erikson's suggestion that "patienthood" is an identity, albeit a largely negative one. A person may choose the patient identity—however unself-consciously—to solve a difficult life problem, especially one that involves a commitment he is about to make or about which he is deeply conflicted (Erikson 1968, 179). "Patienthood," of course, is a rather drastic and inefficient way to solve a problem. The very fact that a psychotic patient may have delusions of grandeur—such as Boisen's perception that he was responsible for the salvation of thousands of souls—may provide a justification, however delusional it may be, for the enormous personal cost involved.

Boisen's view that his psychotic episodes were a form of problem solving would also receive support from cognitive therapists. As Paul French and Anthony P. Morrison (2004) have pointed out, some psychoses may be averted if the individual is provided problem-oriented interventions. These typically involve identifying the problem and translating the problem-identification into a goal. This translation includes assessment of one's interpretations of the problem situation and developing interpretations that are more accurate (that is, are based on truer perceptions of the situation) and more conducive to the solution of the problem.

Thus, Boisen's view that his psychotic episodes were "problem-solving experiences" seems correct, but it may also be said that had he been able to solve these problems in a more normal, less drastic way, he may not have had to experience psychosis. The interpretations that he placed on the problem situation were virtually destined to fail as problem-solving constructions because they were overly complex. His family-of-four concept is a case in point, for he, himself, could not figure out its implications or even relevance to the situation in which he found himself prior to the November, 1930, psychotic episode.

Preadolescent Events and Psychosis

In any event, the underlying cause of his mental illness was, to Boisen, the "sexual hypersensitivity" that arose in his adolescence, and his memoir may thus be viewed as an account of his efforts, largely ineffective, to deal with this perceived problem. Writing in his eighties, he does not believe that he was mistaken about the seriousness of the problem, as he rejects the idea that what he was experiencing was normal for adolescent boys. What he does not do, despite his professed enthusiasm for Freud's writings, is to go back to earlier events in his life, to his preadolescent experiences, to understand his "abnormal" condition.

HIS FATHER'S DEATH

If he were to have done so, it would seem that he would have given greater attention to the two events that occurred within months of one another: the death of his father three months after he turned seven, and the injury to his eye shortly before his eighth birthday. The fact that his father figured quite prominently in his delusions in all three episodes is strong evidence that his father's death had affected him a great deal more than his brief account of the event itself indicates.

He does, however, note that his father's memory "has remained a potent force in my life, one which for me has been associated with my idea of God" (Boisen 1960, 27). He also notes that one effect of his father's death was that his mother "did little with her music afterward" (27). This observation may have relevance to the fact that he was working on a revision of his hymnal when he experienced "a period of uncontrollable sobbing." Subsequently, he experienced himself identifying with his father and inquiring about himself in the third person, as though his father had returned to discover how his son was faring.

LOSING SIGHT IN HIS LEFT EYE

While his loss of sight in his left eye may not seem to have any direct connection with his subsequent mental illness, a growing body of research literature suggests a possible connection. In *Origins of Mental Illness* (1995), Gordon Claridge notes that "the attention defect in schizophrenia appears to be demonstrable as a disorder of eye movements, specifically in the smooth pursuit or tracking movements required when following, say, a swinging pendulum" (184). He notes the work of P. S. Holzman, the author of several of the important studies in this field. Holzman suggests "that the pattern of eye movement in schizophrenia may reflect a weakening of inhibitory controls in the brain" and that this is just one aspect of (quoting Holzman) a "general organismic instability...which manifests itself as inhibition in many spheres, cognitive, perceptual, and affective" (184; Holzman, 1978.)

Boisen minimizes his perceptual difficulties owing to the loss of his left eye ("Its loss may have had an adverse effect upon my skill on the ballfield and the tennis court, but I have not been aware of the difference" [1960, 32]). But these difficulties may have combined with the heightened sexual feelings of adolescence to produce such phenomena as the obscene words leaping out of his Greek dictionary and "hitting" him in the other eye. If so, this experience of unusual or abnormal visual perception when involved with a text may also have influenced him to employ the method of opening the Bible at random (a method his mind told him was "rank superstition"). He may have employed the method of closing his eye and using his index finger to identify the appointed verse. It is also possible that he stared at a page of scripture until a verse leaped off the page, a religious version of obscene words leaping off the pages of his Greek dictionary. Interestingly enough, the "Behold thy mother" verse in John 19:27 is about looking and viewing, and it may, in fact, have excited long repressed feelings relating to seeing her in a state of undress. Alice may have stimulated similar anxieties.

In his article on Boisen as autobiographer, James E. Dittes disputes Boisen's claim that the effects of his eye loss were negligible. He notes that "monocular vision does make a difference: it deprives the person of the principle capacity for depth perception. The author's not noting the difference illustrates the point" (1990, 225). Although Dittes goes on to discuss the relative absence of in-depth interpretations of the experiences that Boisen "unblinkingly" recounts, thus viewing the loss of the left eye metaphorically, it may be that this very loss of depth perception resulted in a different form of perception, that of words and phrases hitting him in the eye and forcing him to pay attention to these and not the other words and phrases on the page. Thus, where depth perception affords background, contextualization, and perspective, the very absence of depth perception may alert a person to the power of the foreground, to *its* ability to leap off the page and force the viewer to pay attention to it and only it. This creates the perceptual conditions for obsessive thinking.[2]

In short, Holzman suggests that "the pattern of eye movement observed in schizophrenia may reflect a weakening of inhibitory controls in the brain." This is just one "aspect of a general organismic instability" manifesting itself as the weakening of inhibitory controls in cognitive, perceptual, and affective spheres. This suggestion seems to have particular relevance in Boisen's case, as he understood his problem to be that of fighting for control of his sexual instincts. These instincts were first aroused in the act of reading French novels, thus, a combination of perceptual (visual) cues and emotional arousal. Perhaps from a neurological standpoint, this was more than his brain could handle, and he suffered a sort of cognitive instability as well, a kind of mental dizziness or panic, as reflected in his sense that ideas came "surging" into his mind.

The Events at Four Years Old

If his father's death and his loss of his left eye had some bearing on Boisen's susceptibility to mental illness later in life, might not the same be said for the two events that occurred in his fourth year of life—the circumcision intended to cure an abnormal "sex-organ excitation" and his being caught in the act of "some mutual explorations with a boy cousin about a year younger"? (24–25).

CIRCUMCISION

The fact that his circumcision took place when he was old enough to know that the operation was taking place but not old enough to know what, in fact, was being cut off or removed suggests that Freud's ideas about "castration anxiety" are neither irrelevant nor extreme. If Boisen read all of Freud's *Introductory Lectures on Psycho-Analysis* (the fact that he cited Freud's comments about a patient transferring his affections onto the doctor, which occurs in the next to last lecture, suggests that he did), then he may well have come across the following quotation from a much earlier lecture:

> It is by no means a rare thing, for instance, for a little boy, who is beginning to play with his penis in a naughty way and is not yet aware that one must conceal such activities, to be threatened by a parent or nurse with having his penis or his sinful hand cut off. Parents will often admit this when they are asked, since they think they have done something useful in making such a threat; a number of people have a correct conscious memory of such a threat, especially if it was made at a somewhat later period. If the threat is delivered by the mother or some other female she usually shifts its performance on to the father—or the doctor. (Freud 1989, 459)

Freud continues, "these events of childhood...are among the essential elements of a neurosis" (461). Of course, Freud would not contend that "castration anxiety" would be a sufficient explanation for a subsequent psychotic breakdown. But, as Claridge argues, anxiety seems to be at the root of all mental disorders (1995, 89ff). The threat of castration would certainly be among the greatest sources of anxiety in a young boy, especially if the medical procedure did not have the desired result (meaning that he continued to do the things that the procedure was intended to inhibit).

SEXUAL EXPLORATIONS WITH HIS COUSIN

The episode involving the boy cousin, following on the heels of his circumcision, is significant not only for the fact that he involved another boy in his sexual explorations but also because it created a special, but highly ambiguous bond between himself and his mother. On the one hand, he still remembers "the horror on my mother's face." On the other, he recalls "her volunteered promise that she would not tell my father" (Boisen 1960, 25).

The word "volunteered" is important, for it indicates that he did not ask that she keep it secret from his father. In fact, he may well have wanted his father to be told so that there could be an openness between them. Moreover, her promise that she would not tell his father was a form of emotional blackmail that he could never pay in full. Again, this episode would not be a sufficient explanation for his subsequent psychotic breakdown, but it created a problematic dynamic in his relations with both parents. This was then exacerbated in the two events of his seventh year, his father's death and his own second psychophysical catastrophe, the loss of his left eye. Interestingly enough, Freud makes an association between anxiety connected to the eyes and the dread of castration (1958, 137–38).

In the final analysis, however, these early childhood experiences–the two related events at age four and the two associated events at age seven–are probably most significant for their bearing on what he felt to be his special burden as the son in the family. The very fact that his "family-of-four" played a major role in his first psychotic episode, when his delusions of grandeur were the most pronounced, suggests that his delusions were not only an attempt at self-cure but also had the purpose of saving–even restoring–his family.

This attempt may be traced to his father's early death, for it was then that the family-of-four (father, mother, brother, sister) was reduced to an asymmetrical, imperfectly balanced family of three. Thus, in addition to their possible role as causal factors in his susceptibility to mental illness, early family dynamics were implicated in his perception that his own family of origin was a problem to be solved. This problem could only be solved, if at all, by addressing the flaws inherent in the whole history of the human family. His psychosis taught him that he was, after all, unequal to the task.

Precursors to Psychosis?

Another approach to the question of how Boisen became mentally ill is to ask whether other diagnoses, less severe than that of schizophrenia, would have applicability in earlier periods of his life, and if so, were these precursors to his eventual psychosis? Two possibilities present themselves.

OBSESSIVE-COMPULSIVE DISORDER

One is that he suffered early in his life from one of the anxiety disorders, most likely obsessive-compulsive disorder, and that this disorder eventually evolved into psychosis (in this case, paranoid schizophrenia). In the article on Boisen cited above, Dittes points out that the "central theme of the book, the lifelong infatuation–*obsession, really*– with Alice Batchelder, cries out for probing analysis" (1990, 226, my emphasis). He contends that there is, in fact, very little of such analysis in Boisen's memoir.

I suggest that this is precisely because Alice Batchelder *was*, in fact, for Boisen, an obsession. Dittes points out that Alice was the object of "a passion heavily and obviously determined by Boisen's inner world, projected onto a figure he never had an opportunity to know well and who steadily discouraged his affection. He fell in love with her at first sight (while she was giving a public lecture) and pursued a relationship which was characterized by distance, geographical and emotional, and by periods of up to several years without even any correspondence" (226–27).

It would not be inaccurate to say, therefore, that he fell in love with the "idea" of Alice Batchelder and held onto this idea even when the real Alice Batchelder deviated from it. As the *DSM-IV* describes an obsessive idea, she became "a recurrent and persistent" thought, one that, despite his own protestations to the contrary, was "intrusive, and inappropriate and that caused marked anxiety or distress" (*DSM-IV*, 418).

If Boisen suffered from obsessive-compulsive disorder, it makes sense to suggest that it had its origins in the traumatic events of his seventh year. Perhaps as a way to demonstrate that he could handle his father's death or any other calamity that might come his way, he compulsively refused to blink when the iron nail approached his eye. The writing of letters to Alice may also have had a sort of compulsiveness about them. Even his selection of Alice may have been based on an obsessional linking of their initials, *A*nton *B*oisen and *A*lice *B*atchelder. And, of course, the fact that he used the method of opening the Bible at random to find a verse meant for him in his current predicament, and did so despite his conscious awareness that this method was "rank superstition," suggests the convergence of obsessional thinking and compulsive behavior.

This suggestion that he was suffering from obsessive-compulsive disorder is relevant to his subsequent psychosis because, according to the *DSM-IV*, an "obsession may reach delusional proportions" (421). The *DSM-IV* also notes that "the ruminative delusional thoughts and bizarre stereotyped behaviors that occur in *Schizophrenia* are distinguished from obsessions and compulsions by the fact that they are not ego-dystonic and not subject to reality-testing. However, some individuals manifest symptoms of both Obsessive-Compulsive Disorder and Schizophrenia and warrant diagnoses" (422).

Thus, the obsessional idea becomes delusional when "reality-testing" is lost. Throughout his memoir, Boisen relates how he drew an inference from something Alice had written in a letter. He responded on the basis of this inference, only to be informed that he had misinterpreted the meaning of the comment. This happened, for example, when he took Alice's comment about her "skill in keeping house and making doughnuts" as "an opening." While he seems justified in coming to this conclusion, this comment of hers as presented in the book is not in context. Thus, his having seized upon it may, perhaps, have been similar to his practice of seeing a particular biblical verse in high relief.

In any event, repeated experiences of this sort could well result in a tendency to doubt or mistrust his inferential capacities, which in turn might lead him to believe that the true meaning of any human interaction is not what it appears on the surface to be. This may well create the conditions for an obsessional idea to reach delusional proportions. The paradox, then, is that as Alice repeatedly informed him that he had misconstrued her meaning, his obsessional idea of her would become more, not less, susceptible to reaching delusional levels.

In their book on early detection of persons at risk of developing psychoses, French and Morrison indicate that persons who are disposed toward obsessional thinking are at high risk for becoming psychotic (2004, 87). This is because obsessional thoughts persist despite the existence of information that challenges or contradicts them. Obsessional thoughts are, therefore, on a continuum with delusional thinking.

If, as suggested, "Alice" was such an obsessional idea, this may explain why Boisen could ignore signals from the real Alice that other men would have accepted as permanent and irrevocable rejection, leading them to direct their attention toward some other "good woman." The very idea that there was only one woman in all the world who could be his is itself a reflection of obsessional thinking. This idea may have then been reinforced by his religious beliefs, which led him to assume that there is more to be discerned in human affairs than readily meets the eye. Thus, when she failed to respond to his letters shortly after their first of many separations, he recognized "that she meant what she said" when she expressed her desire "that our relationship should cease entirely" (Boisen, 1960, 82). His random search for a more authoritative answer, however, produced a very different view: "My eye fell upon the words, 'Ask and ye shall receive...'" (53, Mt. 7:7, Boisen's version).

A man *less* inclined to seek for deeper answers may well have taken Alice's response at face value and moved on from there. In other words, his religious beliefs supported his obsessional thinking, and this contributed to his difficulty in resolving what he refers to as "the question on my mind" as "the thought of her more and more took possession of me" (53). The shift from obsessional to delusional thinking then occurred when he began to assume that she was his to give to another. At this point, he left the sphere of reality altogether.

SCHIZOTYPAL PERSONALITY DISORDER

A second possibility is that Boisen suffered from schizotypal personality disorder. While it is unusual for schizophrenia to emerge prior to late adolescence, schizotypal personality disorder may be apparent in childhood. The *DSM-IV* indicates that only "a small proportion" of individuals with this disorder go on to develop schizophrenia or another psychotic disorder. French and Morrison suggest that persons who have been diagnosed as having schizotypal personality disorder are considered to be at risk of a psychotic disorder, especially if there has been "a recent deterioration in functioning" (2004, 13). As we have seen, Boisen was having difficulty finding a pastorate at the time that he suffered his first major psychotic episode (and was between the professions of forestry and ministry when he had his earlier quasi-psychotic experience in Washington, D. C.).

The essential feature of schizotypal personality disorder is "a pervasive pattern of social and interpersonal deficits marked by acute discomfort with, and reduced capacity for, close relationships as well as by cognitive or perceptual distortions and eccentricities of behavior. This pattern begins by early adulthood and is present in a variety of contexts" (*DSM-IV*, 641). In addition, persons with this disorder often have ideas of reference, which the *DSM-IV* describes as "incorrect interpretations of casual incidents and external events as having a particular and unusual meaning for the person" (641). These ideas of reference should be distinguished, however, from "delusions of reference, in which the beliefs are held with delusional conviction" (641). The very fact that they are distinguishable, however, means that, on occasion, ideas of reference may become delusional. This, it seems, is what occurred to Boisen as the writing of his statement of belief proceeded.

The Enigma of Boisen

Finally, the reader of Boisen's memoir—or of the drastically shortened version presented here—cannot, I think, avoid the feeling that, in the end, there is something very enigmatic about him. Therefore, despite our best efforts to identify the origins of his mental illness, they remain somewhat elusive. Dittes notes that Boisen "did find himself in effective and productive work, if not in satisfying relationships." He concludes: "But the point of view from which he writes never transcends his afflictions; the story is not understood other than in terms of the fear and fantasies which are part of his pathology" (1990, 231).

To put it another way, Boisen views his text as "an autobiographical study of mental disorder and religious experience" (subtitle). He contends that his psychotic episodes were also, in their way, profoundly religious experiences, but the memoir itself presents a picture of a man who lived without God in the world. This may be the consequence of the fact that his image of his father and his idea of God were so closely intertwined. Thus, there is something enormously poignant about the second psychotic episode, where Boisen takes the role of his father and knocks on the door of Dr. Richard Cabot, inquiring about the well-being of Anton, his son. If there is a point at which psychosis and religious experience converge, this, I suggest, is surely it.

NOTES

[1]Boisen notes that reading Professor James's chapters on "Habit" and "Will" did not bring him any comfort. Both chapters are very long and complex, so it is virtually impossible to determine just what it was about these chapters that was upsetting to him. But in his chapter on habit, James emphasized the maxim that one should "never suffer an exception to occur till the new habit is securely rooted in your life" (James 1950, 1:123). Then, in his chapter on will, he discussed the unhealthy will and the explosive will "in which impulses seem to discharge so promptly into movements that inhibitions get no time to arise" (2:537). Boisen may have felt that he had not gotten the good habit securely in place before an exception (sexual weakness) occurred, and that he had been ineffective in inhibiting his unhealthy and explosive wills.

[2]While Dittes emphasizes the effects of the loss of an eye on depth perception, one could also take note of its effect on lateral perception. If monocular vision results in a foreshortening of depth (or, metaphorically, "coming up short"), it also involves a reduction of lateral vision on the side where the eye no longer functions. Metaphorically, then, we might view his memoir as an account of how he was continually "blindsided," surprised, or attacked from an unseen or unexpected direction. He frequently notes that he was stunned by Alice's response to a letter from him, and certainly he was ill-prepared for his psychotic episodes. Since the loss of his eye occurred shortly after his father's death, the following comment concerning his father's death from heart failure is relevant: "There had been two previous attacks, but apparently the gravity of the situation was not recognized" (Boisen 1960, 27). Ill-prepared for the loss of his father, we may say that this was his first major experience of being "blindsided."

2

A HOWLING TEMPEST IN THE BRAIN

▓ WILLIAM STYRON

When Vincent Foster, a member of the White House staff, committed suicide, President and Mrs. Clinton visited William Styron at his home on Martha's Vineyard Island off the coast of Massachusetts to gain Styron's insights into why Foster had taken his own life. Styron, the well-known novelist (author of *Lie Down in Darkness, The Confessions of Nat Turner,* and several others) is also the author of an autobiographical account of his depression, which began when he was sixty years old and nearly cost him his life. This account, *Darkness Visible: A Memoir of Madness* (1990), has made Styron a well-known figure in the field of mental illness.

Over the past several decades, depression has become one of the most widely discussed forms of mental illness. This is partly because there is solid evidence that the number of persons in the United States who suffer from it has increased quite dramatically in the latter half of the twentieth century and early years of the twenty-first century. It is also because persons like Styron have had the courage to make their own struggles with depression known.

Categories and Features of Depression

The *DSM-IV* has several diagnostic categories relating to depression:

1. major depressive disorder, single episode

2. major depressive disorder, recurrent
3. major depressive disorder, in partial remission

The essential feature of major depressive disorder is "a clinical course that is characterized by one or more Major Depressive Episodes without a history of Manic, Mixed, or Hypomanic Episodes" *(DSM-IV,* 339). (We will take up manic-depressive illness in the following chapter.) The *DSM-IV* indicates that it is "sometimes difficult to distinguish between a single episode with waxing and waning symptoms and two separate episodes." An episode is considered to have ended, however, "when the full criteria for the Major Depressive Episode have not been met for at least two consecutive months" (339).

Symptoms of Major Depressive Episode

The essential feature of a major depressive episode "is a period of at least two weeks during which there is either depressed mood or the loss of interest in nearly all activities" (320). The person must also experience at least four additional symptoms drawn from the following list:

1. significant weight loss when not dieting or weight gain, or decrease or increase in appetite nearly every day
2. insomnia or hypersomnia nearly every day
3. psychomotor agitation or retardation nearly every day (observable by others, not merely subjective feelings of restlessness or being slowed down)
4. fatigue or loss of energy nearly every day
5. feelings of worthlessness or excessive or inappropriate guilt (which may be delusional) nearly every day (either by subjective account or as observed by others)
6. recurrent thoughts of death (not just fear of dying), recurrent suicidal ideation without a specific plan, or a suicide attempt or a specific plan for committing suicide (327)

For a diagnosis of a major depressive episode to be assigned a partic-ular person, the symptoms need to cause clinically significant distress or impairment in social, occupational, or other important areas of function-ing. Such symptoms cannot be due to the direct physiological effects of a substance (for example, a drug of abuse, or medication) or a general med-ical condition (for example, hypothyroidism) and are not better accounted for by normal bereavement. If the depression occurs after the loss of a loved one, the symptoms must persist for longer than two months or be characterized by marked functional impairment, morbid preoccupation with worthlessness, suicidal ideation, psychotic symptoms, or psychomotor retardation. In recognition of the fact that many persons experience the presence of their loved one following the loved one's death, this experience is not considered a psychotic symptom.

Dysthymic Disorder

Another diagnostic category relating to depression is dysthymic disorder. This is a disorder without a major depressive episode, but with a depressed mood for most of the day, for more days than most, as indicated either by subjective account or observation by others, for at least two years (345).

For this diagnosis to be assigned, two or more of the following must be present when the individual is depressed:

1. poor appetite or overeating
2. insomnia or hypersomnia
3. low energy or fatigue
4. low self-esteem
5. poor concentration or difficulty making decisions
6. feelings of hopelessness (349)

As with major depressive episode, the symptoms must cause clinically significant distress or impairment in social, occupational, or other areas of functioning, and not be due to the direct physiological effects of a substance or medication or a general medical condition.

Melancholic Features Specifier

As we will see, Styron prefers the word "melancholia" to the word "depression" on the grounds that it has a much richer historical tradition (on this point, see Radden 2000). While Styron has his own views on what "melancholia" means and entails, it is useful to note that the *DSM-IV* includes a "Melancholic Features Specifier." As the term implies, a "Specifier" enables the diagnostician to add a refinement to a larger diagnostic category (in this case, to the current or most recent major depressive episode). For it to be applied, one of the following two conditions must be met: (1) loss of pleasure in all, or almost all, activities; and (2) lack of reactivity to usually pleasurable stimuli (that is, the person does not feel much better, even temporarily, when something good happens). In addition, three or more of the following must be present:

1. distinct quality of depressed mood (that is, the depressed mood is experienced as distinctly different from the kind of feeling experienced after the death of a loved one)
2. depression regularly worse in the morning
3. early morning awakening (at least two hours before usual time of awakening)
4. marked psychomotor retardation or agitation

5. significant anorexia or weight loss
6. excessive or inappropriate guilt

Melancholic features are encountered equally in both genders but are more likely in older persons, are more likely to occur in more severe major depressive episodes, and in those with psychotic features (384).

Not being versed at the time in psychiatric diagnoses, Styron's preference for the word "melancholia" was not based on his awareness of the melancholic features specifier, but he would almost certainly have qualified for its addition to the diagnosis of a major depressive episode.

Giving Depression a Face

This brief survey of the *DSM-IV* categories and criteria provides a good picture of how depression affects the life of the individual who suffers from it. It also provides, albeit indirectly, a general idea of how family members may be affected by a loved one's depression either for a shorter or a longer period of time.

A book like Styron's *Darkness Visible,* however, is especially valuable in showing how the illness presses down upon the individual, causing excruciating pain, and how it can therefore lead a person to want to end it all. Styron's account of his plunge into depression gives the clinical term "depression" a face, and the face is a terrifying one. We may see something romantic, even oddly appealing, in "the blues" and a certain heroism in undergoing the "dark night of the soul," but there is little that is either romantic or heroic about depression.

Those who have suffered from it and are now more or less recovered talk about how it is excruciatingly painful. The pain is all the greater for the fact that its causes, unlike physical illnesses and disabilities, are invisible and often inexplicable. As the *DSM-IV* makes clear, for example, a diagnosis of depression is *not* appropriate if the person's symptoms can be explained in terms of bereavement. Thus, depression seems to lack an obvious cause, and this may make it more difficult for the sufferer—and loved ones—to understand why it is happening. Why me? Why now?

In the following presentation of Styron's battle with depression, I will follow the trajectory of his own account in *Darkness Visible.* Given his obvious gifts as a writer, this chapter-by-chapter account could hardly be improved upon.

So Unaware of the Trouble and Peril that Lay Ahead

In the "Author's Note" placed at the beginning of *Darkness Visible,* Styron indicates that the book began as a lecture given in Baltimore in May 1989 at a symposium on affective disorders. The Department of Psychiatry of Johns Hopkins University Medical School sponsored the symposium. (In her reflections on his illness, his wife, Rose Styron, tells about the time that her future husband came to Johns Hopkins University many years earlier to speak to a writing class in which she was enrolled. He talked about his new novel, *Lie Down in Darkness*. He "gave a shy, nervous performance," and Rose, "not very impressed," left "at the end with fellow poets, barely speaking to the acclaimed author" [R. Styron 2001, 127]). The following year, she looked him up in Rome, and they became friends.

Initial Symptoms of Depression

In May 1989, however, he had come to Johns Hopkins to speak on the subject of depression. This lecture, in greatly expanded form, was published in essay form in *Vanity Fair* later that year. The book is a further expansion of the lecture. The first seventeen pages include a narrative of a trip he made to Paris during which he manifested the diminished ability to think or concentrate that is one of the symptoms of a major depressive episode. By placing this narrative at the beginning of *Darkness Visible*, he enables us to see that depression, while an affective or mood disorder, is also a thought disorder, as it typically manifests itself in the inability to think clearly, logically, or rationally. As he relates, this in turn had serious social consequences.

It is also noteworthy that Styron prefaces the book with a quotation from the book of Job: "For the thing which I greatly feared is come upon me, and that which I was afraid of is come unto me. I was not in safety, neither had I rest, neither was I quiet; yet trouble came" (Job 3:25–26, KJV). Although Job's description of himself as being at risk, restless, and disquieted or agitated, applies to mental illness in general, it may be especially noteworthy in the case of depression, because these are states of mind that the word "depression" does not convey, even though they are very much a feature of it. *Darkness Visible* consists of ten untitled sections, ranging from two to seventeen pages in length. The first and longest section, as noted above, recounts his trip to Paris. It begins: "In Paris on a chilly evening late in October of 1985 I first became fully aware that the struggle with the disorder in my mind—a struggle which had engaged me for several months—might have a fatal outcome" (W. Styron 1990, 3). The "moment of revelation" came when the car he was riding in passed a neon sign reading Hotel Washington. He had not seen this sign since the spring of 1952 (when he was in his mid-twenties). He had stayed at Hotel Washington the first several nights on his first trip to Paris during the first months of a year of travel in Europe. It was a hotel for tourists of very modest means. He had stayed at this hotel only a few days when some newly acquired American friends encouraged him to move to an even seedier but more colorful hotel closer to the literary hangouts. He had just published his first novel, *Lie Down in Darkness,* which brought him instant fame in the United States, but Americans in Paris had not heard of it, so in Paris he was received as just another struggling writer.

Loss of Lucidity

Over the years, he had not given any thought to Hotel Washington. But when it reappeared that October night some thirty-three years later, "the recollection of my arrival so many years earlier started flooding back, causing me to feel that I had come full circle" (4). He recalls having said to himself as he left Paris the very next morning for New York that he never expected to see Paris again. This declaration was somehow connected with his impression that he "would never recapture a lucidity that was slipping away from me with terrifying speed" (4).

Only a few days earlier he had concluded that he was suffering from "a serious depressive illness and was floundering helplessly in my efforts to deal with it" (5). He ought to have been cheered by the festive occasion that brought him to France–his acceptance of the Prix Mondial Cino del Duca, given annually to an artist or scientist whose work reflects themes or principles of a certain "humanism"–but he had not been. This, it might be noted, is one of the characteristics of the *DSM-IV* "Melancholic Features Specifier," that is, a lack of reactivity to usually pleasurable stimuli; the person does not feel much better, even temporarily, when something good happens.

Excessive, Inappropriate Feelings

There were also the excessive or inappropriate feelings of guilt, low self-regard, and worthlessness characteristic of a major depressive episode, especially one warranting the "Melancholic Features Specifier." He points out in this connection:

> Of the many dreadful manifestations of the disease, both physical and psychological, a sense of self-hatred–or, put less categorically, a failure of self-esteem–is one of the most universally experienced symptoms, and I had suffered more and more from a general feeling of worthlessness as the malady had progressed. (5)

He found his "dank joylessness" all the more ironic in light of the fact that his four-day trip to Paris to receive an award "should have sparklingly restored my ego" (5).

The prize itself was established in honor of Ciro del Duca by his widow, Simone. He was an immigrant to France from Italy who had amassed a large fortune before and after World War II by printing and distributing cheap magazines, mainly comic books. He also produced movies and owned racehorses. In time, his publishing firm became "prestigious enough for there to be scant memory of its comic-book origins when del Duca's widow, Simone, created a foundation whose chief function was the annual bestowal of the eponymous award" (6). The prize itself was approximately $25,000 which, to Styron, was a nice sum of money. It was the type of prize that did not, as so many other awards do, induce "an unhealthy uprising of false modesty" for the winners and "backbiting, self-torture and envy" from the losers. The prize "was to me so straightforwardly nice that any extensive self-examination seemed silly, and so I accepted gratefully, writing in reply that I would honor the reasonable requirement that I be present for the ceremony" (7).

The Pleasure-robbing Nature of Depression

At the time he accepted the invitation in early summer, he thought he would make a leisurely trip out of it. As it turned out, however, the trip was "a fast turnaround," four days including travel between New York and Paris. If he had been able to foresee his "state of mind" as the date of the award ceremony approached, he would not have accepted the prize at all. His depression had by this time robbed him of the pleasure of a leisurely trip to France and of enjoying this moment in the limelight.

In an attempt to describe what he was going through at the time, he provides a description of depression and of its utter incomprehensibility to those who have not experienced it personally:

> Depression is a disorder of mood, so mysteriously painful and elusive in the way it becomes known to the self—to the mediating intellect—as to verge close to being beyond description. It thus remains nearly incomprehensible to those who have not experienced it in its extreme mode, although the gloom, "the blues" which people go through occasionally and associate with the general hassle of everyday existence are of such prevalence that they do give many individuals a hint of the illness in its catastrophic form. (7)

By the time he arrived in Paris, he "had descended far past those familiar, manageable doldrums" (7). In fact, in retrospect, he is able to see that, in Paris, he "was at a critical stage in the development of the disease, situated at an ominous way station between its unfocused stirrings earlier that summer and the near-violent denouement of December which sent me into the hospital" (8).

The award ceremony was to take place at noon and be followed by a formal luncheon. He woke up at midmorning in his room at the Hotel Pont-Royal commenting to himself that he felt "reasonably sound." He passed this hopeful word along to his wife, Rose, who had accompanied him on the trip. Aided by the minor tranquilizer Halcion,™ he had managed to defeat his insomnia (one of the key features of depression) and get a few hours of sleep: "Thus I was in fair spirits" (8). This, however, was not entirely encouraging, for he also knew that he was "certain to feel ghastly before nightfall" (8).

The Deteriorating Condition

At this point in time, he was carefully monitoring each phase of his "deteriorating condition." Following several months of denial, during which he ascribed his malaise, restlessness, and sudden fits of anxiety to withdrawal from alcohol (having abruptly quit drinking whiskey and given up all intoxicants in June), he had accepted the fact that he was ill. During the course of his worsening condition, he had done some reading on the subject of depression, both in books tailored for the layperson and in weightier professional books, including the *DSM-III.*

Having developed the habit of informing himself about many medical matters over the years (as we will see later, Rose Styron suggests that this was more than a normal habit of information acquisition, that it was an obsession with him), it "came as an astonishment" to him that he "was close to a total ignoramus about depression, which can be as serious a medical affair as diabetes or cancer" (9). He supposes that "as an incipient depressive," he had "always subconsciously rejected or ignored the proper knowledge; it cut too close to the psychic bone, and I shoved it aside as an unwelcome condition to my store of information" (9).

In any event, during the few hours in the course of a day when the depressive state eased up long enough so that he could concentrate, he "had recently filled this vacuum with fairly extensive reading." He "had absorbed many fascinating and troubling facts, which, however, I could not put to practical use" (9). Where personal knowledge about the nature and symptoms of some mental disorders may be a helpful remedy (as has been shown by the effectiveness of cognitive therapy with persons afflicted with an anxiety disorder), this seems not to be the case where depression is concerned. In fact,

> [t]he most honest authorities face up square to the fact that serious depression is not readily treatable. Unlike, let us say, diabetes, where immediate measures taken to rearrange the body's adaptation to glucose can dramatically reverse a dangerous process and bring it under control, depression in its major stages possesses no quickly available remedy: failure of alleviation is one of the most distressing factors of the disorder as it reveals itself to the victim, and one that helps situate it squarely in the category of grave diseases. (9–10)

Thus, while "proper knowledge" of the disease of depression could have been helpful before it began to take control, the knowledge he was now acquiring was "not encouraging" (10):

Frighteningly, the layman-sufferer from major depression, taking a peek into some of the many books currently on the market, will find much in the way of theory and symptomatology and very little that legitimately suggests the possibility of a quick rescue. Those that do claim an easy way out are glib and most likely fraudulent. (10)

True,

[t]here are decent popular works which intelligently point the way toward treatment and cure, demonstrating how certain therapies—psychotherapy or pharmacology, or a combination of these—can indeed restore people to health in all but the most persistent and devastating cases; but the wisest books among them underscore the hard truth that serious depressions do not disappear overnight. (10–11)

The Mysterious Nature of Depression

This, in Styron's view, simply points to "an essential though difficult reality" that needs to be stated at the outset of his own chronicle. "The disease of depression remains a great mystery. It has yielded its secrets to science far more reluctantly than many of the other major ills besetting us" (11). The very factionalism that exists in present-day psychiatry—the schism between the believers in psychotherapy and the adherents of pharmacology—is itself a reflection of "the inexplicable nature of depression and the difficulty of its treatment" (11).

Depression affects individuals differently, and there are many exceptions as far as symptoms are concerned. For example, while most people who begin to suffer from the illness are laid low in the morning (one of the characteristics of the "Melancholic Features Specifier") but feel better as the day wears on, Styron, himself, atypically, experienced the reverse pattern. He could rise and function almost normally during the earlier part of the day. But he would begin to sense the onset of the symptoms at midafternoon or a little later as gloom crowded in upon him and he experienced "a sense of dread and alienation, and, above all, stifling anxiety" (12).

This very fact enabled him to proceed "without mishap" through the award ceremony itself. He made his acceptance speech "with what I felt was passable aplomb." He promised he would donate the bulk of his prize money to various organizations fostering French-American goodwill, then added, jokingly, that there was a limit to altruism, so he hoped it would not be taken amiss if he held back a small portion for himself. What he did not reveal was no joking matter. The amount he was keeping for himself was to pay for two tickets the next day on the Concorde so that he and Rose could return speedily to the United States "where just a few days before I had made an appointment to see a psychiatrist" (13).

Having been reluctant the past few weeks to seek psychiatric aid, he eventually concluded that he could not delay the confrontation indefinitely. He finally made contact by telephone with a therapist who had been highly recommended to him. The therapist advised him to take the Paris trip and come to see him as soon as he returned. Once in Paris, Styron felt a great need to get back, and fast. Even as he delivered his remarks, he felt a pressing desire for the day to be over with so that he could return home and have his appointment with the psychiatrist who, he hoped at the time, "would whisk my malaise away with his miraculous medications" (13). Looking back, he is "hardly able to believe that I possessed such ingenuous hope, or that I could have been so unaware of the trouble and peril that lay ahead" (14).

The Illness's Embarrassing Progression

What happened following the ceremony was an indication of how far the illness had progressed. He informed Simone del Duca that he could not join her and the dozen or so members of the Academie Française who had chosen him for the prize. Why? Because he had arranged instead to have lunch at a restaurant with his French publisher. She was understandably incredulous, and then enraged, for this decision on his part was completely outrageous.

It had been announced months before to him and everyone else concerned that a luncheon in his honor was part of the day's pageantry, but he had made the date to have lunch with his publisher the previous evening, having forgotten his obligation to Simone del Duca and the others. His behavior "was really the result of the illness, which had progressed far enough to produce some of its most famous and sinister hallmarks: confusion, failure of mental focus and lapse of memory" (14). At a later stage in his illness, his "entire mind would be dominated by anarchic disconnections," but at this stage there was "something that resembled bifurcation of mood: lucidity of sorts in the early hours of the day, and gathering murk in the afternoon and evening" (14–15). He had made the date to have lunch with his publisher in the murky distractedness of the previous evening, completely forgetting his del Duca obligations. That decision continued to "completely master" his thinking so that he was able to "blandly insult" the donor of the prize (15).

When she realized that he was adamant in his determination to honor the lunch engagement agreed upon the evening before, her face flushed angrily as she did an about-face and said goodbye. At that moment, he was suddenly "flabbergasted, stunned with horror at what I had done" (15). He fantasized a luncheon table at which she and the other members of the Academie Française were sitting, while the guest of honor was having lunch at a nearby restaurant. He immediately implored her assistant, who was standing by, wearing an austere, mortified expression, to try to make amends, indicating that he would cancel the other engagement, that it had all been a terrible mistake, a mix-up. Then, he blurted out words that "a lifetime of general equilibrium and a smug belief in the impregnability of my psychic health" had prevented him from believing he could or would ever utter. He felt a chill as he heard himself say to a perfect stranger, "I'm sick, a psychiatric problem" (15).

Madame del Duca accepted his apology and the luncheon proceeded without further strain, but he could not completely rid himself of the suspicion that she was still disturbed by his conduct and "thought me a weird number" (16). Moreover, the luncheon was a long one. When it was over, he felt himself "entering the afternoon shadows with their encroaching anxiety and dread" (16). To make matters worse, a television crew, which he had also forgotten about, was waiting to take him to the newly opened Picasso Museum, where he was supposed to be filmed looking at the exhibits and exchanging comments with Rose.

The Pain of Depression

This turned out to be "a demanding struggle, a major ordeal" (16). By the time they arrived at the museum, it was past four o'clock, and his "brain had begun to endure its familiar siege: panic and dislocation." He had a sense that his "thought processes were being engulfed by a toxic and unnameable tide that obliterated any enjoyable response to the living world" (16). Instead of the pleasure he should have been experiencing as the focus of affirmation and acclaim, he was instead feeling in his mind "a sensation close to, but indescribably different from, actual pain" (16).

His phrase "indescribably different" prompts further reflection on the elusive nature of the distress that depression produces, for

if the pain were readily describable, most of the countless sufferers from this ancient affliction would have been able to confidently depict for their friends and loved ones (even their physicians) some of the actual dimensions of their torment, and perhaps elicit a comprehension that has been generally lacking; such incomprehension has usually been due not to a failure of sympathy but to the basic inability of healthy people to imagine a form of torment so alien to everyday experience. (17)

For himself, "the pain is most closely connected to drowning or suffocating—but even these images are off the mark" (17). He invokes William James at this point, noting that James, "who battled depression for many years, gave up the search for an adequate portrayal, implying its near-impossibility when he wrote in *The Varieties of Religious Experience:*

'It is a positive and active anguish, a sort of psychical neuralgia wholly unknown to normal life'" (17).[1]

Because of the mix-up, his day did not end with the television filming at the museum. The lunch with his publisher was rescheduled for evening dinner. When he and Rose met his publisher, her son, and another friend at the restaurant, rain was descending in torrents. Someone in the group who sensed the state of his mind apologized for the terrible weather. He recalls having thought that even had the weather been perfect, he would still have responded like the zombie he had become. Then, halfway through the dinner, he discovered he had lost the prize check for $25,000. He had tucked it in the inside breast pocket of his jacket, but when his hand strayed idly to that place he discovered it was gone. What had happened to it? And did he unconsciously "intend" to lose the money? After all, he had been bothered recently by the thought that he was not deserving of the prize. So the idea that he "meant" to lose it was not at all far-fetched:

> I believe in the reality of the accidents we subconsciously per-petuate on ourselves, and so how easy it was for this to be not loss but a form of repudiation, offshoot of that self-loathing (depression's premier badge) by which I was persuaded that I could not be worthy of the prize, that I was in fact not worthy of any of the recognition that had come my way in the past few years. (19)

The loss of the check was consistent with his other failures during the course of dinner, including his lack of appetite, incapacity for even forced laughter, and, finally, "virtually total failure of speech" (19). He seemed to have turned "wall-eyed" and "monosyllabic" and sensed that his French friends were becoming uneasily aware of his predicament. Then, of course, there was the embarrassing scene of all of them down on the floor searching for the lost check, which had somehow slipped out of his jacket pocket and fluttered under an adjoining table, discovered there by his publisher's son. As the car took them back to the hotel, passing Hotel Washington on the way, he found himself thinking of two men who died before their time, Albert Camus and Romain Gary, two French writers.

In the Absence of Hope We Must Still Struggle

Styron breaks off his personal story to explain why these two men entered his mind at the time. Profoundly impressed and influenced by Camus when he was a young writer, Styron never met Camus. The disappointment of never having done so was compounded by the fact that it was such a near miss. The other man would later become a cherished friend. But at the time Styron knew Romain Gary only slightly. Gary had offered to arrange a meeting with Camus when Styron was planning a trip to France in 1960, eight years after his first trip to France. Gary had informed him that Camus had read his *Lie Down in Darkness* and had greatly admired it.

But before Styron arrived in France, he learned that forty-six-year old Camus had been killed in an automobile accident. Although he did not know Camus, he "pondered his death endlessly":

> Although Camus had not been driving, he supposedly knew the driver, who was the son of his publisher, to be a speed demon; so there was an element of recklessness in the accident that bore overtones of the near-suicidal, at least of a death flirtation. (22)

It was therefore inevitable that conjectures about Camus's death would reach back to the theme of suicide in his own work and especially to his *The Myth of Sisyphus* (Camus, 1955), which begins: "There is but one truly serious philosophical problem, and that is suicide. Judging whether life is or is not worth living amounts to answering the fundamental question of philosophy" (Styron 1990, 23).

Innocence of Depression

At the time he first read *The Myth of Sisyphus,* however, Styron had found the essay puzzling. Despite its persuasive logic and eloquence, there was a great deal that eluded Styron. He "always came back to grapple vainly with the initial hypothesis, unable to deal with the premise that anyone should come close to wishing to kill himself in the first place" (23). When he later read Camus's *The Fall,* he experienced the same reservations, for he felt that "the guilt and self-condemnation of the lawyer-narrator, gloomily spinning out his monologue in an Amsterdam bar, seemed a touch clamorous and excessive" (23).

What he was unable to perceive at the time was that "the lawyer was behaving very much like a man in the throes of clinical depression. Such was my innocence of the very existence of this disease" (23). This, of course, implies that whether or not the wish to kill oneself is the fundamental question of philosophy, it is a psychological reality, and, on this basis alone, it merits our most serious consideration. In fact, when Gary informed Styron that Camus often spoke of suicide and joked about committing suicide himself, Styron came to view *The Myth of Sisyphus* very differently:

> Despite its abiding tone of melancholy, a sense of the triumph of life over death is at the core of *The Myth of Sisyphus* with its austere message: in the absence of hope we must still struggle to survive, and so we do—by the skin of our teeth. It was only after the passing of some years that it seemed credible to me that Camus' statement about suicide, and his general preoccupation

with the subject, might have sprung at least as strongly from some persistent disturbance of mood as from his concerns with ethics and epistemology. (24)

Later, Gary came to visit Styron in the United States. He again discussed Camus's depression, and as they talked together, Styron "felt that some of [Gary's] suppositions about the seriousness of Camus's recurring despair gained weight from the fact that he, too, had begun to suffer from depression, and he freely admitted as much" (24). Gary insisted that it was not incapacitating, and that he had it under control. "But he felt it from time to time," and he was able therefore "to perceive a flicker of the desperate state of mind which had been described to him by Camus" (28).

While staying at Styron's guest cottage in Roxbury, Connecticut, Gary was joined by his former wife, Jean Seberg. An American actress, she came to see their son at a nearby tennis camp. When Styron came down from his summer home on Martha's Vineyard Island to visit Gary, he was surprised to find her there. He was even more surprised by her terrible appearance: "She moved like a sleepwalker, said little, and had the blank gaze of someone tranquilized (or drugged, or both) nearly to the point of catalepsy" (25).

Styron understood how devoted they still were and was touched by Gary's solicitude toward her. Gary explained that she was being treated for depression. He mentioned something about her antidepressant medications, but none of this registered very strongly with Styron, and it also meant very little to him. Styron's memory of his "relative indifference is important because such indifference demonstrates the outsider's inability to grasp the essence of the illness" (26). Camus's depression—and now Gary's and certainly Seberg's–"were abstract ailments" to him. In spite of his sympathy, he "hadn't an inkling of its true contours or the nature of the pain so many victims experience as the mind continues in its insidious meltdown" (26).

Styron's Revelation

In Paris that October night, he knew that he, too, was in the process of meltdown. On the way back to the hotel, he had "a clear revelation" (26). He saw that a disruption in one's circadian cycle–the metabolic and glandular rhythms that are central to our workaday life–is involved in many, if not most, cases of depression. This is why brutal insomnia so often occurs and why each day's pattern of distress exhibits fairly predictable alternating periods of intensity and relief.

For him, the relief, an incomplete but noticeable letup, came in the hours after dinnertime and before midnight. During this letup, the pain lifted a little and his mind became lucid enough to focus on other matters besides the immediate upheaval convulsing his system. In the car, he felt a semblance of clarity returning, along with the ability to think rational thoughts. But his reminiscences about Camus and his friend Romain Gary were not very consoling, and he proceeds to explain why.

A year or so after his brief encounter with Seberg, she took an overdose of pills. Her body was found several days later in a car parked in a cul-de-sac off a Paris avenue. One year later, in a Paris restaurant over a long lunch, Gary told him that despite the difficulties between himself and Seberg, the loss of her had so deepened his own depression that from time to time he felt nearly helpless. But even then, Styron "was unable to comprehend the nature of his anguish" (27). He noticed, however, that Gary's hands trembled and that his voice "had the wheezy sound of very old age" that "was, or could be, the voice of depression" (27). He was aware that in the vortex of his own severest pain, he had begun to develop that ancient voice himself. This was the last he saw of Romain Gary. In 1980, Gary, then in his mid-sixties, went home after a composed, casual, even light-hearted lunch with the father of Styron's publisher and put a bullet through his brain.

During these musings, Styron saw the Hotel Washington sign, which brought back memories of his first arrival in Paris and "the fierce and sudden realization that I would never see Paris again" (28). The certitude of this realization was astonishing to him and filled him with a new fright. Although "thoughts of death had long been common during my siege, blowing through my mind like icy gusts of wind, they were the formless shapes of doom that I suppose are dreamed of by people in the grip of any severe affliction" (28). This, however, was different, for now he had "the sure understanding that tomorrow, when the pain descended once more, or the tomorrow after that—I would be forced to judge that life was not worth living and thereby answer, for myself at least, the fundamental question of philosophy" (28).[2]

One Is Drawn to Contemplate One's Childhood

At this point, Styron breaks off his account of his worsening depression in October, 1985, and jumps forward to the spring of 1989. This was three years after his recovery and the time when the 1960s political activist Abbie Hoffman took his own life.

Troubling Suicides

Styron was troubled that Hoffman was just past the age of fifty, "too young and apparently too vital for such an ending" (29). He was even more troubled by the predictable reaction from many, "the denial, the refusal to accept the fact of the suicide itself, as if the voluntary act—as opposed to an accident, or death from natural causes—were tinged with a delinquency that somehow lessened the man and his character" (30).

Abbie's brother had appeared on television, "grief-ravaged and distraught " (30). Styron could not help feeling compassion for this man as he tried to deflect the idea of suicide, insisting that Abbie had always been careless with pills and would never have left his family bereft. This denial, however, did not square with the coroner's report that Hoffman had taken the equivalent of 150 phenobarbitals. Styron next cites the case of the poet, Randall Jarrell, who was struck by a car near his home in Chapel Hill, North Carolina, one night in 1965. Jarrell's presence on that particular stretch of road, at an odd hour of the evening, was puzzling. Since some evidence indicated that he had deliberately let the car strike him, the early conclusion was that his death was suicide. But Jarrell's wife, plus many of his friends and supporters, protested; and a coroner's jury eventually ruled the death was accidental. This ruling flew in the face of evidence that Jarrell had been suffering from extreme depression, had been hospitalized for it, and while there only a few months before his death had slashed his wrists. Jarrell, Styron insists, "almost certainly killed himself. He did so not because he was a coward, not out of any moral feebleness, but because he was afflicted with a depression that was so devastating that he could no longer endure the pain of it" (32).

Finally, he cites the case of Primo Levi, the Italian writer and survivor of Auschwitz, who, in 1987, at the age of sixty-seven, threw himself down a stairway. A 1988 *The New York Times* account about a symposium on Levi and his work appalled Styron. According to the article, many of the participants seemed mystified and disappointed by Levi's suicide: "It was as if the man whom they had all so greatly admired, and who had endured so much at the hands of the Nazis—a man of exemplary resilience and courage—had by his suicide demonstrated a frailty, a crumbling of character they were loath to accept" (32). Their reaction was one of helplessness and "a touch of shame" (33).

Making His Privacy Public

Styron's annoyance was so intense that he wrote an op-ed piece for *The New York Times*. He argued that the pain of severe depression is unimaginable to those who have not suffered it. In many instances, it kills because its anguish can no longer be endured. He also noted that the prevention of many suicides will continue to be hindered until the general public becomes aware of the very nature of this pain. He added:

> Through the healing process of time—and through medical intervention or hospitalization in many cases—most people survive depression, which may be its only blessing; but to the tragic legion who are compelled to destroy themselves there should be no more reproof attached than to the victims of terminal cancer. (33)

Having set down his thoughts rather hurriedly and spontaneously, Styron was unprepared for the response, equally spontaneous and enormous. It had required no special originality or boldness on his part to speak out frankly about suicide and the impulse toward it. But he had underestimated "the number of people for whom the subject had been taboo, a matter of secrecy and shame" (34). The overwhelming reaction made him feel that inadvertently he had "helped unlock a closet from which many souls were eager to come out and proclaim that they, too, had experienced the feelings" that he had described (34). This was the first time he had felt it worthwhile to have invaded his own privacy and to make that privacy public.

Spurred by the momentum of the response to his op-ed article in *The New York Times,* he began to think seriously about trying to "chronicle some of my own experiences with the illness and in the process perhaps establish a frame of reference out of which one or more valuable conclusions might be drawn" (34). But the very fact that these conclusions would be based on the events that happened to one man needs to be underscored, for he does not intend that his ordeal would stand "as a representation of what happens, or might happen, to others" (34). After all,

> [d]epression is much too complex in its cause, its symptoms and its treatment for unqualified conclusions to be drawn from the experience of a single individual. Although as an illness depression manifests certain unvarying characteristics, it also allows for many idiosyncrasies; I've been amazed at some of the freakish phenomena—not reported by other patients—that it has wrought amid the twistings of my mind's labyrinth. (34–35)

The idiosyncrasies of each sufferer's experience stand out against the background of the fact that depression is so "assertively democratic"—like a Norman Rockwell poster (35). It "strikes indiscriminately at all ages, races, creeds and classes, though women are at considerably higher risk than men" (35). If there is any other "at risk" group, it appears that "artistic types (especially poets) are particularly vulnerable to the disorder—which, in its graver, clinical manifestations takes upward of twenty percent of its victims by way of suicide" (35). As proof, Styron provides a listing of some twenty artistic types. He notes that they include a Russian poet who criticized the suicide of another poet a few years prior to his own suicide. This, Styron observes, "should stand as a caveat for all who are judgmental about self-destruction" (36).

Following this "roll-call," Styron concludes this appeal for understanding on a note that reasserts itself later on, when he seeks to account for his own susceptibility to depression, namely, its roots in childhood. He notes: "When one thinks of these doomed and splendidly creative men and women, one is drawn to contemplate their childhoods, where, to the best of anyone's knowledge, the seeds of the illness take strong root; could any of them have had a hint, then, of the psyche's perishability, its exquisite fragility? And why were they destroyed, while others–struggled through?" (36).

I Have Felt the Wind of the Wing of Madness

Resuming his account of his own struggle, Styron notes that when he first became aware that this disease had "laid" him "low," he felt a need to register a strong protest against the word "depression." Depression, he observes, used to be called "melancholia."

Melancholia Instead of Depression

In his view, melancholia still appears "to be a far more apt and evocative word for the blacker forms of the disorder" (37). Unfortunately, "it was usurped by a noun with a bland tonality and lacking any magisterial presence, used indifferently to describe an economic decline or a rut in the ground, a true wimp of a word for such a major illness" (37). As this part of the book originated in the lecture at Johns Hopkins University Department of Psychiatry, Styron seems to take some pleasure in noting that it was "a Johns Hopkins Medical School faculty member, Adolf Meyer," who is "generally considered responsible for the currency of this wimpish word in modern times." For the past seventy-five years, this word *depression* "has slithered innocuously through the language like a slug," its very insipidity preventing "a general awareness of the horrible intensity of the disease when out of control" (37).

As one who has suffered the extreme forms of this malady, Styron would like to lobby for a truly arresting designation. Unfortunately, "brainstorm" is unavailable, as it describes an intellectual inspiration that is not necessarily hard won or even particularly reliable. Even so, why not tell others that someone's mood disorder "has evolved into a storm– a veritable howling tempest in the brain, which is indeed what a clinical depression resembles like nothing else" (38). Then even the uninformed layperson might think twice before registering the standard reaction that the word "depression" evokes, something akin to "You'll pull out of it," or "We all have bad days." Styron observes that the phrase "nervous breakdown" seems to be on its way out, and deservedly so, as it seems to insinuate "a vague spinelessness" (38). So, we "seem destined to be saddled with 'depression' until a better, sturdier name is created" (38).

Seeking the Cause or Trigger

Styron guesses that his age–sixty–when the illness struck may account for the fact that his depression was not of the manic type–the one accompanied by euphoric highs. Instead, his was of the "unipolar" form, "which leads straight down" (38). As for what "caused" it, he doubts that he will ever know. He suspects that the search for any definitive answer will forever prove an impossibility, "so complex are the intermingled factors of abnormal chemistry, behavior, and genetics. Plainly, multiple components are involved—perhaps three or four, most probably more, in fathomless permutations." This is why the belief that there is a single immediate answer—or combined answer—to why someone committed suicide is so fallacious (39).

But did something in his own life trigger it, something that, as it were, set it off? He points to a "manifest crisis" in his own case. It began in June, four months before the Paris experience and six months before he ended up in the hospital. He freely acknowledges that, like a great many American males, he used alcohol "as the magical conduit to fantasy and euphoria, and to the enhancement of the imagination" (40). While he never wrote under its influence, he did use it, often in conjunction with music, "as a means to let my mind conceive visions that the unaltered, sober brain has no access to" (40). But besides being "an invaluable senior partner of my intellect," alcohol was also "a friend whose ministrations I sought daily—sought also, I now see, as a means to calm the anxiety and incipient dread that I had hidden away for so long somewhere in the dungeons of my spirit" (40).

The "manifest crisis," then, was his sudden loss of this friend and its calming presence. This loss left him vulnerable to hidden anxiety and dread. In June, he suddenly, almost overnight, discovered that he could no longer drink alcohol: "It was as if my body had risen up in protest, along with my mind, and had conspired to reject this daily mood bath which it had so long welcomed and, who knows? perhaps even come to need" (41). Noting that many other drinkers experience this intolerance as they grow older, he suspects that, for him, the crisis was at least partly metabolic, "the liver rebelling, as if to say, 'No more, no more'" (41). Alcohol, even in miniscule amounts, caused nausea, "a desperate and unpleasant wooziness, a sickly sensation and ultimately a distinct revulsion." The comforting friend had abandoned him, "not gradually and reluctantly, as a true friend might, but like a shot" (41). By neither will nor choice, he had become an abstainer. The situation was puzzling and also traumatic. He dates "the onset of my depressive mood from the beginning of this deprivation" (41).

In a sense, he should have been overjoyed that his body had rejected in such absolute fashion a substance that was undermining its own health. Instead, he began to experience "a vaguely troubling malaise, a sense of something having gone cockeyed in the domestic universe I'd dwelt in so long, so comfortably" (42). While depression is not uncommon when people stop drinking, this is usually on a scale that is not menacing. But it became menacing in Styron's case, illustrating "how idiosyncratic the faces of depression can be" (42).

His Crisis Response

At first, the changes he was experiencing did not alarm him. He did notice that his surroundings took on "a different tone at certain times" (42). The shadows of nightfall seemed more somber, his mornings were less buoyant, and walks in the woods were less zestful. Then in a moment during his late afternoon working hours "a kind of panic and anxiety overtook me, just for a few minutes, accompanied by a visceral queasiness" (42). This "seizure" was slightly alarming, but since he was ignorant of mood disorders, he did not realize that he was already in the grip of the onset of one.

He also attributes his lack of recognition to the fact that alcohol had one last perverse trick to play on him as they said farewell to one another. This was the fact that while alcohol is a major depressant, it had never truly depressed him during his drinking career, "acting instead as a shield against anxiety" (43). So when the friend who was a depressant for others left him, it left him vulnerable to a depression that alcohol, in his own case, had held at bay:

> Suddenly vanished, the great ally which for so long had kept my demons at bay was no longer there to prevent those demons from beginning to swarm through the subconscious, and I was emotionally naked, vulnerable as I had never been before. Doubtless depression had hovered near me for years, waiting to swoop down. Now I was in the first stage—premonitory, like a flicker of sheet lightning barely perceived—of depression's black tempest. (43)

As the summer months continued, he responded indifferently to the pleasures of Martha's Vineyard Island. He felt an odd fragility in his body, as if it had become frail, hypersensitive, and somehow disjointed and clumsy, lacking normal coordination. Soon he became hypochondriacal, feeling something wrong with his corporeal self. Twitches and pains seemed to presage all sorts of dire infirmities. He observes in this connection that for centuries melancholia and hypochondria have been thought to be related (see Jackson, 1986, chap. 11). He thinks that the hypochondria is part of the psyche's apparatus of defense: "Unable to accept its own gathering deterioration, the mind announces to its indwelling consciousness that it is the body with its perhaps correctable defects—not the precious and irreplaceable mind—that is going haywire" (44).

Strange Behavior Pattern

Another "strange behavior pattern" began at this time (one that is listed among the criteria for "Melancholic Features Specifier" for major depressive episode in the *DSM-IV*). He experienced "a fidgety restlessness that kept me on the move, somewhat to the perplexity of my family and friends" (44). In late summer, he made the mistake of downing a scotch and soda on an airplane trip to New York. This first taste of alcohol in months caused his body to react so powerfully that the very next day he saw a Manhattan internist, who inaugurated a long series of tests. After three weeks of very expensive, high-tech tests, the doctor pronounced him totally fit. Normally, he would have been elated to receive such good news, and for a couple of days he was happy. Then once again came the rhythmic daily erosion of his mood. The anxiety, agitation, and unfocused dread returned.

It was now early October. He and Rose had moved back to their home in Connecticut. One unforgettable feature of this stage of his disorder was the way in which his own farmhouse, his beloved home for thirty years, took on "an almost palpable quality of ominousness" (45). He wondered how this friendly place, teeming with such wonderful memories, "could almost perceptibly seem so hostile and forbidding" (48). It was not as though he was alone, for Rose was there. In fact, she "was present and listened with unflagging patience to my complaints" (45–46). But he felt "an immense and aching solitude" (46). Moreover, he had lost his powers of concentration. The act of writing became more and more difficult and exhausting until it ceased altogether.

He also suffered "dreadful, pouncing seizures of anxiety" (46). One bright day on a walk with his dog through the woods, he heard a flock of Canada geese honking high above the trees, which were ablaze with foliage. Ordinarily such a sight and sound would have exhilarated him. This time, however, "the flight of birds caused me to stop, riveted with fear, and I stood stranded there, helpless, shivering, aware for the first time that I had been stricken by no mere pangs of withdrawal but by a serious illness whose name and actuality I was able finally to acknowledge" (46). On the way home, he could not rid his mind of a line from the French poet, Charles Baudelaire, dredged up from the distant past, "I have felt the wind of the wing of madness"(46).

On the Wing of Madness

Styron knows, of course, that the word "madness" (like insanity, lunacy, and so forth) has been banished from modern usage. But, as one who knows what it is like to be in the grips of depression, he does not want to let the word go. "Never let it be doubted," he writes, "that depression, in its extreme form, is madness" (46–47). This madness, he goes on to say,

> results from an aberrant biochemical process. It has been established with reasonable certainty (after strong resistance from many psychiatrists, and not all that long ago) that such madness

is chemically induced among the neurotransmitters of the brain, probably as the result of systemic stress, which for unknown reasons causes a depletion of the chemicals norepinephrine and serotonin, and the increase of a hormone, cortisol. With all of this upheaval in the brain tissues, the alternate drenching and deprivation, it is no wonder that the mind begins to feel aggrieved, stricken, and the muddied thought processes register the distress of an organ in convulsion. (47)

He finds that sometimes, though infrequently, such a disturbed mind will turn to violent thoughts regarding others: "but with their minds turned agonizingly inward, people with depression are usually dangerous only to themselves" (47). In fact, "the madness of depression" is "the antithesis of violence. It is a storm indeed, but a storm of murk" reflected "in slowed-down responses, near paralysis, psychic energy close to zero. Ultimately, the body is affected and feels sapped, drained" (47).

Circuits Conk Out

As the disorder gradually took possession of his system, Styron began to view his mind as similar to one of those outmoded small-town telephone exchanges being gradually inundated by flood waters. One by one, the normal circuits began to drown, causing some of the functions of the body and nearly all of those of instinct and intellect to slowly disconnect. His circuits "conked out" fairly close to the known schedule.

He especially recalls the near disappearance of his voice: "It underwent a strange transformation, becoming at times quite faint, wheezy and spasmodic—a friend observed later that it was the voice of a ninety-year-old" (48). Sexual interest "also made an early exit" (48). While most sufferers lose all appetite, his remained fairly normal; but he found himself eating only for subsistence. Like everything else within the scope of sensation, food was utterly without savor. Most distressing of all was sleep disruption "along with a complete absence of dreams" (48). Exhaustion combined with sleeplessness "is a rare torture" (48).

The little sleep he got—two or three hours—was accomplished with the aid of a tranquilizer. Consulting the *Physicians' Desk Reference* after his illness subsided, he read that the medicine he had been ingesting for two years prior to his illness (first Ativan,™ then Halcion™) was three times the normally prescribed strength. These medicines were not advisable as a medication for more than a month or so, and people of his age should use them with special caution. The benzodiazepine family of tranquilizers is capable of depressing mood and even precipitating a major depression. So it "seems reasonable to think that this was still another contributory factor to the trouble that had come upon me. Certainly, it should be a caution to others" (49). When he was hopitalized in December, the staff psychiatrist informed him that he was taking three times the normal dosage of Halcion™ and switched him to Dalmane,™ a longer-acting medication (71).

His few hours of sleep ended at three or four in the morning, when he "stared up into yawning darkness, wondering and wrenching at the devastation taking place in my mind, and awaiting dawn, which usually permitted me a feverish, dreamless nap" (49). It was during one of these "insomniac trances," he thinks, that there came over him "the knowledge— a weird and shocking revelation, like that of some long-beshrouded metaphysical truth—that this condition would cost me my life if it continued on such a course" (50). Death "was now a daily presence," blowing over him "in cold gusts." He had not yet thought about suicide. The possibility was still around the corner. But he would soon meet it face to face.

At this point, just before his trip to Paris, he had begun to discover that depression "takes on the quality of physical pain" (50). It is not an immediately identifiable pain, like that of a broken limb. It is more like the physical discomfort of being imprisoned in a fiercely overheated room: "And because no breeze stirs in this cauldron, because there is no escape from this smothering confinement, it is entirely natural that the victim begins to think ceaselessly of oblivion" (50).

Loss Is the Touchstone of Depression

Continuing his narrative, Styron focuses on his relationship with the psychiatrist he began to visit immediately after his return from Paris. He remembered that before Emma, the heroine of Emile Zola's *Madame Bovary*, committed suicide, she consulted the village priest, who was only able to offer "Christian platitudes." Styron thus points out that our society is so structured that "Dr. Gold [a pseudonym], or someone like him, is the authority to whom one is forced to turn in crisis" (52). Like Emma, who doubted that the priest could do much for her at this point (and was proven right), Styron had serious doubts that a "conversation with another mortal, even one with professional expertise in mood disorders, could alleviate the distress" (51–52).

A Psychiatrist's Value

In retrospect, he thinks he was essentially correct in harboring such doubts. He acknowledges that such a person may "offer consolation if not much hope, and become the receptacle for an outpouring of woes" (52). Basically, however, his illness had progressed to the point where psychotherapy was ineffectual. Thus, while he "would never question the potential efficacy of psychotherapy in the beginning manifestations or milder forms of the illness—or possibly even in the aftermath of a serious onslaught—its usefulness at the advanced stage I was in has to be virtually nil" (52). His more specific purpose in consulting Dr. Gold was to obtain help through pharmacology, though he found that this, too, was "a chimera for a bottomed-out victim such as I had become" (52).

Dr. Gold asked him if he were suicidal, and he reluctantly responded yes. He did not, however, reveal that many of the artifacts in his house had become potential devices for his own destruction. He had identified the attic rafters and a couple of maple trees outside for hanging himself, the garage for inhaling carbon monoxide, the bathtub to receive the flow from his opened arteries, and the kitchen knives for stabbing himself to death. He also toyed with the idea of self-induced pneumonia—a long frigid, shirt-sleeved hike through the rainy woods. Or perhaps he would stage an accident, a la Randall Jarrell, by walking in front of a truck on the highway nearby. Of course, "These thoughts may seem outlandishly macabre—a strained joke—but they are genuine. They are doubtless especially repugnant to healthy Americans, with their faith in self-improvement. Yet in truth such hideous fantasies, which cause well people to shudder, are to the deeply depressed mind what lascivious daydreams are to persons of robust sexuality" (53).

He and Dr. Gold "chatted" twice a week, but Styron had little to tell him except to try, vainly, to describe his desolation. Nor could the doctor say much of value in response. His "platitudes were not Christian" but were "almost as ineffective," being drawn from the pages of the *DSM-III* which Styron had already read.

Trying Medications

The solace he offered was an antidepressant medication called Ludiomil.™ Upon informing Dr. Gold of adverse side effects (edginess, hyperactivity, urinary retention), he learned that ten days must pass to allow this drug to clear his system before starting a new drug. Ten days to someone in his condition was like ten centuries, and this does not begin to take account of the fact that when a new drug is inaugurated, several weeks must pass before it becomes effective. And its effectiveness is not guaranteed in any case.

Styron goes on to say that he has no doubt that depression responds to medications. "In certain moderate cases and some chronic forms of the disease (the so-called endogenous depressions) medications have proved invaluable, often altering the course of a serious disturbance dramatically" (54). But, for whatever reasons, neither medications nor psychotherapy "were able to arrest my plunge toward the depths" (54–55). In a very real and horrible sense, he was too far gone to be able to profit from the methods (for example, cognitive therapy) and medications that work in earlier stages of the disease. He compares the medications in use for severe cases of depression to the drugs that were available to treat massive bacterial infections before the discovery of antibiotics.

Loss as the Touchstone of Depression

On the other hand, he believes that, despite its still-faltering methods of treatment, psychiatry has contributed a great deal, both analytically and philosophically, to "an understanding of the origins of depression" (56). Much remains to be learned, and a great deal will doubtless remain a mystery. But certainly one psychological element has been established beyond reasonable doubt, and that is the concept of loss: "Loss in all of its manifestations is the touchstone of depression—in the progress of the disease and, most likely, in its origin" (56).

He adds, "At a later date I would gradually be persuaded that devastating loss in childhood figured as a probable genesis of my own disorder" (56). (He expands on this conclusion toward the end of his memoir.) In the meantime, as he monitored his retrograde condition, he felt loss at every turn. Besides his physical losses described earlier, his "sense of self" had all but disappeared, "along with any self-reliance" (56). This loss "can quickly degenerate into dependence, and from dependence into infantile dread. One dreads the loss of all things, all people close and dear. There is an acute fear of abandonment. Being alone in the house, even for a moment, caused me exquisite panic and trepidation" (56–57).

He continues:

> Of the images recollected from that time the most bizarre and discomfiting remains the one of me, age four and a half, tagging through a market after my long-suffering wife; not for an instant could I let out of my sight the endlessly patient soul who had become nanny, mommy, comforter, priestess, and, most important, confidante—a counselor of rocklike centrality to my existence. (57)

As he will indicate later, "the devastating loss in childhood" that was the probable genesis of his disorder concerned his mother. So it is not surprising that in the depths of his depression he experienced himself as a small boy unable to let his wife—who had become, among other things, his "mommy"—out of his sight. What motivated this behavior was "an acute fear of abandonment."

As his sense of loss progressed, he began to develop "fierce attachments": "Ludicrous things—my reading glasses, a handkerchief, a certain writing instrument—became the objects of my demented possessiveness. Each momentary misplacement filled me with a frenzied dismay, each item being the tactile reminder of a world soon to be obliterated" (57).

As November wore on, his condition worsening, a photographer and his assistants came to take pictures for an article to be published in a national magazine. He believes he obeyed the photographer's request to smile, but a couple of days later the magazine's editor telephoned Rose, asking if her husband would submit to another session, for the photos of him, even the ones with smiles, were "too full of anguish" (58).

Loss of Hope

Six months after the initial onset of the disorder, he had reached that phase where "all sense of hope had vanished" along with the idea of futurity. His brain, "in thrall to its outlaw hormones," had become less "an organ of thought than an instrument registering, minute by minute, varying degrees of its own suffering" (58). Mornings were bad. Afternoons were worse, forcing him into bed around three o'clock. There he would remain for as long as six hours, "gazing at the ceiling and waiting for that moment of evening when, mysteriously, the crucifixion would ease up just enough to allow me to force down some food and then, like an automaton, seek an hour or two of sleep again" (58–59). He aska the seemingly obvious question: "Why wasn't I in a hospital?" (59).

The Sound Pierced My Heart like a Dagger

His narrative shifts, however, to an account of a notebook that he had kept for years. While it contained nothing scandalous, he would not have wanted others to see its contents. He had intended to make some use of it professionally and then destroy it when he became a candidate for the nursing home. The destruction of the notebook had now come to be the act that would, instead, eliminate the last obstacle to "putting an end to myself" (59). One evening in early December the moment for its destruction came.

A Bad Day

The day itself had gone badly. As he could no longer drive, Rose had driven him to Dr. Gold's office. Dr. Gold informed him that he had decided to put him on the antidepressant Nardil,™ an older medication that had the advantage of not causing the urinary retention of the other two drugs he had prescribed. But it too had certain drawbacks. It would take the medicine four to six weeks to take effect. He would have to obey certain dietary restrictions to avoid a clash of incompatible enzymes that could cause a stroke. Furthermore, the pill at optimum dosage would have the side effect of impotence.

Up to this point Styron had had some trouble with his psychiatrist's personality, but "had not thought him totally lacking in perspicacity" (60). If the doctor's comment that the medicine would take four to six weeks to take effect was not enough to undermine his belief in his psychiatrist's understanding of his condition, his straight-faced allusion to sexual impotence was the last straw. "Putting myself in Dr. Gold's shoes, I wondered if he seriously thought that this juiceless and ravaged semi-invalid with the shuffle and the ancient wheeze woke up each morning from his Halcion sleep eager for carnal fun" (60).

In any event, the day's session had been "so comfortless" that he returned home in "a particularly wretched state" (60). A few guests were coming over for dinner, a prospect that he viewed with total indifference. But the expectation that he would be present for this occasion (presumably planned by Rose in hopes that a gathering of a few friends would lift his spirits) is itself a peculiarity of this type of illness.

> For in virtually any other serious sickness, a patient who felt similar devastation would be lying flat in bed, possibly sedated and hooked up to the tubes and wires of life-support systems, but at the very least in a posture of repose and in an isolated setting. His invalidism would be necessary, unquestioned and honorably attained. However, the sufferer from depression has no such option and therefore finds himself, like a walking casualty of war, thrust into the most intolerable social and family situations. There he must, despite the anguish devouring his brain, present a face approximating the one that is associated with ordinary events and companionship. (62–63)

That December evening, he could have remained in bed or agreed to attend the dinner party; but, in any case, "the very idea of a decision was academic," as either option was sheer torture. At dinner, he was barely able to speak, but the guests, all good friends, were aware of his condition and politely ignored his "catatonic muteness" (63). Then, after dinner, sitting in the living room, he experienced "a curious inner convulsion" that he can now describe only as "despair beyond despair." It "came out of the cold night; I did not think such anguish possible" (63).

The Irreversible Decision

While his friends chatted quietly in front of the fire, he excused himself and went upstairs, where he retrieved his private notebook from its special place. Then he went to the kitchen. With the "gleaming clarity" of one who knows he is involved in "a solemn rite," he noted all the trademarks on the articles that he assembled for its disposal: the Viva™ paper towels for wrapping the book, the Scotch™ tape to encircle it, and the empty Post Raisin Bran™ box in which he put the parcel before taking it outside and stuffing it deep down into the garbage can, which would be emptied the next morning. Fire, of course, would have destroyed it faster, "but in garbage there was an annihilation of self appropriate, as always, to melancholia's fecund self-humiliation. I felt my heart pounding wildly, like that of a man facing a firing squad, and knew I had made an irreversible decision" (64).

As he engaged in this act of self-humiliation, he had the sense (observed by others in the throes of deep depression) of being accompanied by "a second self—a wraithlike observer who, not sharing the dementia of his double, is able to watch with dispassionate curiosity as his companion struggles against the oncoming disaster, or decides to embrace it" (64). There is a theatrical quality about all this. During the next several days as he went about preparing for his own extinction, he could not shake off a sense of melodrama, one in which he, the victim-to-be of self-murder, was both the solitary actor and lone member of the audience. He had not yet chosen his method, but he knew that this step would come next and would come soon, "as inescapable as nightfall" (65). This second self watched in mingled terror and fascination as he began to make his necessary preparations. He went to see his lawyer to rewrite his will and spent a couple of afternoons in a muddled attempt to write a letter of farewell.

It turned out that putting together a suicide note, which he "felt obsessed with a necessity to compose," was the most difficult task of writing he had ever tackled. He had too many people to acknowledge, to thank, and to bequeath final bouquets, and, in the end,

> I couldn't manage the sheer dirgelike solemnity of it; there was something I found almost comically offensive in the pomposity of such a comment as "For some time now I have sensed in my work a growing psychosis that is doubtless a reflection of the psychotic strain tainting my life" (this is one of the few lines I recall verbatim), as well as something degrading in the prospect of a testament, which I wished to infuse with at least some dignity and eloquence, reduced to an exhausted stutter of inadequate apologies and self-serving explanations. (65)

After struggling with longer versions, he tried a very truncated version. Finally, even a few words seemed too long-winded, and he tore up all his efforts, resolving to go out in silence.

Late one bitterly cold night, knowing he could not get through the next day, he sat in the living room bundled up against the chill. Something was wrong with the furnace. Rose had gone to bed, and he was forcing himself to watch the tape of a movie in which a young actress who had been in a play of his had a small part. At one point in the film, set in late nineteenth-century Boston, the characters moved down the hallway of a music conservatory. In the background, from unseen musicians, came a contralto voice, and "a sudden passage from the Brahms's *Alto Rhapsody*" (66):

> This sound, which like all music—indeed, like all pleasure—I had been numbly unresponsive to for months, pierced my heart like

a dagger, and in a flood of swift recollection I thought of all the joys the house had known: the children who had rushed through its rooms, the festivals, the love and work, the honestly earned slumber, the voices and the nimble commotion, the perennial tribe of cats and dogs and birds. (66–67)

He realized in this moment that all of this "was more than I could ever abandon, even as what I had set out so deliberately to do was more than I could inflict on those memories, and upon those, so close to me, with whom the memories were bound" (67). No less powerfully, he realized that he would not commit "this desecration" on himself. He "drew upon some last gleam of sanity to perceive the terrifying dimensions of the mortal predicament I had fallen into" (67). He woke up Rose, and soon telephone calls were made. The next day he was admitted to the hospital.

A Kinder, Gentler Madhouse than the One I'd Left

In hindsight, he should have been admitted much earlier. But Dr. Gold, who was called in to arrange for his admission, had earlier brushed aside his admittedly hesitant queries as to whether he should be hospitalized. Dr. Gold advised that he should try to avoid the hospital at all costs due to the stigma he might suffer. Even at the time, this reasoning seemed "extremely misguided," especially since he had thought that psychiatry itself "had advanced long beyond the point where stigma was attached to any aspect of mental illness, including the hospital" (68).

The Hospital as Salvation

Whether another psychiatrist would have discouraged the hospital route is impossible to say. Styron suggests that many psychiatrists who seem to be able to comprehend the nature and depth of their patients' anguish maintain "their stubborn allegiance to pharmaceuticals in the belief that eventually the pills will kick in, the patient will respond, and the somber surroundings of the hospital will be avoided" (68). In his own case, this view came within a hair's-breadth of costing him his life. For Styron, "the hospital was my salvation, and it is something of a paradox that in this austere place with its locked and wired doors and desolate green hallways—ambulances screeching night and day ten floors below—I found the repose, the assuagement of the tempest in my brain, that I was unable to find in my quiet farmhouse" (68–69).

He identifies three reasons for this. One is that of *sequestration*, or safety. One is removed to a world in which the urge to pick up a knife and plunge it into one's breast disappears "in the newfound knowledge, quickly apparent even to the depressive's fuzzy brain, that the knife with which he is attempting to cut his dreadful Swiss steak is bendable plastic" (69).

Another is *stabilization.* The depressed patient experiences "a transfer out of the too familiar surroundings of home, where all is anxiety and discord, into an orderly and benign detention where one's duty is to try to get well. For me the real healers were seclusion and time" (69).

A third way in which the hospital became his salvation was that it became a *sanctuary.* When he was admitted, his depression was so profound that some of the staff felt he was a candidate for electroconvulsive therapy (or ECT). He wanted to avoid this, though, "because he began to get well, gradually but steadily" (70). He was amazed to discover that the fantasies of self-destruction all but disappeared within a few days after he checked in, a "testimony to the pacifying effect that the hospital can create, its immediate value as a *sanctuary* where peace can return to the mind" (70, my emphasis). Being taken off Halcion also contributed to the decline and disappearance of his suicidal thoughts. As noted earlier, the staff psychiatrist remarked that Styron had been taking three times the usually prescribed dose. He placed him on another sleep-inducing medication. Styron blames himself for overdosing, but notes that another doctor had assured him he could "take as many pills as I wished" (71).

Finding Peace in a Kinder, Gentler Madhouse

Styron remained in the hospital for seven weeks. Given that he was placed on a floor with fifteen other middle-aged men and women "in the throes of melancholia of a suicidal complexion," it was "a fairly laughterless environment" (72). But the peek that the bare recreation room afforded into the outside world—*Dynasty, Knot's Landing,* and *CBS Evening News*—would sometimes make him aware "that the place where I had found refuge was a kinder, gentler madhouse than the one I'd left" (73). Then something occurred that he could not have imagined prior to that December evening when he was convinced he could not endure another day. The depression began to capitulate: "Even those for whom any kind of therapy is a futile exercise can look forward to the eventual passing of the storm. If they survive the storm itself, its fury almost always fades and then disappears. Mysterious in its coming, mysterious in its going, the affliction runs its course, and one finds peace" (73).

As he got better, he noticed the distractions of the hospital's routines, which he describes as "its own institutionalized sitcoms" (73). Group therapy proved, for him, a complete waste of time, perhaps because it was supervised by "an odiously smug young shrink with a spade shaped dark beard (*der junge Freud?*)" who was "alternately condescending and bullying" (73). The rest of the psychiatric staff were "exemplary in their tact and compassion" (73).

Art therapy, which he describes as "organized infantilism," was not much better; but in time he began to play along with it, having become fond of the instructor in spite of himself. In early February, he sensed that although still shaky, he had emerged into light: "I felt myself no longer a husk but a body with some of the body's sweet juices stirring again. I had my first dream in many months, confused but to this day imperishable, with a flute in it somewhere, and a wild goose, and a dancing girl" (75).

An Insufferable Burden of Rage and Guilt

Having survived his illness, Styron feels he is in a position to offer guidance to those whose loved ones may be afflicted now or in the future. He begins by noting that the great majority of those who go through even the severest depression survive it and "live ever afterward at least as happy as their unafflicted counterparts" (75). Except for the awfulness of certain memories, acute depression inflicts few permanent wounds. True, many–perhaps half–will be struck again, but most victims live through these relapses, often coping better the second time because they have become psychologically tuned by past experience to deal with it better. (While Styron does not mention his own second episode, Rose Styron discusses it in her reflections on his illness; I will take this up later in the chapter.)

Guidance for Depression Sufferers

If the great majority of sufferers survive it, those who are caught in its grip, especially first-timers, need to be told by those who are in a position to do so (family, friends, admirers) "that the illness will run its course and that they will pull through" (76). This, of course, is a tough job, as such assurance may seem platitudinous and insensitive to the sufferer's excruciating pain. Still, "it has been shown over and over again that if the encouragement is dogged enough–and the support equally committed and passionate–the endangered one can nearly always be saved" (76).

Most people in the grip of more extreme forms of depression are, "for whatever reason, in a state of unrealistic hopelessness, torn by exaggerated ills and fatal threats that bear no resemblance to actuality" (76). It may require "an almost religious devotion" on the part of loved ones "to persuade the sufferers of life's worth, which is so often in conflict with a sense of their own worthlessness, but such devotion has prevented countless suicides" (76). Note, here, the difference between the "Christian platitudes" that could not avert Emma Bovary's suicide and the "almost religious devotion" that involves persuading the sufferer that life *is* worth living. The operative words here are "convince" and "persuade." Having come so close to terminating his own life, Styron exhibits here the same "almost religious devotion" that he encourages others to exhibit. Such "devotion" goes beyond public "advocacy" for the mentally ill, important as this is, and focuses, more narrowly, on the critical role that loved ones can play in dissuading the depressed person from committing this "desecration" against himself.

Looking for the Cause

Styron moves next to the question of how he came to be visited by such a calamity. It was not until he began to recover that he gave this question any serious thought. He has already cited the "manifest crisis" of his abrupt withdrawal from alcohol as the triggering event. He is open to the idea that the fact his depression and his turning sixty ("that hulking milestone of mortality") occurred simultaneously was more than coincidental. A "vague dissatisfaction" with the way his work was going, while not a new experience for him, may also have magnified the difficulty with alcohol. But the really interesting question for him is this: "What are the forgotten or buried events that suggest an ultimate explanation for the evolution of depression and its later flowering into madness?" (78).

The Buried Events

Before his illness, he had never given much thought to his work as a writer "in terms of its connection with his subconscious." After he returned to health and was able to reflect on the past in light of his ordeal, he "began to see clearly how depression had clung to the outer edges of my life for many years" (78). He recognized, in fact, that suicide had been "a persistent theme" in his books. Three of his major characters killed themselves. Also, for the first time in years, he reviewed sequences in his novels where his heroines lurched down pathways toward doom. He was stunned to perceive how accurately he had "created the landscape of depression" in the minds of these young women, "describing with what could only be instinct, out of a subconscious already roiled by disturbances of mood, the psychic imbalance that led them to destruction" (79). Thus, when depression finally arrived, it was "in fact no stranger, not even a visitor totally unannounced; it had been tapping at my door for decades" (79).

But if this is so, how did he come by this "subconscious" affinity for the mood disturbances that eventuated in his illness and for such an extreme form of it? He identified two major factors, the second of which was the more significant. The first is that his father battled depression for much of his life. He "had been hospitalized in my boyhood after a despondent spiraling down that in retrospect greatly resembled mine. The genetic roots of depression seem now to be beyond controversy" (79). But he is persuaded "that an even more significant factor was the death of my mother when I was thirteen; this disorder and early sorrow— the death or disappearance of a parent, especially a mother, before or during puberty–appears repeatedly in the literature on depression as a trauma sometimes likely to create nearly irreparable emotional havoc" (79). The danger is especially apparent if the young person "is affected by what has been termed 'incomplete mourning'" (79–80). Having been unable to achieve "the catharsis of grief," he "carries within himself through later years an insufferable burden of which rage and guilt, and not only damned-up sorrow, are a part." These "become the potential seeds of self-destruction" (80).

Incomplete Mourning

Styron cites in this connection a book on suicide, *Self-Destruction in the Promised Land,* by Harold I. Kushner. Kushner uses Abraham Lincoln as an example of "incomplete mourning" and suggests that Lincoln's own "suicidal turmoil" in his youth was directly linked to the death of his mother when he was nine years old and to unexpressed grief exacerbated by his sister's death ten years later. Drawing insights from the chronicle of Lincoln's success in avoiding suicide, Kushner, in Styron's view, makes a convincing case for two ideas. First, early loss precipitates self-destructive conduct. Second, this same behavior becomes a strategy through which one comes to grips with his guilt and rage and triumphs over self-willed death. This "reconciliation" may also be entwined with the quest for immortality. One way this quest may express itself is through work honored by posterity. While this is relevant to Lincoln, it is also relevant to "a writer of fiction" (81).

Styron goes on to say that, for him, this theory of "incomplete mourning" has considerable validity. Also, "if it is true that in the nethermost depths of one's suicidal behavior one is still subconsciously dealing with immense loss while trying to surmount all the effects of its devastation, then my own avoidance of death may have been belated homage to my mother" (81). As evidence, he adds: "I do know that in those last hours before I rescued myself, when I listened to the passage from the *Alto Rhapsody*–which I'd heard her sing–she had been very much on my mind" (81).

So We Came Forth and Beheld These Stars

In the closing pages of *Darkness Visible,* Styron discusses the difficulty that writers have had in finding "a vocabulary that might give proper expression to the desolation of melancholia" (82). He suggests, however, that "the vast metaphor which most faithfully represents the fathomless ordeal" is Dante's image in *The Divine Comedy* of the "dark wood": "In the middle of the journey of our life / I found myself in a dark wood, / For I had lost the right path" (83). These lines, which conjure "the ravages of melancholia," have, however, "often overshadowed the last lines of the best-known part of that poem, with their evocation of hope" (83). Styron returns here to the theme that suicide may be averted if loved ones are able to convince the sufferer that the depression will finally relinquish its deadly grip. He concludes that

> one need not sound the false or inspirational note to stress the truth that depression is not the soul's annihilation; men and women who have recovered from the disease—and they are countless—bear witness to what is probably its only saving grace: it is conquerable (84).

Those who have dwelt in depression's "dark wood" have experienced the ascent that Dante also describes, "trudging upward and upward out of hell's black depths and at last emerging into what he saw as 'the shining world'" (84). Whoever has been restored to health "has almost always been restored to the capacity for serenity and joy, and this may be indemnity enough for having endured the despair beyond despair" (84). Styron concludes his memoir with this line from Dante's poem: "And so we came forth, and once again beheld the stars" (83).[3]

Rose Styron's Reflections

A major concern of this book is the effect of mental illness on loved ones. In chapters 4 and 5, I will focus on two books written by family members of mentally ill persons. In Styron's case, however, we are fortunate to have a memoir written by the afflicted one as well as a briefer essay by the person who was closest to him throughout his ordeal. Rose Styron's essay, "Strands" (2001), follows an excerpt from *Darkness Visible* in Nell Casey's *Unholy Ghost: Writers on Depression.* In addition to her own recollections, Rose includes notes their daughter Polly wrote. Polly had come to visit her parents on the day her father decided he could not go on, the day before he was admitted to the hospital.

In "Strands," Rose Styron provides her own perspective on her husband's illness. In her description, his moods had become more erratic over a period of years before his major depressive episode in 1985. Having cherished separate quiet times—after all, he was a writer—

> he came to demand real solitude. He stopped allowing me to invite guests, arrange celebrations. He wrote in the afternoons and then drank tumblers of whiskey till the wee hours while he listened to certain pieces by Mozart and Beethoven over and over. He talked to me less and less, read to me not at all. Increasingly, he became irritated by noise—traffic, excessive conversation, the clatter of dropped utensils. He tried to shut out the sounds even of our four spirited children. Unpredictably, he would lash out at the family he loved. Having been raised by steady, affectionate parents who encouraged my independent

judgment, I was baffled by my spouse's outbursts and need to control me and the children. (R. Styron 2001, 128).

She accepted his behavior on the grounds that there was "no physical violence in him" and of her awareness that "his childhood had not been a happy one: his mother died when he was thirteen; he had no siblings; his sweet, distraught father soon married a nurse who was jealous and disapproving of Bill. So I made allowances for what I tagged Fear of Loss" (129).

Insanely Hypochondriacal

Her love for him, however, did not prepare her for 1985 when this hypochondriacal man (with a *Merck's Manual* at their bedside) became "*insanely* hypochondriacal. He saw THE END on every horizon. Death was on his mind—not only for himself but for others. When his favorite dog was sick, he was certain she would die (she lived three more years to his joy)" (129). When their daughter Polly fell off a horse and their daughter Alexandra was in a car accident, "both requiring stitches in their heads, he assumed death was imminent for them both. Agonized about our daughters, Bill remonstrated *me*. I felt genuinely guilty, that it was my fault that I had not been careful enough with them" (129).

If he did summon the energy to write, "he described characters consumed by their own fears of failing health and fortune, or approaching death. I noted, bemused, that every one of his fictional heroines was a victim of suicide or murder; but I had not understood that it was a disguise for his own apprehensions" (129–30).

She attributed his irritable moods and preoccupation with death to withdrawal from alcohol, recalling an earlier withdrawal from smoking that was compensated by a frenetic need for chocolate. But attempts to ply him with sweets this time were ineffectual. His previous habit of urging her to leave him at home alone and go off on trips by herself was replaced by a sudden desire for her to be there all the time. He "didn't want me out of his sight, *wanted* to talk. He asked me to accompany him on long walks with the dogs, during which he talked about his hatred for the world and winter, his fears about work and aging" (130).

Between Compassion and Despair

She was "sad for him," but also "happy for us" because there was a new closeness in their relationship. At the same time, she "seesawed hopelessly between bafflement and anger, between immediate compassion for Bill and despair for his future" (130). Then, however, she "finally figured out that Bill was depressed—not just moody or in withdrawal or angry at life but *clinically depressed*" (131). She knew "we needed professional help" (131). She contacted friends of his who had experienced mood swings since their youth and asked them to suggest to him that he needed professional assistance.

She also "became the scholar of Bill's moods and behavior, too interested and curious to turn off entirely (remember that this man I had married was never boring, always brilliantly mercurial), even when I could not reach him" (131). She accompanied him to a psychiatrist recommended by a local doctor (their trusted family doctor had died). She overheard him "droning at Bill about age, about lowering his creative expectations—maybe Bill shouldn't write anymore and should think of other things to do—meanwhile instructing him not to think about hospitalization because it would only stigmatize him" (132). When she phoned the psychiatrist to tell him that the medications he had prescribed were not working, he responded by prescribing more medication.

She mentions the trip to Paris and suggests that the luncheon fiasco and the search for the missing check "were much funnier scenes than Bill remembers in *Darkness Visible*" (132). Also, she questions whether the scene of his sitting alone watching the documentary while she slept upstairs could possibly be accurate. In *her* mind, "I never slept if Bill was not in bed beside me" (133). The psychiatrist had, in fact, cautioned her, "Just don't let him out of your sight." But, whether his memory was "skewed by trauma" or the account reflected a novelist's intuitive feeling for "a meaningful ending," she *is* "convinced that 'the piercing of his heart by Brahms,'" which "must have taken place several hours earlier," was "the moment that saved him." She is certain that his thoughts of our family "did finally nullify his resolve to kill himself" (133).

Polly's Perspective

Their daughter Polly's account supports her own recollection that she had not gone to bed that evening, leaving him alone in the living room to struggle over the question whether to take his life. Polly found him in bed, "lying there, with his long gray hair all tangled and wild" (133). She took his trembling hand as he said, "I'm a goner, darling." She continues:

> His eyes had a startled look, and he seemed to be not quite there. His cool, trembling hands kept fumbling over mine. "The agony's too great now, darling. I'm sorry. I'm a goner." For the next hour he raved about his miserable past and his sins and the waste of his life and how, when they published the scandal of his life, we should try not to hate him. "You'll hate me. You'll hate me," he said in a whisper. Everything was repeated over and over. "I love you so much. And the other children. And your mother. You'll hate me for what I am going to do to myself. My head is exploding. I can't stand the agony anymore. It's over

now. I can't stand the agony. Tell the others how much I love them. I've betrayed my life. All my books have been about suicide. What a miserable account of a life. I'm dying! I'm dying! I am dying!" And on and on, and over and over, while grabbing me to come closer, taking my head to his breast, holding me closer. (133–34)

When her mother came upstairs, Polly mouthed the word "hospital" to her; and arrangements were made to take him. As Rose suggests, this is a very different scene from the one he presents in *Darkness Visible*–of taking the initiative himself to wake her up and apparently ask her to take him to the hospital. But this scene has its own drama. As Rose also indicates, this does not affect other features of his account–hearing the sudden soaring passage from Brahms's *Alto Rhapsody* and feeling it pierce his heart like a dagger and realizing that he could not inflict this desecration on the memories he had of all the joys the house had known, on his family, nor on himself.

Rose's Hospital Experience

While Styron suggests that his hospitalization brought almost instant peace–a sense of security–Rose indicates that it "began agonizingly" for her:

Visiting each day, I would listen to hours of his nightmares, sorrows, disorientation, then watch him shuffle down the hall like a figure from *One Flew Over the Cuckoo's Nest*. When I spoke to the doctor, he warned me that electroconvulsive therapy (ECT) might be advisable. Filled with *Cuckoo* images, it didn't occur to me that [these] techniques had been improved, and I protested emphatically. Even at his most medicated, Bill begged me to keep protesting so his creative brain would not be permanently altered. I pursued this mission so annoyingly, the doctors urged me to go on vacation. (134)

"Slowly but surely, with time, therapy, and medication, Bill improved" (134). Note that Rose mentions "therapy" here, whereas his own view was that group therapy was worse than useless and art therapy was rather infantile. Perhaps, though, the young art instructor evoked his paternal feelings toward his loving daughters, and the very infantile nature of the projects–"My House," for example–tapped into long repressed memories of childhood. Polly describes his convalescence in this way: "As his anxiety subsided, he became increasingly goofy and zombielike, but then slowly became more coherent, more animated, and finally more willful. When his temper returned, we let out a collective sigh of relief" (134).

Rose mentions a second episode in early 1988 that Styron did not include in *Darkness Visible*. This second episode fits his observation that if a relapse occurs, most victims often cope better the second time around "because they have become psychologically tuned by past experience to deal with the ogre" (W. Styron 1990, 76). This episode was prompted by his "acute apprehension" concerning a major surgical operation that had been delayed a couple of weeks because of the hospital's busy schedule. His insomnia had returned, and he had persuaded a new local doctor to give him a prescription for Halcion, which he took just prior to a speaking/teaching engagement at Claremont Colleges in California. While there, his gloom returned. He "became alternately obsessed, distracted, or mute before the students" (R. Styron 2001, 135). He phoned Rose, informed her that the Halcion had caused "a chemical commotion" in his brain, and that he was violently suicidal again and very scared. She called a psychiatrist they both admired, who advised her to fly to California and bring him directly back to the hospital where his surgery was planned. Meanwhile, arrangements would be made to admit him to the psychiatric wing until the operation. The "whole stay was a success" (135), testifying to the wisdom of taking immediate action when depression reasserted itself.

Rose's Advice

Rose concludes her account with the observation that "sticking with the person you love through the stressful dramas of mood disorder can eventually be incredibly rewarding" (137). Citing the comment by Johns Hopkins psychiatrist Ray de Paulo that depression "eats at the heart of every relationship," she suggests: "One must be sensitive, nurture the fragile connections, humor the sufferer like a baby" (137). Perhaps the best thing one can do, she concludes, "is to act on intuition. And keep intuition's third eye open forever, after recovery, to note the first trembling turning leaves of a change of season" (137).

Anxiety and Depression

Now that we have brought Rose Styron more clearly into the picture, I would like to return to *Darkness Visible* and conclude with some reflections of my own. I will begin with the connection William Styron draws between anxiety and depression and will then conclude with the origins of melancholia in the vicissitudes of mother-son relationships. The purpose of these reflections is not to question the fact that depression is a brain disorder or disease—I take this fact to be axiomatic—but to consider the equally self-evident fact that depression is an illness that its sufferers experience in very different ways.

Common Features among Depression Sufferers

If so, this raises the question whether certain features of depression are common to most, perhaps all, sufferers? In my view, Styron puts his finger on two such features:

1. the close link between depression and anxiety
2. the equally close link between depression and loss

As Styron notes, his use of alcohol through the years had served the purpose of calming "the anxiety and incipient dread that I had hidden away for so long somewhere in the dungeons of my spirit" (W. Styron 1990, 40). Deprived of alcohol's "ministrations," he was newly vulnerable to the anxiety that the alcohol had calmed and, in fact, had served the purpose of hiding from his conscious mind. He was aware that, for others, alcohol is a major depressant, but, for him, "it had never truly depressed me during my drinking career, acting instead as a shield against anxiety" (43).

Depression is classified in the *DSM-IV* as a mood, not an anxiety disorder (a class of mental disorders that includes agoraphobia, panic disorder with and without agoraphobia, social phobia, specific phobia, obsessive-compulsive disorder, posttraumatic stress disorder, acute stress disorder, and generalized anxiety disorder). But Styron's observation that anxiety was an important feature of his illness is supported by research on depression.

In *Origins of Mental Illness* (1995), Gordon Claridge cites the research of Jeffrey Gray, who has explored in detail the connection between anxiety and depression (1982). According to Claridge, Gray "has argued that differences in the trait of anxiety are due to variations among individuals in their sensitivity to punishment, assumed to exist as a biological characteristic from birth" (Claridge, 109). That is, more anxious individuals react more strongly to events in their environment that signal punishment. Their tendency is to avoid or withdraw from such situations and to develop a heightened fear of them. Thus, they develop a greater tendency to be inhibited than other individuals who have a greater sensitivity to those events in the environment that signal reward (Claridge, 35–36). Gray suggests that both sensitivities have their locus in the limbic system of the brain. As Claridge notes, evidence for this suggestion is especially strong in the case of sensitivity to punishment and the behavioral inhibition that this produces (36–37).

Such inhibition is reflected in anxiety disorders, for one of the effects of a heightened sensitivity to the punishment-inflicting events in the environment is to become fearful to the point of phobia, which is the tendency to exaggerate the capacity of the external world to inflict pain. Agoraphobics fear the world outside their homes, social phobics fear certain social situations, and specific phobics focus on one or another object (for example, snakes, cats, injections) or features of the external world (heights, storms, rivers) and their perceived capacity to cause injury or harm. Cognitive therapy for phobic persons involves encouraging them to make more realistic assessments of the threat involved, assessments that generally lead to the conclusion that their fear is largely or even completely unfounded.

Dysthymic Disorder

Gray points out that such inhibition is also found among dysthymic individuals. According to the *DSM-IV*, the essential feature of dysthymic disorder "is a chronically depressed mood that occurs for most of the day more days than not for at least two years" (*DSM-IV*, 345). Dysthymic persons may have symptoms similar to those who experience a major depressive episode, but these symptoms have typically become "so much a part of the individual's day-to-day experience" that they tend to minimize them, saying, "I've always been this way" or "That's just how I am."

These symptoms are usually not reported unless directly asked about by the interviewer (345–46). Symptoms like low self-esteem, poor concentration or difficulty making decisions, and feelings of hopelessness that a person experiencing a major depressive episode finds unusual and a basis for alarm may seem more routine or normal for the dysthymic person. An accurate diagnosis between dysthymic disorder and major depressive disorder is made particularly difficult by the fact that the two disorders share similar symptoms and the differences between them in terms of onset, persistence, and severity are not easy to evaluate retrospectively.

But major depressive disorder consists of one or more discrete major depressive episodes that can be distinguished from the person's usual functioning, whereas dysthymic disorder is characterized by chronic, less severe depressive symptoms that have been present for many years (343). Styron's observation that a review of his writings revealed that "depression, when it finally came to me, was in fact no stranger, not even a visitor totally unannounced; it had been tapping at my door for years" suggests a dysthymic personality with low to moderate (or subclinical) symptoms until his major depressive episode in 1985.

The fact that dysthymic personalities also have the behavioral inhibitions characteristic of persons who are anxiety-prone leads Claridge to suggest that persons with anxiety disorders and persons who are dysthymic (whether or not the dysthymia reaches clinical levels) share in common a pessimistic worldview. He also argues, however, that the pessimism of dysthymic individuals is qualitatively different, in that anxiety-prone individuals view the world fearfully, as having the ability to hurt, while depression-prone individuals view the world as uncontrollable. Since an anxiety-proneness provides the biological predisposition for depression to develop, these two views may interact. Claridge goes on to argue that depression usually has an additional causal factor that accounts for the sense that what happens in the world outside oneself is beyond one's control. This causal factor is a catastrophic loss in childhood or adolescence (1995, 110).

Early Catastrophic Loss and Depression

In support of the argument that an early catastrophic loss is a key causal factor in the development of depression later in life, Claridge cites the research studies of G. W. Brown and his associates (1978). Their extensive study of the past histories of depressed individuals and of the life events surrounding their illnesses revealed an important vulnerability factor, the loss of a close relative—especially the mother—in childhood or adolescence (1978, 108). They went on to suggest "that such loss is a particularly catastrophic example of the kind of trauma which could lead to a permanent perception that events are uncontrollable" (108–9).

Since many persons who have suffered such catastrophic loss do not experience depression later in life, Claridge believes that those who have been spared are likely not to have had the biological or temperamental predisposition of anxiety-proneness. Conversely, those who have this biological predisposition (which would make them potential candidates for an anxiety disorder) and have experienced a catastrophic loss in childhood or adolescence are uniquely at risk of suffering depression at some point in adulthood. This depression may occur in the more chronic form of dysthymia or the more acute form of major depressive episode.

What Claridge does not address, however, is why a more chronic tendency toward dysthymia reaches clinical levels or why a major depressive episode occurs when it does. Why now rather than earlier or later? In Styron's case, however, we have his own explanation that the "manifest crisis" that triggered his major depressive episode was the fact that his body began to reject alcohol in early June. Significantly, he himself suggests that withdrawal from alcohol left him vulnerable to both anxiety and depression.

This supports Claridge's argument that both biological and experiential factors are involved in depressive disorders. Conversely, Claridge's theoretical discussion enables us to see the importance of Styron's alcohol withdrawal in creating a vulnerability to a major depressive episode. If alcohol had been successful through the years as a means to calm the anxiety and incipient dread that had been hidden away for so long in the dungeons of his spirit, it seems likely that the alcohol successfully addressed the underlying biological component of his vulnerability to depression. He probably began drinking shortly after his mother's death. Alcohol may have immunized him against the chemical processes in the limbic system of the brain (which Claridge refers to as the "lower brain") that causes the biological inhibition reflected in anxiety disorders. (The limbic system also causes the biological excitation found in sensation-seeking, impulsivity, and the like [see Webster and Jackson 1997]).

With this immunization removed, he became vulnerable to the deeper depressions relating to the trauma of his mother's death. As Styron further noted, once this "shield against anxiety" was removed, there was nothing to prevent the "demons" which had hovered around for years "from beginning to swarm through the subconscious, and I was emotionally naked, vulnerable as I had never been before," vulnerable to "depression's black tempest" (W. Styron 1990, 43).

Melancholia as Incomplete Mourning

In Styron's own view, his mother's death when he was thirteen was the origination point of his vulnerability to depression later in life. However, its connection to the full range of emotions that he experienced, prompting him to prefer the term "melancholia" to "depression," remains somewhat unclear. Melancholia of the kind he experienced was more than dammed-up sorrow. It was also dammed-up rage and dammed-up guilt. Why rage? Why guilt? An essay by Sigmund Freud titled "Mourning and Melancholia" (1963; originally published in 1917), is especially relevant in this regard.

In introducing Freud, I am mindful of Styron's observation that the "odiously smug young shrink" who led group therapy during his seven-weeks hospitalization had "a spade-shaped dark beard" that suggested he may have seen himself as "*der junge Freud.*" This does not necessarily mean that Styron has something against Freud. It could just as well mean that he thought the young shrink was a pitiful imitation of Freud. Whatever the case may be, Styron's view that his major depressive episode at age sixty had its experiential roots in his incomplete mourning of his mother receives theoretical support in Freud's "Mourning and Melancholia."

Mourning and Melancholia

In her edited volume of writings on melancholia going back to Aristotle, Jennifer Radden (2000) notes that Freud was the first to suggest that "loss" is the primary cause of melancholia. For Freud, "Melancholia represents loss of the 'object,' that is, the beloved parent whose love has been perceived to be withdrawn. Self-accusation and self-hatred, which Freud describes as central characteristics of the melancholic patient, are a form of rage redirected from the loved object to the self" (Radden 2000, 282). If Freud's essay provides theoretical support for Styron's view of the primary cause of his depression, we can well imagine that if Freud had had access to Styron's book, he would have cited it in support of his argument in the essay. A brief summary of this classic essay will enable us to see the connection between Freud's theory, based on his clinical experiences with melancholiacs, and Styron's own experience.

Noting that the study of dreams has enabled him to shed light on narcissistic mental disorders, Freud wonders if similar light might be shed on the disorder of melancholia by comparing it with the normal process of mourning "the loss of a loved person, or the loss of some abstraction which has taken the place of one, such as fatherland, liberty, an ideal, and so on" (Freud 1963, 164). Although grief involves "grave departures from the normal attitude to life, it never occurs to us to regard it as a morbid condition and hand the mourner over to medical treatment" (165). Rather, "We rest assured that after a lapse of time it will be overcome, and we look upon any interference with it as inadvisable or even harmful" (165).

This is not the case with melancholia, which results from the same influences but expresses itself in such a way that we suspect "a morbid pathological condition" (165). (As Rose Styron indicates, she became convinced that her husband was "clinically depressed.") The distinguishing mental features of melancholia are "a profoundly painful dejection, abrogation of interest in the outside world, loss of the capacity to love, inhibition of all activity, and a lowering of the self-regarding feelings to a degree that finds utterance in self-reproaches and self-revilings, and culminates in a delusional expectation of punishment" (165). (Consider in this regard Polly's account of Styron's self-reproaches and self-revilings the evening that arrangements were made for him to be hospitalized). Freud notes that several of these mental features are also found in grief, with the notable exception of the fall in self-esteem that finds utterance in self-reproach and expectations of punishment. This exception is a clue to why mourning eventually completes itself and "the ego becomes free and uninhibited again," while melancholia continues to fester.

Thus, melancholia takes a different course from that of mourning, and the question is why? The primary reason, in Freud's view, is that there is an *unconscious* aspect to the loss in melancholia. (Recall Styron's observation that he was vulnerable to the "demons" that had hovered around for years in his "subconscious" mind.) This unconscious aspect is present in cases in which the loss is similar to the loss incurred in grief, but is not due to death per se. It is also present in cases where the other person has not actually died but has become lost as an object of love (for example, in cases of marital desertion or divorce), or when one feels justified in declaring that a loss has occurred but cannot see clearly what has been lost. In the latter case, one may know whom one has lost but not *what* one has lost in losing this person (166).

Freud concludes: "This would suggest that melancholia is in some way related to an unconscious loss of a love-object, in contradistinction to mourning, in which there is nothing unconscious about the loss" (166). Thus, in mourning, one is very conscious not only of whom one has lost but also what one has lost in losing this person. Because one is conscious of both, there can eventually be a sense of finality to the experience of mourning. One knows full well the reality and the nature of one's loss. In melancholia, one does not know what one has lost or does not realize the extent of one's loss.

If the primary reason that melancholia takes a different course from normal mourning is that there is some *unconscious* aspect to the loss (something that one is not consciously aware of), how does this explain the fact that melancholia manifests itself in reduced self-esteem, in self-reproaches, and in expectations of punishment? Freud believes the answer lies in the self-reproaches: "The patient represents his ego to us as worthless, incapable of any effort and morally despicable; he reproaches himself, vilifies himself and expects to be cast out and chastized. He abases himself before everyone and commiserates his own relatives for being connected with someone so unworthy" (167). The patient "does not realize that any change has taken place in him, but extends his self-criticism back over the past and declares that he was never any better. This picture of delusional belittling—which is predominantly moral—is completed by sleeplessness and refusal of nourishment, and by an overthrow, psychologically very remarkable, of that instinct which constrains every living thing to cling to life" (167). Freud adds that "in the clinical picture of melancholia dissatisfaction with the self on moral grounds is far the most outstanding feature; the self-criticism much less frequently concerns itself with bodily infirmity, ugliness, weakness, social inferiority" (169).

Excessive Self-reproach

Why this self-reproach? And why such excessive self-reproach? Why such "delusional belittling" of oneself? Freud believes that these self-reproaches are "reproaches against a loved object which has been shifted on to the patient's own ego" (169). In Freud's view, we have compelling evidence that melancholic persons are actually reproaching the loved object, namely the fact that melancholic persons can reproach themselves so mercilessly and yet are not ashamed and do not hide their heads. Instead of adopting "the attitude of humility and submission that would alone befit such worthless persons," they "give a great deal of trouble, perpetually taking offense and behaving as if they had been treated with great injustice" (169–70). The unconscious element in melancholia, then, is due to ambivalent feelings—negative as well as positive—toward the lost loved object and to the inability to acknowledge the negative feelings.

The illness of melancholy has been developed "so as to avoid the necessity of openly expressing [one's] hostility against the loved one" (172).

Negative Feelings

But why would one have negative feelings in the case of someone who has died? If such feelings are understandable in cases of marital desertion or divorce, where, as Freud says, the "lost object" is "to be found among those in his near neighborhood" (173), why would they occur in the case of the physical death of the loved one? The answer seems to be that the loved one, such as a mother, is subject to reproach because she is viewed as having abandoned oneself—not voluntarily, perhaps, as in the case of suicide, but, nonetheless, leaving one bereft and defenseless all the same.

This redirection of negative feelings onto oneself also provides an explanation for cases of melancholia that end in suicide. The hostility toward the lost loved object may, in extreme cases, assume a sadistic form, and "it is this sadism, and only this, that solves the riddle of the tendency to suicide which makes melancholia so interesting and so dangerous" (173). Freud continues:

> It is true we have long known that no neurotic harbors thoughts of suicide which are not murderous impulses against others redirected upon himself, but we have never been able to explain what interplay of forces could carry such a purpose through to execution. Now the analysis of melancholia shows that the ego can kill itself only when...it can treat itself as an object, when it is able to launch against itself the animosity relating to an object [that is, the object that it has lost]. (173)

Thus, the same mechanism that prompts self-reproach is responsible for suicide as well. Suicide, however, puts an end to the ambivalently-experienced object by putting an end to the ego itself.

Freud and Styron

How does Freud's analysis of melancholia relate to Styron? Not all cases of melancholia involve the physical death of the loved one (in fact, the more normative experience is that the lost loved one is still in "the near neighborhood"). But some do, and because they do, the same instigating event is present as in the instance of mourning. But instead of the more normal route of mourning, these cases take the path of melancholia. Styron's observation that his was an example of "incomplete mourning" is therefore a very accurate one.

Melancholia for Styron was the failure to complete the mourning process following his mother's death, because he could not at that time acknowledge–admit into his conscious mind–that he had negative feelings toward her that were related to the loss itself. He does not specifically acknowledge such feelings in *Darkness Visible*. We may assume, however, that they would have been feelings of having been abandoned, left perhaps with the task of having to take care of a depressed father while also having to deal with the inevitable challenges of adolescence. As his major depressive episode in 1985 included feelings not only of sorrow but also of guilt and rage, we may also, perhaps, assume that some of these feelings were related to guilt that he felt as a boy of thirteen for not having saved his mother from an untimely death. The feelings were also related to anger or rage at himself for not anticipating her death and for any negative feelings he may have harbored against her prior to her death, and so forth. That is, the self-reproaches that are also expressed by those in mourning–but in a milder form than in cases of melancholia–may also have been present, though also unacknowledged, at the time of her death.

Defense against Ambivalence Removed

His major depressive episode therefore reflected the fact that his defense against these ambivalent feelings reaching his conscious mind was removed. The "friend" he turned to after her death had also abandoned him, leaving him to face the original loss alone. Now the melancholy was free either to run its course toward eventual suicide or to make way for the completion of the mourning process. As suicide was averted that critical evening in December, we may assume that the second course has taken place and that the writing of *Darkness Visible* has itself contributed to the mourning process. The primary agency in the mourning process, however, was the major depressive episode itself. Its severity is testimony to the unsettling power of long-repressed emotions once they are allowed to surface.

As we have seen, Styron draws attention to the connection between hearing Brahms's *Alto Rhapsody* the night (or was it earlier in the day?) that he believed he could not live another day and the fact that he had heard his mother sing this haunting piece when he was a boy. He also suggests that his own avoidance of death may have been "related homage" to his mother (after all, he owed his very existence to her).

To help us understand the more ambivalent feelings he had toward her, however, his image of himself as a four-and-a-half-year-old boy tagging after his long-suffering wife through a market is especially revealing. His mention of this "bizarre and discomfiting" image occurs immediately after his observation that, in a major depressive episode such as his, "there is an acute fear of abandonment. Being alone in the house, even for a moment, caused me exquisite panic and trepidation" (W. Styron 1990, 57). In various writings (Capps 1997, 2002) I have suggested that male melancholia has its origins in the emotional separation between a boy and his mother around three-to-five years of age. This is the time when boys are expected to gain independence from their mothers so that they may identify with their fathers, and their mothers are expected to help them accomplish this transfer. For many, if not all, boys this is a traumatic experience, but the fact that it is traumatic is insufficiently recognized because it is considered natural and, indeed, is partially self-initiated.

I have suggested that boys and men relive this trauma in subsequent life experiences of real or perceived abandonment. If Styron experienced the death of his mother at age thirteen, this, in my view, reawakened the earlier trauma and the emotions that typically accompany it (guilt, dread, longing, and so forth). Thus, while he finds this image "bizarre and discomfiting," it may be explained as a manifestation of his "regression" to the very origins of the melancholic disposition in the small boy. As he himself recognized, his wife had become "mommy," and he feared that she would abandon him; therefore, he did not dare let her out of his sight.

Madame del Duca as Victim

Another clue to his ambivalent feelings toward his mother is provided by the account of his trip to Paris to receive the del Duca Prize. He added this account to his original essay because the trip "had special significance for me in terms of the development of the depressive illness from which I had suffered" (1). He does not, however, make a direct link between his melancholia as it related to his mother and his behavior in relation to Madame del Duca, whom he describes as "a large dark-haired woman of queenly manner" (14).

Precisely because he views his behavior toward her as a manifestation of his illness, we may assume that this behavior was the work of his unconscious mind and thus of his repressed ambivalence toward his mother. His behavior was the sort of rudeness we might expect, and find somewhat forgivable, from a young boy. As he says, his "refusal" to join her and the others at the luncheon "was both emphatic and simple-minded." It was also insulting, for his inability to attend her elaborately planned luncheon was due to the fact that he had decided, on the spur of the moment, to have a casual lunch with another woman who, we may assume, was considerably younger.

I suggest, therefore, that even as Rose Styron became the "mother" from whom he could not bear to be separated, Madame del Duca became the object—and victim—of long stored-up ambivalent feelings toward his mother, the one who had abandoned *him*. The message from deep in his unconscious mind—over which he had lost control—was something like, "Let me show *you* how it feels to be the recipient of rejection, of callous disregard for one's love and attachment, of being the one left in the lurch, condemned to make the best of an uncontrollable situation."

It is also noteworthy that his account in *Darkness Visible* of how the prize came into existence is itself somewhat damaging, in a humorous way, to Madame del Duca's stature as a cultured woman and benefactress. While noting that the prize itself "has become greatly respected in France," he mentions that her husband acquired his wealth through the publication of comic books, and that the foundation Madame del Duca had created was designed in part to obscure the "comic-book origins" of her husband's "multi-fold empire." If there is now "scant memory" of these "comic-book origins," Styron's mention of them in *Darkness Visible* brings them back into the open. Perhaps there is a parallel here between the fact that his depression marked the reemergence of long-repressed feelings that are much more ambiguous than his comment about his "belated homage to my mother" implies and the fact that *Darkness Visible* reveals a truth about Madame del Duca's background that somewhat sullies her own queenly bearing.

Dealing with Melancholia

His allusion to comic-books (the type of literature that appeals to young boys and immature men) also suggests that humor was one of the ways Styron had learned to deal with his melancholia and its origins in the mother-son relationship. He made a heroic attempt at humor in his acceptance speech, and, as Rose Styron notes, the scene involving her husband's attempts to make amends with Madame del Duca was much funnier than it seems in his book. From his point of view, however, it was anything but funny, suggesting that if dreams are the first casualty of depression, humor is not far behind. (Perhaps it was not coincidental that Freud's first major book was *The Interpretation of Dreams* [1965, originally published in 1900] and his second major book was *Jokes and Their Relation to the Unconscious* [1960, first published in 1905]. If Styron's dream life returned with a flute, a wild goose, and a dancing girl, his humor life has also returned, if not with his account of the mix-up with Madame del Duca, then certainly in his account of his destruction of his private notebook.

The very fact that his humor failed him in the luncheon mix-up with Madame del Duca, however, is also revealing of the degree to which she had become, in a sense, a stand-in for his own mother. When he became conscious of how he had offended her, he apologized, and asked to be reinstated. Throughout the luncheon, however, he sensed that his "benefactress was still disturbed by my conduct" and that he had not, therefore, been able to repair the wrong that he had committed or the damage that this wrong had done to their relationship.

On the other hand, through his "unintentionally" boorish behavior toward Madame del Duca, he began to allow long-repressed ambivalent feelings toward his mother to come, at last, to expression. What Freud says about manic episodes that sometimes accompany melancholia is relevant here. As Freud points out, in mania "a man finds himself in a position to throw off at one blow some heavy burden, some false position he has long endured" (1963, 175). Styron says that his depression lacked the manic features that would probably have been present if it had happened much earlier in his life. His insulting behavior toward Madame del Duca also had none of what Freud calls the "high spirits" or "elation" of mania. Still, his rude behavior did enable him to begin the long and dangerous process of ending "a long-sustained condition of great mental expenditure, or one established by long force of habit" (175), namely, the repression of ambivalent feelings toward his own mother.

While his rudeness toward Madame del Duca was a manifestation of the confusion that typically occurs in major depressive episodes, it was also, as Freud suggests regarding mania, "a triumph" of a sort, as the confusion in this case was caused by long-repressed feelings of ambivalence breaking through. Significantly, Freud also suggests that "alcoholic intoxication" is similar to manic outbursts insofar "as it consists in a state of elation; here there is probably a relaxation produced by toxins of the expenditure of energy in repression" (175). Thus, alcohol, which for Styron was never a depressant, had served through the years as a means to relax a mind overtaxed by the exertion of repressed ambivalent feelings toward his mother.

Styron's Self-loathing

Although Styron does not make the link between Madame del Duca and his own mother that I have suggested here, he does wonder if his subsequent "loss" of the prize check was "intended." He believes "in the reality of the accidents we subconsciously perpetuate on ourselves, and so how easy it was for the loss to be not loss but a form of repudiation" (W. Styron 1990, 19). He sees the loss of the check as the "offshoot of that self-loathing (depression's premier badge) by which I was persuaded that I could not be worthy of the prize, that I was in fact not worthy of any of the recognition that had come my way in the past few years" (19).

What he does not say—or recognize—is that the "self-loathing" was itself an "offshoot" of ambivalent feelings toward his mother. These feelings originated in the emotional separation of mother and son in early childhood (age four-and-a-half stands out for him) followed by their physical separation when he was thirteen. I think that her death prohibited him from expressing these ambivalent feelings in his adolescent years, a time when boys typically contend with their conflicting feelings toward their mothers. When one's mother is dead, the expression of negative thoughts and feelings toward her seems an unfeeling attack on her sacred memory. This problem may be compounded when one's father, as in Styron's case, remarries, leaving the son—in Styron's case, the only child—to be the one who maintains an absolute loyalty to his mother.

Given the son's inevitable ambivalent feelings toward her, however, this act of psychic sacrilege is necessary if he is also to pay "belated homage" to her, the homage, as Styron observes, of preserving the life that she had given him and of finally completing the mourning process. When the contralto voice—also a stand-in for his mother's voice—pierced his heart like a dagger, melancholia had become mourning, and there was no need to do the desecration to himself—and to her—that would end the howling tempest in his brain.

NOTES

[1]This quotation is from James's chapter in *The Varieties of Religious Experience* (1982; originally published in 1902) on "The Sick Soul" (147). In this chapter, James suggests that "many kinds of pathological depression" (145) can be distinguished. He discusses three kinds. The first is "mere passive joylessness and dreariness, discouragement, dejection, lack of taste and zest and spring" (145). The second is the "much worse form" that Styron cites. He describes a "positive and active anguish, a sort of psychical neuralgia wholly unknown to healthy life," an anguish that "may partake of various characters, having sometimes more the quality of loathing; sometimes that of irritations and exasperation; or again of self-mistrust and self-despair; or of suspicion, anxiety, trepidation, fear. The patient may rebel or submit; may accuse himself, or accuse outside powers; and he may or may not be tormented by the theoretical mystery of why he should so have to suffer" (148). The third and "worst kind of melancholy is that which takes the form of panic fear" (159–160). Instead of providing characteristics of this type, James provides a case example that is widely known to be himself (disguised as a Frenchman). This case is too long to cite here, but his "informant" notes that "In general I dreaded to be left alone. I remember wondering how other people could live, how I myself had lived, so unconscious of that pit of insecurity beneath the surface of life" (161). As Styron's memoir reveals, he experienced all three kinds of "pathological depression."

[2]In light of Styron's earlier citation of William James's characterization of melancholia, it is interesting to note that James also wrote an essay, "Is Life Worth Living?" (1956a; originally published in 1895) and concluded that it all depends "on you *the liver*" (60). He appeals to one's "unconquerable subjectivity" that proves to be the match for whatever "evils crowd upon you" (60). He concludes the essay with the following benediction: "These, then, are my last words to you: Be not afraid of life. Believe that life *is* worth living, and your belief will help create the fact" (62). The double entendre—"You *the liver*"—would have special appeal to Styron's sense of humor, as he notes that when his body reacted against alcohol, it was as if his liver rebelled, "as if to say, 'No more, no more'" (W. Styron 1990, 41).

[3]Styron's quotations from Dante's *The Divine Comedy* are from the first part, "The Inferno" (Alighieri 1993). The first quotation is the first three lines of Canto 1; the second quotation is the last line of Canto 34 and the last line of the poem itself.

3

IT NEVER OCCURRED TO
ME THAT I WAS ILL

■ KAY JAMISON

In chapter 1 on Anton Boisen, I discussed the fact that Boisen's diagnosis has been a matter of some controversy over the years. Specifically, the original diagnosis of schizophrenia, catatonic type, was challenged in 1981 by Carol North and William M. Clements. They concluded that he more likely suffered from bipolar affective disorder. While I indicated my belief that the proper diagnosis would have been that of paranoid schizophrenia, I also cited statements from the *DSM-IV* indicating that it is often difficult to differentiate the two mental disorders.

In this chapter, I will discuss Kay Redfield Jamison's *An Unquiet Mind: A Memoir of Moods and Madness* (1995). This is her personal account of her lifelong struggles with what she prefers to call manic-depressive illness (rather than the official term, "bipolar disorder"). This was the original diagnosis, and no one, including Jamison herself, has challenged its accuracy. But the diagnostic question is less interesting in her case than the fact that she was a psychologist specializing in psychopathology, the study and treatment of mental disorders. She had also done research on mood-altering drugs. Still, it took her several years to realize that she was mentally ill herself, suffering from one of the major mood disorders.

Bipolar I Disorder

According to the *DSM-IV*, the essential feature of bipolar I disorder (the type that Kay Jamison had) is a clinical course that is characterized by the occurrence of one or more manic episodes or mixed episodes (that is, episodes that have both manic and depressive features). It is a recurrent disorder; more than 90 percent of individuals who have a single manic episode go on to have future episodes. Roughly 60 to 70 percent of manic episodes occur immediately before or after a major depressive episode, and manic episodes often precede or follow the major depressive episodes in a characteristic pattern for a particular person. For Jamison, this pattern was a manic episode followed by a depressive episode. The number of lifetime episodes (both manic and major depressive) tends to be higher for bipolar I disorder than for major depressive disorder, recurrent.

Studies of the course of bipolar I disorder prior to lithium maintenance treatment suggested that, on average, four episodes occur in ten years. Approximately 5 to 15 percent of individuals with bipolar I disorder have multiple (four or more) mood episodes that occur within a given year. Although the majority of individuals with bipolar I disorder return to a fully functional level between episodes, some (20 to 30 percent) continue to display mood liability and interpersonal or occupational difficulties. Psychotic symptoms may develop after days or weeks in what was previously a nonpsychotic manic or mixed episode. When an individual has manic episodes with psychotic features, subsequent manic episodes are more likely to have psychotic features. Incomplete recovery between episodes is more common when the current episode is accompanied by mood-incongruent psychotic features (*DSM-IV*, 350–53). Mood-incongruent psychotic features are delusions that are essentially unrelated to the depression itself. When a depressed person believes, falsely, that she is responsible for the illness of someone else, this is mood-congruent, as depressed persons tend to blame themselves for negative circumstances that are not their own fault. But when a depressed person believes that someone else is inserting thoughts into her mind, this is considered a mood-incongruent psychotic feature, because this belief has no direct connection to the depressed mood itself (377).

Jamison was born in 1946 and was therefore forty-nine years old when *The Unquiet Mind* was published. At the time she wrote it, she had been living with the awareness of her mental illness for almost twenty years. In the following account, I will refer to her as "Kay" when relating her personal experiences. I will call her "Jamison" when discussing her comments and observations as author.

An Enemy and a Companion

The prologue begins: "When it's two o'clock in the morning, and you're manic, even the UCLA Medical Center has a certain appeal. The hospital—ordinarily a cold clotting of uninteresting buildings—became for me, that fall morning not quite twenty years ago, a focus of my finely wired, exquisitely alert nervous system" (Jamison 1993, 3). I "took in everything around me. I was on the run. Not just on the run but fast and furious on the run, darting back and forth across the hospital parking lot trying to use up a boundless, restless, manic energy. I was running fast, but slowly going mad" (3).

She had been with a male colleague from the medical school earlier that evening, but he had stopped running an hour earlier, complaining of exhaustion. Suddenly a police car pulled up. While she was in a "less-than-fully-lucid state of mind," due, in part, to inebriation, she could see that the officer had a hand on his revolver as he got out of the car: "What in the hell are you doing running around the parking lot at this time?" Not an unreasonable question! Her thought processes, though not especially clear or coherent, told her that this particular situation was going to be hard to explain.

But then her colleague came to the rescue, "We're both on the faculty in the psychiatry department" (4). The officer looked at them, smiled, and returned to his squad car and drove away. Evidently, being pro-fessors of psychiatry explained everything. To her colleague, this was an evening of uninhibited excess. For her, it was a manic episode, one of many that would mark the beginning of yet another plunge into insanity.

Criteria for a Manic Episode

The *DSM-IV* provides a clear set of criteria for a manic episode. The primary criterion is "a distinct period of abnormally and persistently elevated, expansive, or irritable mood, lasting at least 1 week (or any duration if hospitalization is necessary)" (*DSM-IV,* 332). A secondary criterion is that during the period of mood disturbance, three (or more) of the following symptoms have been present (four if the mood is only irritable):

1. inflated self-esteem or grandiosity
2. decreased need for sleep
3. more talkative than usual or pressure to keep talking
4. flight of ideas or subjective experience that thoughts are racing;
5. distractibility (that is, attention is too easily drawn to unimportant or irrelevant external stimuli)
6. increase in goal-directed activity (either socially, at work or school, or sexually) or psychomotor agitation
7. excessive involvement in pleasurable activities that have a high potential for painful consequences (such as engaging in unrestrained buying sprees, sexual indiscretions, or foolish business investments) (322)

An additional criterion is that the mood disturbance "is sufficiently severe to cause marked impairment in occupational functioning or in usual social activities or relationships with others, or to necessitate hospitalization to prevent harm to self or others, or there are psychotic features" (332).

Jamison notes that within a month of signing her appointment papers to become an assistant professor of psychiatry at UCLA, she was "well on my way to madness" (1993, 4). It was 1974, and she was twenty-eight:

> Within three months I was manic beyond recognition and just beginning a long, costly personal war against a medication that I would, in a few years' time, be strongly encouraging others to take. My illness, and my struggles against the drug that ultimately saved my life and restored my sanity, had been years in the making. (4)

The Mania's Origins

Her mania did not happen overnight. On the contrary, "For as long as I can remember I was frighteningly, although often wonderfully, beholden to moods. Intensely emotional as a child, mercurial as a young girl, first severely depressed as an adolescent, and then unrelentingly caught up in the cycles of manic-depressive illness by the time I began my professional life, I became, both by necessity and intellectual inclination, a student of moods" (5). This, she observes, has been the only way she has been able to understand, and to accept, her illness, and the only way she has been able to try to make a difference in the lives of others (5).

Her own experience with manic-depressive illness has taught her that it is a fascinating, albeit deadly, enemy and companion: "I have found it to be seductively complicated, a distillation of what is finest in our natures, and of what is most dangerous" (5). It is something that needs to be contended with. To do so, she "first had to know it in all of its moods and infinite disguises, understand its real and imagined powers" (5). Initially, her illness seemed simply to be an extension of herself, of her "ordinarily changeable moods, energies, and enthusiasms." Consequently, she now believes that she gave it too much license and should have done more to rein it in and control it. Moreover, she believed that she ought to be able to handle her increasingly violent mood swings by herself. So, for the first ten years she did not seek treatment. Even after her condition became a medical emergency, she still intermittently resisted the medication "that both my training and my clinical research expertise told me was the only sensible way to deal with the illness I had" (5).

Resisting Medication

The primary reason she resisted the medications was that her manias, "at least in their early and mild forms, were absolutely intoxicating states that gave rise to great personal pleasure, an incomparable flow of thoughts, and a ceaseless energy that allowed the translation of new ideas into papers and projects" (5–6). Medications inhibited these "fast-flowing, high-flying times." They also brought with them seemingly intolerable side effects. It took her far too long to realize "that lost years and relationships cannot be recovered, that damage done to oneself and others cannot always be put right again, and that freedom from the control imposed by medication loses its meaning when the only alternatives are death and insanity" (6).

Her resistance to medications is not uncommon. In fact, she notes that the major clinical problem in treating manic-depressive illness is not the lack of effective medications but the fact that patients so often refuse to take them. Moreover, for a variety of reasons (lack of information, poor medical advice, stigma, or fear of personal and professional reprisal), many sufferers do not seek treatment despite the fact that it is a highly destructive illness:

> Manic-depression distorts moods and thoughts, incites dreadful behaviors, destroys the basis of rational thought, and too often erodes the desire and will to live. It is an illness that is biological in its origins, yet one that feels psychological in the experience of it; an illness that is unique in conferring advantage and pleasure, yet one that brings in its wake almost unendurable suffering and not infrequently, suicide. (6)

Jamison counts herself fortunate that she has not died from her illness, has had the best medical care available, and has benefited from supportive friends, colleagues, and family. Because of this, she has tried to use her own experiences of the disease to inform her research, teaching, clinical practice, and advocacy work. She has especially tried to persuade her professional colleagues of the "paradoxical core" of an illness "that can both kill and create" (7). She has tried, along with many others, "to change public attitudes about psychiatric illnesses in general and manic-depressive illness in particular" (7). A special difficulty in her case has been the attempt "to weave together the scientific discipline of my intellectual field with the more compelling realities of my own emotional experiences" (7). On the other hand, the genuine freedom that she now experiences to live the kind of life that matters to her derives from this binding together of "raw emotion" and "the more distanced eye of clinical science" (7).

Jamison concludes the prologue to *An Unquiet Mind* with the observation that she has "many concerns" about writing a book that so explicitly describes her own attacks of mania, depression, and psychosis, as well as her problems acknowledging her need for ongoing medication. Clinicians have been reluctant to make their own psychiatric problems known to others, as these disclosures often affect licensing and hospital privileges. But she has weighed the possible professional consequences of writing the book against the personal cost of continuing to be silent: "I am tired of hiding, tired of misspent and knotted energies, tired of the hypocrisy, and tired of acting as though I have something to hide" (7).

Everything in My World Began to Fall Apart

The Unquiet Mind has four parts, each containing two to four chapters. Part 1, "The Wild Blue Yonder," consisting of two chapters, "Into the Sun," and "An Education for Life," covers her childhood, adolescence, university and graduate school training, and her appointment as an assistant professor in the UCLA Department of Psychiatry. It concludes three months prior to her first major psychotic episode at the age of twenty-eight.

Into the Sun

She begins "Into the Sun" with an account of a routine experience for a young girl whose elementary school was near Andrews Air Force Base just outside of Washington, D. C. She was watching a jet flying overhead, as she had often done before. But this time something was different. The noise from the plane was unusually loud because the plane was lower than usual. She knew that the pilot couldn't see her, despite the fact that he was flying low, but she waved just the same for he just might be her father. A career Air Force officer, her father was first and foremost a scientist–a meteorologist–and only secondarily a pilot. But he loved to fly, so his professional work and his love of flying meant that "both his mind and his soul ended up being in the skies." Like him, Kay tended to "look up rather more than I looked out" (11).

When she mentioned to her father that the Army and Navy have much more tradition and legend than the Air Force, he would respond that the Air Force is the future, adding, "we can fly." Then, on occasion, he would burst into an enthusiastic rendition of the Air Force hymn, "fragments of which remain with me to this day, nested together, somewhat improbably, with phrases from Christmas carols, early poems, and bits and pieces of the Book of Common Prayer" (12). When she heard the words, "Off we go into the wild blue yonder," she would think that "wild" and "yonder" were the most wonderful words she had ever heard. The phrase, "Climbing high, into the sun" evoked such a "total exhilaration" that she knew, instinctively, that she was "a part of those who loved the vastness of the sky" (12).

On this occasion, however, the jet approaching Andrews Air Force Base was flying much too low. As it streaked past, it barely missed the playground and the merry-go-round she was standing near. She and her second-grade classmates "stood there clumped together and absolutely terrified." The plane flew into the trees, exploding directly in front of them: "The ferocity of the crash could be heard in the plane's awful impact; it could also be seen in the frightening yet terrible lingering loneliness of the flames that followed" (12).

Within minutes, mothers were rushing out on the playground to reassure the children that the pilot was not their father. Over the next few days, it became clear, from the public release of the young pilot's final message to the control tower before he died, that he knew he could save his own life by bailing out. To do so, however, would risk that his unpiloted plane would crash onto the playground and kill the children and the teachers there. Thus, "the young pilot became a hero, transformed into a scorchingly vivid, completely impossible ideal for what was meant by the concept of duty. It was an impossible ideal, but all the more compelling and haunting because of its very unobtainability" (13). The memory of the crash came back to her many times over the years. It was "a reminder both of how one aspires after and needs such ideals, and of how killingly difficult it is to achieve. I never again looked at the sky and saw only vastness and beauty. From that afternoon on I saw that death was also and always there" (13).

Jamison's Family

From this harrowing experience, Jamison moves to a description of her family as she was growing up. Like all military families, they moved a lot. By fifth grade she had attended four different elementary schools. But her parents, especially her mother, kept life as secure, warm, and constant as possible. Her brother was the eldest and the strongest. Despite their three years' difference in age, he was her "staunchest ally." She idolized him and often trailed along after him and his friends. He was smart, fair, and self-confident. She always felt that whenever he was around, she would be protected.

Sister

Her relations with her sister, only thirteen months older than herself, were more complicated. Her sister was the truly beautiful one in the family, and she had a charismatic manner about her. She also had "a fierce temper, very black and passing moods, and little tolerance for the conservative military lifestyle that she felt imprisoned us all" (14). She was defiant and broke out with abandon whenever possible. When the family was living in Washington, she would frequently skip high school classes to go to the Smithsonian and Army Medical Museums or just to smoke and drink beer with her friends. She also resented Kay, whom she called "the fair-haired one," because she felt that friends and schoolwork came too easily for her younger sister. Sandwiched between her brother, a natural athlete and exceptional student, and Kay, who loved school and was vigorously involved in sports, friends, and class activities, her sister stood out "as the member of the family who fought back and rebelled against what she saw as a harsh and difficult world. She hated military life, hated the constant upheaval and the need to make new friends, and felt the family politeness was hypocrisy" (14).

Looking back, Kay believes that her sister was deprived of the experience of the essentially happy childhood that she herself enjoyed, the "solid base of warmth, friendship and confidence" that proved to be "an extremely powerful amulet, a potent and positive countervailing force against future unhappiness" (15). When, years later, both of them had to deal with their "respective demons," her sister "saw the darkness as being within and part of herself, her family, and the world," whereas Kay saw this darkness "as a stranger." However lodged within her mind and soul this darkness became, "it almost always seemed an outside force that was at war with my natural self" (15). (Her acknowledgments indicate she had two other sisters, but she does not mention them in the text itself).

Her Father

Her father, when he was involved with the family, was often only marginally involved. He was "ebullient, funny, curious about almost everything, and able to describe with delight and originality the beauties and phenomena of the natural world. When times were good and his moods were at high tide, his infectious enthusiasm would touch everything" (15). Music would fill the house, wonderful new pieces of jewelry would appear, and he would discourse on his latest passion, ranging from windmill power to Russian poetry. Looking back, Kay could see that it was like having Mary Poppins for a father.

Her mother has said, many times, "that she always felt she was in the shadow of my father's wit, charm, intensity, and imagination. Her observation that he was a Pied Piper with children certainly was borne out by his charismatic effect upon my friends and the other children in whatever neighborhood we found ourselves" (17). But her mother was the one her friends wanted to sit down and talk with.

Her Mother

The book is dedicated to her mother. The inscription reads, "Who gave me Life not once, but countless times," is "kind, fair, and generous," and "has the type of self-confidence that comes from having been brought up by parents who not only loved her deeply and well, but who were themselves kind, fair, and generous people" (17). Kay's maternal grandfather, who died before she was born, was a college professor trained in physics, a witty man who was inordinately kind to students and colleagues. Her maternal grandmother, whom she knew well, was a warm and caring woman with a deep and genuine interest in people.

Daughter of these two kind and gracious parents, Kay's mother was a popular student in high school and college. Pictures in her photograph albums portray an obviously happy young woman, usually surrounded by friends and a series of good-looking suitors: "There were no foreboding shadows, no pensive or melancholic faces, no questions of internal darkness or instability" (18). Kay guesses that her mother's belief "that a certain predictability was something that one ought to be able to count upon" had its roots "in the utter normality of the people and events captured in these pictures, as well as in the preceding generations of her ancestors who were reliable, stable, honorable, and saw things through" (19). "Such seeming steadiness in the genes" of her mother's family "could only very partially prepare Kay's mother "for all the turmoil and difficulties that were to face her once she left her parents' home to begin a family of her own." This same "persevering steadiness" that her mother exhibited was to be the single most important factor in helping Kay herself to remain alive "through all of the years of pain and nightmare that were to come" (19).

HOSPITAL EXPERIENCES

Kay notes that both of her parents strongly encouraged her academic interests and did not object to her desire to keep dogs, cats, birds, fish, turtles, lizards, frogs, and mice in the house. They drew the line, though, when she expressed interest in having a sloth for a pet. They realized that she was probably more enamored of the *idea* of owning a sloth than actually having one around. When she was twelve, they bought her dissecting tools, a microscope, and a copy of Gray's *Anatomy*. The ping-pong table in the basement became her laboratory.

When she began working as a candy striper, a volunteer program for high school girls, at the hospital at Andrews Air Force Base, doctors encouraged her medical interests by giving her scalpels, hemostats, and bottles of blood for her homemade experiments. She went with the doctors on their rounds, holding instruments, peering into wounds, and, on one occasion, removed stitches from a patient's abdominal incision. Once, she was allowed to witness an autopsy. It

> was extraordinary and horrifying. I stood at the side of the steel autopsy table, trying hard not to look at the dead child's small,

naked body, but being incapable of not doing so. The smell in the room was vile and saturating, and for a long while only the sloshing of water and the quickness of the pathologist's hands were saving distractions. (21)

To keep from seeing what she was seeing, she "reverted back to a more cerebral, curious self, asking question after question, following each answer with yet another question" (21). Why did the pathologist make the cuts that he did? Where did all the body parts go? Why were some parts weighed and others not? Initially, this reversion to "a more cerebral, curious self" was "a way of avoiding the awfulness of what was going on in front of me." But, before long, "curiosity became a compelling force in its own right." She focused on the questions and stopped seeing the body:

> As has been true a thousand times since, my curiosity and temperament have taken me to places I was not really able to handle emotionally, but the same curiosity, and the scientific side of my mind, generated enough distance and structure to allow me to manage, deflect, reflect, and move on. (22)

VISITING A MENTAL HOSPITAL

If the autopsy of the small, naked child was horrifying to her, even more horrifying was her visit with her sister candy stripers to St. Elizabeths Hospital in Washington, D. C., when she was fifteen.[1] She recalls that all of them were dreadfully nervous during the bus ride to the hospital, "giggling and making terribly insensitive school-girlish remarks in a vain effort to allay our anxieties about the unknown and what we imagined to be the world of the mad" (22). She thinks they were especially afraid of the strangeness, of possible violence, and what it would be like to see someone completely out of control. Like English children who were warned that their behavior would land them in Bedlam, "You'll end up in St. Elizabeths" was one of the taunts of her own childhood. So, despite the fact that she had no reason at the time to doubt her sanity,

> irrational fears began to poke away at my mind. I had a terrible temper, after all, and though it rarely erupted, when it did it frightened me and anyone near its epicenter. It was the only crack, but a disturbing one, in the otherwise vacuum-sealed casing of my behavior. God only knew what ran underneath the fierce self-discipline and emotional control that had come with my upbringing. But the cracks were there, I knew it, and they frightened me. (22–23)

When they arrived at the hospital, Kay and the other candy stripers were in for a big surprise, at least initially. Far from being the grim place they imagined it would be, the grounds were vast, quite beautiful, and filled with magnificent old trees. They discovered extraordinary views of the city. The lovely antebellum buildings conveyed the Southern graciousness that was once such an integral part of the capital city. Appearances, however, can be deceiving, and perhaps especially so in the setting of a mental hospital.

Entering the wards abolished the illusion created by the architecture and landscaping. Immediately, they faced the dreadful reality of the sights, sounds, and smells of insanity. At Andrews Air Force Base hospital, she was accustomed to seeing relatively large numbers of nurses on the wards, but here, there were ninety patients for each psychiatric nurse. Enter the curious self: Kay asked their nurse escort how one person could be expected to control so many potentially violent patients? She responded that drugs would control most of them, but, now and again, it became necessary to "hose them down." This response left Kay incredulous: "How could anyone be so out of control that they would require such a brutal method of restraint? It was something I couldn't get out of my mind" (23).

Much worse, however, was entering the dayroom of one of the women's wards, standing dead still, and looking around her at the bizarre clothes, the odd mannerisms, the agitated pacing, strange laughter, and occasional heartbreaking screams. She recalls that one woman stood like a stork, one leg tucked up, and giggled to herself all the time they were there. Another patient stood in the middle of the room talking to herself, braiding and unbraiding her long reddish hair, and tracking with her quick eyes the movements of anyone who attempted to come anywhere near her. At first frightened by her, Kay was also intrigued and somehow captivated. She slowly walked toward the woman. After standing several feet away from her for a few minutes, she gathered up her nerve to ask her why she was in the hospital? "By this time I noticed out of the corner of my eye that all of the other candy stripers were huddled together, talking among themselves, at the far end of the room. I decided to stay put, however; my curiosity had made strong inroads on my fears" (24).

The woman stared through her for a very long time, then turning sideways so that she would not see Kay directly, she explained why she was there:

> Her parents, she said, had put a pinball machine inside her head when she was five years old. The red balls told her when she should laugh, the blue ones when she should be silent and keep away from other people; the green balls told her that she should

start multiplying by three. Every few days a silver ball would make its way through the pins of the machine. (24)

At this point she turned her head and stared at Kay, who assumed she was checking to see if Kay was still listening. Kay asked, "What does the silver ball mean?" She looked at Kay intently, and then everything went dead in her eyes. She stared off in space, caught up in some internal world: "I never found out what the silver ball meant" (25).

Fascinated by what she saw, Kay "was primarily frightened by the strangeness of the patients" and the "perceptible level of terror in the room" (25). What impressed itself upon her the most, however, "were the expressions of pain in the eyes of the women. Some part of me instinctively reached out, and in an odd way understood the pain, never imagining that I would someday look in the mirror and see their sadness and insanity in my own eyes" (25). Little did she know that she would have her own version of the story that the patient whose parents had put a pinball machine in her head had related to her that day.

A DISINTEGRATING FAMILY

Except for this account of her visit to St. Elizabeths, Jamison's portrayal of her adolescence focuses on her life as the daughter of a military man. She had great friends and a full and active life of swimming, riding, softball, parties, and boyfriends. In the midst of this she experienced "a gradual awakening to the reality of what it meant to be an intense, somewhat mercurial girl in an extremely traditional and military world" (27). While she wanted her independence, she also felt the appeal of the world of tradition. The military world was "a society built around a tension between romance and discipline: a complicated world of excitement, stultification, fast life, and sudden death, and it afforded a window back in time to what nineteenth-century living, at its best, and at its worst, must have been: civilized, gracious, elitist, and singularly intolerant of personal weakness" (29).

Just as she was beginning to get used to the paradoxes of coming of age in a military society, "and for the first time feeling firmly rooted in Washington" (30), her father retired from the Air Force. He took a position as a scientist at the Rand Corporation in California. It was 1961; she was fifteen years old, "and everything in my world began to fall apart" (30).

Being the daughter of a retired Air Force officer was a damning mark against her at Pacific Palisades High School. Longing for the "conservative military lifestyle" that she had known, she began to lose her moorings. Outwardly adjusting well, she was "deeply unhappy," and "was furious" at her father for having taken a job in California instead of retiring in Washington. Moreover, her brother had gone off to college before their move to California, "leaving a huge hole in my security net" (34). Her relationship with her sister, "always a difficult one, had become at best fractious, often adversarial, and, more usually, simply distant" (34).

Worst of all, her parents, "although still living together, were essentially estranged" (34). Her mother was busy teaching and attending graduate school. Her father was caught up in his scientific work, but his moods were increasingly erratic. Occasionally, they soared. When they did, "the sparkle and gaiety that flew out of them created a glow, a warmth and a joy that filled all the rooms of the house" (34). But his emotional flights also, at times, pushed the limits of reason and of the tolerance of the Rand Corporation. His scheme for assigning IQ scores to hundreds of individuals, most already deceased, while ingenious, was "disturbingly idiosyncratic." And, worse, it had absolutely nothing to do with the meteorology research that he was being paid to conduct. More ominously, "the blackness of his depressions filled the air as pervasively as music did in his better periods" (34).

Within a year or so of the move to California, his dark moods worsened, and dramatically so. At times he "was immobilized by depression, unable to get out of bed, and profoundly pessimistic about every aspect of his life and future. At other times, his rage and screaming would fill me with terror" (35). This was something new, for Kay had never known her father—a soft-spoken and gentle man—to raise his voice. Now there were days, even weeks, when she was frightened to show up for breakfast or come home from school. He began drinking heavily, and this made matters worse.

NEED TO ESCAPE

Her mother was as bewildered and frightened as Kay was, and both of them increasingly sought escape through work and friends. They went everywhere together. Her mother slept in Kay's bed at night, listening for hours to Kay's tales of woe. Kay would cry herself to sleep with her arms around her mother's neck. For a year or so, her father's black moods were the focus of Kay's concern. By the time she was sixteen or seventeen, it became clear "that my energies and enthusiasms could be exhausting to the people around me, and after having weeks of flying high and sleeping little, my thinking would take a downward turn toward the really dark and brooding side of life" (35).

Her two closest friends, both male, were a bit inclined to the darker side as well. While they were able to navigate the more normal and fun-loving side of high school life, the three of them met in the after hours together to drink, smoke, and engage in pessimistic discussions about life and death. They also debated "the melancholic and existential readings" they had set for themselves (36). They were later to learn that two of them had manic-depressive illness in their immediate families, and the mother of the third had shot herself through the heart.

THE FIRST MANIC-DEPRESSIVE ATTACK

This chapter concludes with an account of her first attack of manic-depressive illness as a senior in high school. Here is how she describes it:

> Once the siege began, I lost my mind rather rapidly. At first, everything seemed so easy. I raced about like a crazed weasel, bubbling with plans and enthusiasms, immersed in sports, and staying up all night, night after night, out with friends, reading everything that wasn't nailed down, filling manuscript books with poems and fragments of plays, and making expansive, completely unrealistic plans for my future. The world was filled with pleasure and promise; I felt great. Not just great, I felt *really* great. (36)

Her mind seemed clear, fabulously focused. Not only did everything make perfect sense, but it all began to fit into "a marvelous kind of cosmic relatedness" (36–37). She shared with her friends her sense of enchantment with the laws of the natural world and of the sheer beauty of it all, but they were "less than transfixed by my insights into the webbings and beauties of the universe" (37). On the other hand, they were more than impressed by how exhausting it was to be with her and listen to her enthusiastic ramblings. They begged her to slow down, not to talk so fast. Unlike the very severe episodes that occurred a few years later, "this first sustained wave of mild mania was a light, lovely tincture of true mania; like hundreds of subsequent periods of high enthusiasm it was shortlived and quickly burned itself out" (37). It had probably been tiresome to her friends, and certainly both exhilarating and exhausting to herself, but it was not "disturbingly over the top" (37).

Then, however, came the inevitable collapse. Her mind did not merely slow down. It came to a grinding halt. "The bottom began to fall out of my life and my mind. My thinking, far from being clearer than a crystal, was tortuous" (37). She would read the same passage over and over again only to realize that she could not remember any of it. Unable to follow the material presented in class, she found herself staring out the window with no idea of what was going on around her. This "was very frightening" (37). It was as if her mind had begun to turn against her. Now, all of a sudden, it mocked her for her vapid enthusiasms, laughed at all of her foolish plans, and was incapable of concentrated thought except on the subject of death: "I was going to die, what difference did it make? Life's run was only a short and meaningless one, why live?" (38).

Exhausted, she had difficulty pulling herself out of bed in the morning. It took twice as long to walk the same distance as before, and she wore the same clothes over and over again because it was too much trouble to decide what to wear. She avoided friends and, instead, sat in the school library when not in class, "virtually inert, with a dead heart and a brain as cold as clay" (38). This unnatural tiredness was filled with a bleak preoccupation with death. She dragged her exhausted body around a local cemetery, ruminating on how each of its inhabitants had lived before death came. She sat on graves, writing long, dreary, and morbid poems. At times, she had periods of frenetic and horrible restlessness," but "no amount of running brought relief" (39). For several weeks, she drank vodka in her orange juice before setting off for school and thought obsessively about killing herself. In *Night Falls Fast* (Jamison 1999) she provides a detailed account of her suicidal thoughts over several months in her senior year of high school.

DISGUISING DEPRESSION

Kay was able to disguise from her family the way she felt inside. Two friends who expressed concern were sworn to secrecy when they asked to talk with her parents. One teacher noticed, as did the parent of a friend, but she assured them both that she was fine. She knew "something was dreadfully wrong," but had no idea what. She "had been brought up to believe that you kept your problems to yourself" (39). She concludes the chapter with the observation that she "aged rapidly during those months, as one must with such loss of one's self, with such proximity to death, and such distance from shelter" (40).

An Education for Life

The second chapter in Part 1, "An Education for Life," covers the years from the beginning of her undergraduate studies to her appointment as an assistant professor in the UCLA Department of Psychiatry. She had wanted to go to the University of Chicago, both because it had a reputation for encouraging nonconformity and because her father and her mother's father had gone there to graduate school. This proved financially impossible because her father's erratic behavior had cost him his job at Rand. She ended up applying to and being accepted by UCLA. This turned out to be the best place for her as it "provided an excellent and idiosyncratic education, an opportunity to do independent work, and the wide berth that perhaps only a large university can afford a tempestuous temperament" (42).

UNIVERSITY YEARS

This is not to say, however, that college was a period of emotional stability. Following on the heels of her depression in her senior year in high school, it was, for the most part, "a terrible struggle, a recurring nightmare of violent and dreadful moods spelled only now and then by weeks, sometimes months, of great fun, passion, high enthusiasms, and long runs of very hard but enjoyable work" (42). This pattern of shifting moods and energies had its sadistic side, largely because she experienced "fitful reinfusions of the intoxicating moods" that she had enjoyed in high school (42). These filled her with a "cataract of ideas and more than enough energy to give me at least the illusion of carrying them out" (42).

During these periods of exaltation, her classwork seemed very straightforward and she breezed through the examinations, laboratory work, and term papers. But then her mood would crash, and, as in her senior year in high school, her mind would grind to a halt. She would wake up in the morning with a profound sense of dread that she would somehow have to drag herself through another day. She would sit for hour after hour in the library, unable to muster enough energy to attend class. In her room, she would stare out the window, stare at her books, rearrange them, shuffle them around, and think about dropping out of college. Thoughts about death as the only release from the overwhelming sense of inadequacy and blackness around her were her constant companions. Otherwise, she felt utterly alone, and the animated conversations of her fellow students only made her feel more alone and utterly hopeless.

As before, bouts of terrible agitation made these periods of total despair even worse. Her mind would race from subject to subject, and, unlike the times when it was filled with exuberant and cosmic thoughts, it would be "drenched in awful sounds and images of decay and dying: dead bodies on the beach, charred remains of animals, toe-tagged corpses in morgues" (45). In these periods of restless agitation, she was angry and irritable. The only way she could reduce the agitation was to run along the beach or pace back and forth across her room "like a polar bear at the zoo" (45). To make matters worse, she "had no idea what was going on, and I felt totally unable to ask anyone for help. It never occurred to me that I was ill; my brain just didn't put it in those terms" (45).

"Visiting" a Psychiatrist

After hearing a lecture on depression in her abnormal psychology class, however, she finally went to the student health center to ask to see a psychiatrist. But she got only as far as the stairwell outside the clinic. Paralyzed by fear and shame, unable to enter and unable to leave, she sat there for what must have been an hour, head in hands, and sobbing. She left, and never returned. Eventually, the depression went away of its own accord, "but only long enough for it to regroup and mobilize for the next attack" (45).

Then, however, she was blessed with "a stroke of good luck" (45). In a class on personality theory, the professor was demonstrating different ways of assessing cognitive and personality structures. He held up several

Rorschach cards, asked the class to write down their responses to them, and then told them to pass the responses forward. Her mind "was flying high that day, courtesy of whatever witches' brew of neurotransmitters God had programmed into my genes" (46). Needless to say, this very description of her mind is itself an example of her ability to integrate many different conceptual models and modes of thought.

The professor proceeded to read aloud from a random selection of the responses. Midway through she heard "a recital of somewhat odd associations, and I realized to my great horror that they were mine. Some of them were humorous, but a few of them were simply bizarre. Or so they seemed to me. Most of the class was laughing, and I stared at my feet in mortification" (46). After he finished reading her responses, he asked the student who had written these responses to remain after class to talk with him for awhile. Kay was convinced that, because he was a psychologist, he could see straight into what she refers to in the text as her "psychotic underpinnings" (46). She was terrified. But as she walked back to his office with him, he said that in all of his years of teaching he had never encountered such "imaginative" responses to the Rorschach. In retrospect, she suspects that he saw in her Rorschach responses a student who was very intense, serious, and determined, and probably rather troubled; but he "was kind enough to call creative that which some, no doubt, would have called psychotic" (47). This was her first lesson "in appreciating the complicated, permeable boundaries between bizarre and original thought." To this day, she remains "deeply indebted to him for the intellectual tolerance that cast a positive rather than a pathological hue over what I had written" (47).

The professor asked her about her background, gently pointed out that as a freshman she was not supposed to be in an upper level course, and then offered her a position as a lab assistant for his research on the structure of human personality. The research life allowed an independence and flexibility that she found exhilarating. Her undergraduate transcript was riddled with failing grades and incomplete courses, but her research papers offset her often dreary grades. While not attempting to justify or rationalize the inconsistencies during the first two undergraduate years, she notes that the university schedule, like the rest of the world's schedules, is based on the assumption of steadiness and consistency in moods and performance. Thus, it fails to consider the changes in behavior and abilities that are integral to the lives of most manic-depressives.

Student at St. Andrews

Aware that her life had been in turmoil the first two years of college, Kay decided to take a year off to study at the University of St. Andrews in Scotland. Her brother and a cousin were studying at English universities at the time, and they encouraged her to come over and join them. She chose Scotland, however, because she had been "deeply affected by the Scottish music and poetry that her father loved, and there was something very appealing to me in the Celtic melancholy and fire that I associated with the Scottish side of my ancestry" (48). Despite her desire to get away from her father's black, unpredictable moods, she had "a vague notion that I might better understand my own chaotic feelings and thinking if I returned in some sense to the source" (48). A federal grant enabled her to do just that.

Her assignment to the program in invertebrate zoology provided a certain respite from her focus, at UCLA, on the human personality. But, more importantly, St. Andrews was "a mystical place":

> That year I walked for long hours along the sea and through the town and sat for hours mulling and writing among the ancient ruins of the city. I never tired of imagining what the twelfth-century cathedral must once have been, what glorious stained glass must once have filled its now-empty stone-edged windows; nor could I escape the almost archetypal pullings of Sunday services in the college chapel which, like the university itself, had been built during the early fifteenth century. The medieval traditions of learning and religion were threaded together in a deeply mystifying and wonderful way. (51)

She especially recalls the "ravishingly beautiful Christmas services at the end of term," with their old and beautiful carols, the hanging lamps of gold-chained crowns, the deeply carved wooden chair stalls, and the recitation of lessons in gentle, lyrical Scottish accents. She remembers leaving the chapel late that winter night "to enter onto an ancient scene, the sight of scarlet against snow, the ringing of bells, and a clear, full moon" (52).

St. Andrews "provided a gentle forgetfulness over the preceding painful years." "It remains a haunting and lovely time," a "marrow experience" (52). Like her fundamentally happy childhood, St. Andrews, too, was an "amulet against all manner of longing and loss, a year of gravely held but joyous remembrances. Throughout and beyond a long North Sea winter, it was the Indian summer of my life" (52).

New Career Plans

As she returned to UCLA, she realized that, given her temperament, her earlier plan to enter medical school on graduation from college was not a good idea. She loved research and writing, but the thought of being chained to the kind of schedule that medical school required was increasingly repugnant. "As important, I had read William James' great psychological study, *The Varieties of Religious Experience,* during my year in

St. Andrews. I was completely captivated by the idea of studying psychology, especially individual differences in temperament and variations in emotional capacities, such as mood and intense perceptions" (53).

She began working with a second professor on his research grant, a study of the psychological and physiological effects of mood-altering drugs. Mutually aware of their own fluctuating moods, they would occasionally talk about the possibility of taking antidepressant medications, but were deeply skeptical of their effectiveness and wary of potential side effects. "Somehow, like so many people who get depressed, we felt our depressions were more complicated and existentially based than they actually were. Antidepressants might be indicated for psychiatric patients, for those of weaker stock, but not for us. It was a costly attitude; our upbringing and pride held us hostage" (54).

The work she was doing with him and with the professor she had worked with since her freshman year, the strong influence of William James, and the instability and restlessness of her temperament combined to help her make up her mind to study for a Ph.D. in psychology. She applied for admission at UCLA and began her doctoral studies in 1971. She was twenty-five years old.

Graduate School

Graduate school was a continuation, in some respects, of the "Indian summer" she had enjoyed in St. Andrews. Looking back, she realizes that she was enjoying a remission, a common occurrence in the early years of manic-depressive illness. This provided "a deceptive respite from the savagely recurrent course that the untreated illness ultimately takes" (56). At the time, however, she assumed she was simply back to her normal self. She was also married to an exceedingly kind and gentle man, a talented painter, whom she met at a brunch given by mutual friends. With her variability in moods and his steadiness, they complemented one another's temperaments.

Several months of clinical studies at the Maudsley Hospital in London prior to meeting her husband led her to switch, midway in her doctoral studies, to clinical psychology. Psychopathology, the scientific study of mental disorders, proved enormously interesting to her. She was being taught how to make clinical diagnoses, but she did not make any connection in her own mind between the problems she had experienced and what was described as manic-depressive illness in the textbooks. "In a strange reversal of medical-student syndrome, where students become convinced that they have whatever disease it is that they are studying, I blithely went on with my clinical training and never put my mood swings into any medical context whatsoever" (58–59).

Looking back, her "denial and ignorance seem virtually incomprehensible" (59). On the other hand, she noticed that she was more comfortable treating psychiatric patients than were many of her colleagues, a repetition, perhaps, of the day she stood alongside the psychotic woman at St. Elizabeths while the other candy stripers huddled together in a group.

In her view, her doctoral dissertation on heroin addiction was "uninspired," but after a vigorous oral defense, she received her degree and was immediately hired as an assistant professor in the UCLA Department of Psychiatry. She had "a glorious—as it turned out, too glorious—summer, and, within three months of becoming a professor, I was ravingly psychotic" (63).

Missing the "Friendly Things"

Part 2, "A Not So Fine Madness," consisting of four chapters, begins with the chapter entitled, "Flights of the Mind." Her appointment in July, 1974, began normally enough. She was assigned to one of the adult inpatient wards for her clinical and teaching responsibilities. She also supervised psychiatric residents and clinical psychology interns on diagnostic techniques, psychological testing, psychotherapy, and, given her background in psychopharmacology, some issues related to drug trials and medications.

Flights of the Mind

At this time, she had no particular interest in mood disorders. Since she had been almost entirely free of serious mood swings for more than a year, she assumed that these problems were behind her. Stimulated by her faculty status, not to mention the "invigorating difference in salary" in the transition from intern to faculty, she settled into her new job with great optimism and energy. She worked very hard that summer and, in retrospect, slept very little. "Decreased sleep is both a symptom of mania and a cause" (69), but she did not know this at the time. It probably would not have made any difference to her if she had. Summer had often brought longer nights and higher moods, "but this time it pushed me into far higher, more dangerous and psychotic places than I had ever known" (69–70).

THE FIRST DIAGNOSIS

The university chancellor had a garden party each year to welcome new faculty members. By coincidence, the man who was to become her psychiatrist was also there because he had recently joined the adjunct medical school faculty. Her recollection of the event was of herself zipping around and talking with lots of people, including a long conversation with the chancellor himself, believing herself to be irresistibly charming and captivating. A "bit high," perhaps, but "a fabulous, bubbly, seductive, assured time" (71).

Not so, her future psychiatrist recalled. She was dressed in a remarkably provocative manner, totally unlike her normally conservative dress, and far too talkative. "Kay looks manic," he said to himself (71). This, however, was merely the beginning. As time went on, her mind "was beginning to have to scramble a bit to keep up with itself." She had "a neuronal pileup on the highways of my brain" (72). The more she tried to slow down her thinking, the more she realized she could not. One day she made thirty to forty copies of Edna St. Vincent Millay's poem, "Renascence," an article on religion and psychosis from the *American Journal of Psychiatry,* and another article on why case conferences are an enormous waste of time. Convinced that the poem and two articles had profound meaning and relevance for the clinical staff on the ward, she passed them out to everyone she encountered that day.

What strikes her now is not that her behavior was rather manic but that she had a sense, a prescience, of incipient madness. The poem, which she had read as a child, was, of the three, the most important clue. While she was just beginning her "journey into madness," this poem "described the entire cycle that she was about to go through. It began with normal perceptions of the world, continued through ecstatic and visionary states to unremitting despair, and finally to reemergence into the normal world, but with heightened awareness" (73). Millay was nineteen years old when she wrote the poem. Although Jamison did not know it at the time, Millay later survived several breakdowns and hospitalizations. Somehow, then, "in the strange state I was in, I knew that the poem had meaning for me; I understood it perfectly" (73).[2]

MARRIAGE DISINTEGRATES

During this same period of feverish behavior at work, her marriage "was falling apart." She separated from her husband ostensibly because she wanted children and he did not, "but it was far more complicated than this" (73). She was increasingly restless, irritable, and craving excitement. She began to rebel against the very things she most loved about him: his kindness, stability, warmth, and love. She found herself a very modern apartment in Santa Monica; and, despite her love for warm and old-fashioned things, she purchased cool and modern furniture. This was a move she could ill-afford: "Spending a lot of money that you don't have—or, as the formal diagnostic criterion so quaintly put it, 'engaging in unrestrained buying sprees'—is a classic part of mania" (74).

As her bills mounted, her brother came to her rescue. He obtained a personal loan from the World Bank where he worked as an economist. With this money they were able to cover the thousands and thousands of dollars of her outstanding bills. She estimates that her two major manic episodes—this one and a later one when she was in London—cost over thirty thousand dollars.

FIRST PSYCHOTIC DELUSIONS

One of her least expensive purchases, however, was especially ominous. Aware that she was in serious trouble, she had gotten a prescription for lithium from a colleague whom she had been dating following her separation from her husband. She went to the pharmacy to have it filled. After paying for it, she also purchased twelve snakebite kits and other absurd, useless, and bizarre items. She had a feeling that the pharmacist, having just filled the lithium prescription, could appreciate the humor in this. But he, of course, was completely unaware of "the life-threatening problem created by rattle-snakes in the San Fernando Valley," and of the fact that "God had chosen me, and apparently only me, to alert the world to the wild proliferation of killer snakes in the Promised Land" (76). As she scurried up and down the aisles of the drug store, she had devised a plan to alert the *Los Angeles Times* to the danger but was far too manic to tie her thoughts together into a coherent battle plan. This experience in the drugstore is her first account in *An Unquiet Mind* of truly delusional, psychotic ideation.

Meanwhile, her apartment was a place of increasing chaos. Books were strewn everywhere, clothes were piled up in mounds in every room, and unwrapped packages and unemptied shopping bags lay cluttered all over the place. Hundreds of scraps of paper filled every conceivable place. One paper contained an incoherent and rambling poem titled, "God is a Herbivore," apparently inspired by her constantly expanding spice collection. Her sensitivity to sounds in general and music in particular was intense. Individual notes from a horn, oboe, or cello were exquisitely poignant. Certain notes, either alone or in combination, carried a piercing beauty and clarity. Soon, however, the intensity and sadness of classical music became unbearable as she became impatient with the pace and overwhelmed by the emotion. She switched abruptly to rock music and played it as loud as possible. Soon her rooms were filled with records, tapes, and album jackets as she continued her search for "the perfect sound" (79).

This search was the prelude to the loss of control of her mind:

> The chaos in my mind began to mirror the chaos of my rooms; I could no longer process what I was hearing; I became confused, scared, and disoriented. I could not listen for more than a few minutes to any particular piece of music; my behavior was frenetic, and my mind more so. Slowly the darkness began to weave its way into my mind, and before long I was hopelessly out of control. (79)

She could not follow the path of her own thoughts. Sentences flew around in her head and fragmented first into phrases, then words.

Finally, only sounds remained. Then, one evening she stood in the middle of her living room and looked out at the blood-red sunset spreading over the horizon of the Pacific Ocean. She suddenly felt "a strange sense of light at the back of my eyes and almost immediately saw a huge centrifuge inside my head" (80). And then,

> I saw a tall figure in a floor-length evening gown approach the centrifuge with a vase-sized glass tube of blood in her hand. As the figure turned around, I saw to my horror that it was me and that there was blood all over my dress, cape, and long white gloves. I watched as the figure carefully put the tube of blood into one of the holes in the neck of the centrifuge, closed the lid, and pushed a button on the front of the machine. The centrifuge began to whirl. (80)

Then suddenly, the image that had been inside of her head was completely outside of it, and she was paralyzed by fright:

> The spinning of the centrifuge and the clanking of the glass tube against the metal became louder and louder, and then the machine splintered against the windowpanes, against the walls and paintings, and soaked down into the carpets. I looked out toward the ocean and saw that the blood on the window had merged into the sunset; I couldn't tell where one ended and the other began. (80)

She screamed at the top of her lungs, unable to "get away from the sight of the blood and the echoes of the machine's clanking as it whirled faster and faster. Not only had my thoughts spun wild, they had turned into an awful phantasmagoria, an apt but terrifying vision of an entire life and mind out of control. I screamed again and again" (80). Slowly, "the hallucination receded." She retained the presence of mind to telephone the colleague she had been dating to tell him what had happened. He came right over.

MANIC-DEPRESSIVE ILLNESS DIAGNOSED

When he arrived, he said he was certain she had manic-depressive illness and persuaded her to make an appointment to see a psychiatrist. In addition to lithium, her friend prescribed other antipsychotic medications on a short-term, emergency basis until she could see the psychiatrist. He spent hours talking with her family about her illness and how they might best handle it. He also insisted that she take a short time off from work. This ultimately saved her from losing her job and her clinical privileges. He arranged for her to be looked after at home during the times when he was unable to be there.

For Jamison, this episode, her first in which she was psychotically manic, was the "most dreadful" experience of her life. She had been mildly manic before, but these had never been frightening experiences—ecstatic at best, confusing at worst. Moreover, she had developed mechanisms of self-control that enabled her "to keep down the peals of singularly inappropriate laughter, and set rigid limits on my irritability" (82). She had also learned to pretend she was paying attention when her mind was off chasing rabbits in a thousand directions. But this time none of these tactics was of any avail. Moreover, nothing prepared her for this attack of insanity. In time, endless and terrifying days of drugs—lithium, Thorazine,™ Valium,™ and barbituates—began to take effect. She could feel her mind being reined in and slowed down: "But it was a very long time until I recognized my mind again, and much longer until I trusted it" (83).

Jamison's account continues with a testimony to the critical role that her psychiatrist played in her life from that time onward. He insisted on a combination of drug treatments (lithium) and psychotherapy. He listened to her convoluted, alternative explanations for her breakdown—the stress of a dissolving marriage, of joining the psychiatry faculty, of overwork. Still he remained firm in his judgment, shared with the colleague she had been dating, that she had manic-depressive illness and was going to have to be on lithium, probably indefinitely. She credits the combination of lithium and psychotherapy with enabling her to live a fairly normal life. Lithium prevents her seductive but disastrous highs, diminishes her depressions, clears out the "wool and webbing" from her "disordered thinking," and slows her down. But psychotherapy does the work of healing by making some sense of the confusions, reining in the terrifying thoughts and feelings, and returning "some control and hope and possibility of learning from it all" (89).

Missing Saturn

The second chapter in Part 2, "Missing Saturn," is largely an account of her lack of judgment about the necessity of taking lithium. A common reaction that follows in the wake of early episodes of manic-depressive illness is the terrible sense of loss one experiences when the medications cause the departure of high flights of mind and mood. For Jamison, the feeling that she was now less productive, lively, and energetic was depressing to her. Friends tried to reassure her that "now, you're just like the rest of us"; but in comparing herself with her former self, she felt "far removed from when I have been my liveliest, most productive, most intense, most outgoing and effervescent" (92).

Her "war" with lithium began not long after she started taking it. Within months, she went against medical advice and stopped taking it.

For one thing, it had very negative side effects, including frequent nausea, vomiting, physical trembling, walking into walls, and slurred speech, causing her to appear inebriated. (All of this changed very much for the better when she later switched to a time-released form of lithium.) Worse, the medication seriously affected her ability to read, comprehend, and remember what she had read. She was unable to read a serious work of literature or nonfiction cover to cover. She threw books against the wall in blind fury. Journal articles came somewhat easier because they were short, but she needed to read the same lines repeatedly and take copious notes before she could comprehend what she was reading.

Needlepoint came to her rescue and, poetry "remained within my grasp." "I now fell upon it with a passion that is hard to describe" (95). Also, children's books, shorter and larger print than adult books, "were relatively accessible" to her, and she read over and over again the classics of childhood. Kenneth Graham's *The Wind in the Willows* (1989; first published in 1908) was especially overwhelming: "Once I remember, I broke down entirely at a particular passage describing Mole and his house. I cried and cried and could not stop" (96).

Mole, who had been away from his underground home for a very long time exploring the world of light and adventure with his friend Ratty, was walking along one evening and suddenly and powerfully smelled his old home. He begged Ratty to join him in revisiting his home. After a nightcap of mulled ale in front of the fire, Mole reflected on how much he has missed the warmth and security of what he once had known, all of those "friendly things which had long been unconsciously a part of him" (96). This passage made her weep: "I missed my home, my mind, my life of books and 'friendly things,' my world where most things were in their place, and where nothing awful could come in to wreak havoc" (96–97).

The Charnel House

In the next chapter, "The Charnel House," Jamison focuses on the prolonged depression, lasting more than a year and a half, which followed her second "floridly psychotic mania" (110), a manic episode that was due to her failure to take her medications. Severely depressed, she was seeing her psychiatrist two or three times a week and had resumed taking her lithium on a regular basis. But her depression continued, and she was very suicidal.

SEEKING SUICIDE

Her psychiatrist recommended a voluntary confinement in a psychiatric hospital but she refused, "horrified at the thought of being locked up," but mostly "concerned that if it became public knowledge that she had been hospitalized, my clinical work and privileges at best would be suspended; at worst, they would be revoked on a permanent basis" (112). Since she opposed voluntary confinement, her psychiatrist did not consider involuntary confinement, knowing that the state confinement code was written in such a way that it would have been relatively easy for her to counteract it. After the experience, Jamison drew up a clear arrangement with her psychiatrist and family that if she ever again became severely depressed they had the authority to approve, against her will if necessary, both electroconvulsive therapy (ECT), an effective treatment for certain types of severe depression, and hospitalization.

While severely depressed, she yanked the bathroom lamp out of the wall one evening and banged her head over and over again against the bathroom door, pleading with God to make her insanity stop. She then devised a plan that would turn lithium into her killer. She obtained an antiemetic prescription from a hospital emergency room so that she would not vomit up the overdose of lithium pills. Then she removed the telephone from her bedroom so that she would not inadvertently pick it up, took several handfuls of pills, and curled up in her bed, waiting to die. When the telephone *did* ring, a call from her brother from Paris to find out how she was doing, she instinctively, in her semiconscious state, crawled to the telephone in the living room. Her brother concluded from her slurred speech that something was terribly wrong and called her psychiatrist immediately.

She was in and out of a coma for several days, but another friend, who happened to be working as an emergency room physician on weekends, kept a constant watch on her. This friend drew her blood for lithium and electrolyte levels and walked her repeatedly to pull her out of her drugged state (117).

SEEKING TO RECONCILE

After her suicide attempt, she had to "reconcile her image of herself as a young girl filled with enthusiasms, high hopes, great expectations, enormous energy, and dreams and love of life with that of a dreary, crabbed, pained woman who desperately wished only for death and took a lethal dose of lithium in order to accomplish it" (121). Similarly, after each of her violent psychotic episodes, she had to reconcile, as best she could, her sense of herself "as a reasonably quiet-spoken and highly disciplined person, one at least generally sensitive to the moods and feelings of others, with an enraged, utterly insane, and abusive woman who lost access to all control or reason" (121).

The discrepancies between these selves is exacerbated "for a woman brought up in a highly conservative and traditional world" (121):

> For the most important and shaping years of my life I had been brought up in a straitlaced world, taught to be thoughtful of

others, circumspect, and restrained in my actions. We went as a family to church every Sunday....The independence encouraged by my parents had been of an intellectual, not socially disruptive, nature. Then, suddenly, I was unpredictably and uncontrollably irrational and destructive. This was not something that could be overcome by protocol or etiquette. God, conspicuously, was nowhere to be found. Navy Cotillion, candy-striping and *Tiffany's Table Manners for Teenagers* could not, nor were they ever intended to be, any preparation or match for madness. Uncontrollable anger and violence are dreadfully, irreconcilably, far from a civilized and predictable world. (122–23)

Furthermore, depression is much more in line with society's notions of what women are all about: passive, dependent, confused, rather tiresome, and with limited aspirations. In contrast, manic states seem more characteristic of men: restless, aggressive, volatile, impulsive, grandiose, and visionary. When anger or irritability occur under such circumstances, it is more quietly tolerated in men. This places women, who are equally at risk of manic-depressive illness, at a certain disadvantage. If not condemned for their unladylike behavior, they are misdiagnosed, receive poor, if any, psychiatric treatment, and are at high risk for suicide, alcoholism, drug abuse, and violence (123).

Tenure

The final chapter of Part 2, "Tenure," focuses on Jamison's career (1974–1981) leading up to the granting of tenure. As the years marked by her struggle to stay sane went by, she became more and more determined to realize "some good from all of the pain." Tenure became a symbol of the stability she craved and the ultimate recognition she sought for having competed and survived in the normal world. She began to narrow her interests to the study and treatment of mood disorders, and, more specifically, to manic-depressive illness. Her personal and professional interest, together with the interest of two colleagues who had considerable clinical and research experience with mood disorders, led to the development of the UCLA Affective Disorders Clinic. This clinic stressed the combined use of medications and psychotherapy rather than medications alone. Despite these professional successes, the picture that she paints of these years is one of fear that her illness would be discovered by persons who would not be supportive and that she might be deprived of her clinical work and teaching. When she received tenure and promotion to the rank of associate professor, family and friends who gathered one evening for her tenure party understood that it was not only a celebration of the major rite of academic passage, but also of her struggle against severe mental illness itself.

Low-key and Reassuring

Part 3, "This Medicine, Love," is the shortest section of the memoir, but it provides compelling evidence that if lithium stabilizes, love truly heals.

An Officer and a Gentleman

The first chapter, "An Officer and a Gentleman," is a poignant account of a love relationship that played a vital role in the healing of the self torn asunder by her devastating illness. She met David Laurie the year she was appointed to the UCLA faculty. He was a visiting professor, a psychiatrist on leave from England's Royal Army Medical Corps. She discouraged his attentions that year because she and her husband were attempting to repair their marriage after she had moved out. The attempt eventually failed, due, she believes, to the fact that it never "really had a chance after I had impulsively left during my first major manic episode" (142).

THE LONDON EXPERIENCE

Two years later, however, David returned to UCLA and invited her to stay with him a few weeks in London. She was still recovering from her long suicidal depression, but she accepted his invitation. In his company, "the exhaustion, wariness, and black faithlessness" that she had been experiencing began to lift, and she began to remember how important love is to the sense that one is truly alive. One day, however, while David was at work, she decided to visit the cathedral at Canterbury. On a previous visit several years earlier, she had experienced a sense of ecstasy as she viewed "the dark gorgeous stained glass" and "the intense, transient light patterns on the cathedral floor" (143). This time, still suffering the after-effects of her long depression, she "kneeled without ecstasy, prayed without belief, and felt as a stranger" (143). All the same, it was a quieter and gentler sense of Canterbury than the previous one. In the midst of this "godless kneeling," though, she remembered that she had forgotten to take her lithium tablet the night before and reached into her purse for the medication. As she opened the bottle, the contents spilled out onto the cathedral floor, which was filthy. Furthermore, she was too embarrassed to bend over and pick them up. So she left the cathedral without them.

As she returned to London, she knew that this was a moment of reckoning, for it meant that she would have to ask David to write a prescription for her, and this meant that he would learn about her illness. Realizing that she could lose him over this self-disclosure, she also knew that she could not afford not to obtain her medications. The last time she had stopped taking her lithium she had gotten manic almost immediately, and her long depression followed in its wake: "I could not survive another year like the one I had just gone through" (144).

That evening she told David about her illness, dreading his reaction and furious with herself for not having told him earlier. He was silent for a very long time, and she sensed that his silence meant that he was sorting through all the implications, medical and personal, of what she had told him. She was certain of his love for her, but, a psychiatrist himself, he would know how uncertain the course of her illness would be. Moreover, "He was an army officer, his family was extremely conservative, he desperately wanted to have children, and manic-depressive illness was hereditary" (144). She fully expected him to tell her that their relationship could not continue. Instead, he put his arms around her and said, simply, "Rotten luck."

Overcome with relief, she explained to him that "rotten luck" sounded like something out of a P. G. Wodehouse novel. This reminded him of a Wodehouse character who acknowledged that while he was not "disgruntled," he was not "gruntled" either. They both laughed, "somewhat nervously to be sure, but some of the awful ice was broken" (148). Beginning that very night, he began to ask her what she had been through and what he could do to help her when she was ill. She left London "with a terrible sense of apprehension," but he wired and called often. Later in the year they spent time together in Washington, D. C., and "as I was feeling myself again, I enjoyed life in ways that I hadn't in years" (147). He returned to London, and she went back to Los Angeles.

Sudden Loss

Some months later, she returned to England for two weeks. One Sunday morning, after church, as they walked up into the hills to listen to the ringing of the church bells, Kay noticed that David had stopped. He was standing still and breathing heavily. He made a joke about it; they laughed, and let it go at that. Shortly thereafter, he was assigned to the British Army Hospital in Hong Kong and made plans for her to visit him there. But it was not to be. One night, not long before she was to join him, she heard a knock on the door. It was an odd time, and she wasn't expecting anyone. Even stranger was the fact that she remembered what her mother had said about how pilots' wives dreaded the chaplain's knock on the door. She opened it, only to see a diplomatic courier with a letter from David's commanding officer saying that David had died very suddenly of a massive heart attack. He was forty-four; Kay was thirty-two.

One thing that helped her deal with her grief was the unbelievable tenderness of the British Army and the healing that comes from their traditions. The rituals of military funerals are themselves "predictable, reassuring, dignified, religious, and dreadfully final" (149–50). During the funeral, David's commanding officer insisted that she join in the singing of the hymns. He laughed out loud when she made a joke in reference to the somewhat overdone eulogy about "officers and gentlemen" and pushed her forward when she felt an overwhelming desire to remain back from the gravesite. During the rest of the time she spent in England, her mind was filled with memories and regrets "for lost opportunities" and "unnecessary and damaging arguments"; but "grief, fortunately, is very different from depression: it is sad, it is awful, but it is not without hope" (150). His death did not plunge her into unendurable darkness, and suicide never crossed her mind.

On her return home, she continued to receive letters from him, long delayed in the mail, and then, of course, they ceased. Years later, when she was asked to speak about his death, she concluded with a poem by Edna St. Vincent Millay. It began with the lines, "Time does not bring relief; you have all lied / Who told us time would ease me of my pain?" (Fuller 2000, 271). In fact, however, "Time finally did bring relief. But it took its own, and not terribly sweet, time in doing so" (Jamison 1993, 152).

They Tell Me It Rained

The second chapter in Part 3, "They Tell Me It Rained," focuses on her sabbatical year in England four years after David Laurie's death. On visiting his grave in Dorset, she was taken aback by the tranquility and beauty of the churchyard in which he was buried. As she placed a bouquet of long-stemmed violets on his grave and sat, tracing the letters of his name in the granite, she felt his presence next to her, as when they knelt together at the communion rail in St. Paul's Church in London. She wished more than anything that he could see that she was well and that she could somehow repay him for his kindness and belief in her:

> But mostly, as I was sitting there in the graveyard I thought of all of the things David had missed by dying young. And then, after an hour or more of being lost in my thoughts, I was caught up short by the realization that I had been thinking, for the first time, about how much David had missed, rather than what we together would miss. (158–59)

She adds, "David had loved and accepted me in an extraordinary way; his steadiness and kindness had sustained and saved me, but he was gone. Life—because of him, and despite his death—went on" (159). If mourning can ever be said to have completed itself, this was true for her, and this, too, testified to the role that David had played in her own healing.

During this year in England, after consultation with her psychiatrist in Los Angeles and her doctor in London, she began, very slowly, reducing the amount of lithium she was taking. The effect was dramatic: "It was as though I had taken the bandages off my eyes after many years of partial blindness" (161). Walking in Hyde Park one day, she realized that her steps were literally bouncier than they had been before. She was taking in sights and sounds that had previously been filtered as though through thick layers of gauze, and the quacking of ducks was more insistent, and more intense. Most significant, she could once again read without effort: "It was, in short, remarkable" (162).

Love Watching Madness

The third and final chapter of Part 3, "Love Watching Madness," tells how she met Dr. Richard Wyatt at a Christmas party in Washington, D. C. A well-known schizophrenia researcher, Wyatt was chief of neuro-psychiatry at the National Institute of Mental Health. Theirs was "a short but very convincing courtship." After a year or so, they were married. She resigned her position at UCLA and moved to Washington. At the time of writing *The Unquiet Mind,* they had been husband and wife for nearly a decade.

MARRIED AGAIN

Temperamentally, they "could not have been more different" (171). Richard was low-key, slow to anger, and "the world registered gently upon him, sometimes not at all," whereas she "was fast to feel both pleasure and pain" (171–72). In terms of interests, habits, lifestyle, they were "a complete mismatch"; yet "not once in the years we have been together have I doubted Richard's love for me, nor mine for him. Love, like life, is much stronger and far more complicated than one is brought up to believe" (173). She likens her life with Richard to reaching "a safe harbor" (173).

During their courtship, she inevitably had to tell him about her illness. When she did so, he looked genuinely stunned. He put down the hamburger he was eating, stared into her eyes, and said rather dryly, "That explains a lot." This response was not the "Rotten luck" and hug that David Laurie had offered, but, in his own way, Richard, too, was "remarkably kind." Like David, he asked many questions of a medical nature and was, "as ever, low-key and reassuring" (174). She knew, however, that it is one thing to have an understanding of how an illness works and quite another to have to live with it on a day-to-day basis. She remains deeply skeptical "that anyone who does not have this illness can truly understand it" (174).

DEALING WITH MANIA

Richard's difficulty in understanding it has been reflected in his tendency to view her occasional "black manias" as being "willful, angry, irrational, or simply tiresome" rather than as the effect of an illness that is not always controllable. Clearly, the manias of manic-depressive illness put love to its greatest test: "The sadder, sleepier, slower, and less volatile depressions are more intuitively understood and more easily taken in stride. A quiet melancholy is neither threatening nor beyond ordinary comprehension; an angry, violent, vexatious despair is both" (174).

Yet experience and love have taught both of them a great deal about dealing with manic-depressive illness. For her own part, she has come to believe that her husband's imperturbability is worth three hundred milligrams of lithium per day! "Sometimes, in the midst of one of my dreadful, destructive upheavals of mood, I feel Richard's quietness nearby and am reminded of Byron's wonderful description of the rainbow that sits 'Like Hope upon a death-bed' on the verge of a wild, rushing cataract; yet, 'while all around is torn / By the distracted waters,' the rainbow stays serene: 'Resembling, 'mid the torture of the scene, / Love watching madness with unalterable mien'" (175).[3] Her return to the Washington area has also been important, for Los Angeles "had never been the City of Angels to me." After all, it had been "filled with near death, a completely shattered innocence, and a recurrently lost and broken world" (171).

Given a Choice, Would I Choose It?

Part 4 of *The Unquiet Mind* focuses on the more technical side of manic-depressive illness and does not add significantly to the personal account presented in the first three sections of the book. It *is*, however, worth noting Jamison's preference for the term "manic-depressive illness" over "bipolar I disorder." She reasons that the tendency of the latter term to polarize the two clinical states "flies in the face of everything that we know about the cauldronous, fluctuating nature of manic-depressive illness" (182). It also "ignores the question of whether mania is, ultimately, simply an extreme form of depression" (182). Also significant is a conversation with Danish psychiatrist, Morens Scou, the man most responsible for the introduction of lithium as a treatment for manic-depressive illness. From the conversation she came to realize that manic-depressive illness occurred repeatedly throughout the last three generations on her father's side of the family (189).

In the epilogue, Jamison asks if she, given the choice, would choose to have manic-depressive illness. If lithium were not available to her, or did not work for her, the answer would be a simple no. So the fact that it does work for her means that she can afford to pose the question and, in fact, come down on the side of choosing it. On the one hand, she has nothing good to say for depression. But "the countless hypomanias, and mania itself, all have brought into my life a different level of sensing and feeling and thinking" (218–19). Even when she has been most psychotic–delusional, hallucinating, frenzied–she has "been aware of finding new corners in my mind and heart," some of which "were incredible and beautiful and took my breath away and made me feel as though I could die right then and the images would sustain me" (219).

Reliving the Childhood Trauma

Readers of *The Unquiet Mind* often comment on the overwhelming power of Jamison's first major psychotic episode in her apartment in Santa Monica. They take particular note of the fact that the huge centrifuge that was originally inside her head suddenly spun outside of her head, eventually splintering against the windowpanes, the walls, and the paintings. There was blood everywhere. As she looked out toward the ocean, she saw that the blood on the window had merged with the sunset, and this caused her to scream. She tried in vain to escape from the sight of the blood and from the echoes of the machine's clanking as it whirled faster and faster. But she was "paralyzed by fright" and was unable to move (80). In comparison with this huge centrifuge that was whirling and spattering blood everywhere, the image of the pinball machine inside the head of the woman at St. Elizabeths Hospital was relatively benign.

While Jamison does not comment further on the images that whirled around in her head and then spun outside, it seems as though she had a purpose in beginning her memoir with the scene of a seven-year-old girl witnessing the horrifying crash of the jet plane near her elementary school playground. The relatedness of the two scenes is, in fact, suggested in her chapter titles. "Into the Sun" is the title of the chapter in which she recounts her childhood experience, while "Flights of the Mind" is the title of the chapter in which she recounts her psychotic episode. The psychotic episode itself began as she was looking into the sun along the Santa Monica harbor, watching as its redness turned to blood. The spinning of the centrifuge machine and the clanking of the glass tube against the metal became louder and louder–like the unusually loud sound of the low-flying jet–and then splintered into a thousand pieces, leaving blood everywhere. This terrifying experience as she stood in the seeming safety of her living room was, it seems, a repetition of the earlier one when she, as a child, stood in the playground, "absolutely terrified," as the plane "flew into the trees, exploding directly in front of us" (12).

Other experiences from childhood may also have figured into the hallucination, such as the tubes of blood that the doctors at Andrews Air Force Base hospital provided her for her experiments on animals and birds. These became the "vase-sized glass tube of blood" that she was carrying as she approached the centrifuge. A possible self-identification with the child whose naked body she witnessed in the autopsy room may also be evident in the fact that she experienced herself as the threatened one, the one who would have lost her life had not the pilot sacrificed his life instead.

These associations raise the question of how earlier traumas are stored in the brain and reemerge in psychotic delusions many years later. Ruth Leys, a professor of humanities at Johns Hopkins University (where Kay Jamison is currently located), investigates the history of the concept of trauma in her book *Trauma: A Genealogy* (2000). In her discussion of current research on the neurobiology of trauma, Leys expresses deep skepticism over claims that the brain "takes pictures" of an earlier traumatic experience and is therefore capable of "representing" or "reproducing" it later. She refers to these as "literalistic" models of brain transmission. On the other hand, she believes that if the claim of a literal representation of the earlier experience is abandoned, this makes way for the view that an earlier traumatic experience may be reexperienced, but in a significantly modified way. She notes, for example, that the repetition may have language elements–speech–that are superimposed on the original trauma (Leys 2000, 231–65). While her book focuses on post-traumatic stress syndrome and not on psychotic episodes per se, such episodes may perhaps be examples of the "nonliteralistic" repetition of earlier traumas.

The fact that speech may be superimposed on the original trauma could explain, for example, the hearing of "voices" in some psychotic episodes. A nonliteralistic repetition of earlier traumas also allows for the role of current environmental cues (the blood-red sun, the whirling phonograph machine) in the hallucination, as well as for the integration of several traumatic episodes into a single psychotic episode. The very fact that Kay Jamison's childhood was a happy one would also cause this traumatic experience at age seven to loom larger by way of contrast. In a paradoxical way, her sister, who had a more mistrustful temperament, was less vulnerable than Kay to such traumatizing external events. As Kay points out, she experienced her own mental illness as a "stranger" from without. In effect, it came on the wings of a jet plane that invaded the tranquility of the playground.

Following her psychotic episode, Kay found that she could read children's books. This may also indicate that her psychotic episode was an attempt, however troubling, to come to terms with the childhood trauma of the plane crash. If her psychotic breakdown reflected the traumas of her childhood that had been "stored" in the reservoirs of her brain, then her reading of *The Wind in the Willows* brought back the pleasant scenes of her childhood home near *Andrews* Air Force Base, memories rekindled during her year in St. *Andrews* (the similarity in their names seems more than coincidental). If so, she, like Mole, longed for the warmth and security of what she had known as a child. She had briefly reexperienced such warmth and security that Christmas evening in St. Andrews when she participated in the singing of "the old and beautiful carols," then walked out into the evening and witnessed that ancient scene, the sight of scarlet gowns against the snow, the ringing of bells, and a clear, full moon. Note the contrast between the red blood splattered everywhere in her psychotic experience and the sight of scarlet gowns against the snow, the contrast between the clanking sound of the whirling centrifuge and the ringing of the bells, and the contrast between the blood-red sun over the Santa Monica harbor and the clear, full moon outside the university chapel.

The fact that the pilot in the plane crash could have been her father, and that her father did, in fact, experience his own emotional crash when Kay was in high school, leads to another important theme of *The Unquiet Mind,* that of father-loss.

The Underlying Theme of Father-Loss

Personal memoirs are much more than a mere factual account of "what happened." They are *interpretations* of the events and experiences of one's life. As interpretations, they usually involve an effort to make sense of one's life, to discover its meaning and discern its overall coherence, or, if such coherence seems missing or lacking, to present an explanation for why this is so. Kay Jamison's *The Unquiet Mind* is no exception. The central, unifying theme of her book is not the mere fact of her mental illness but her effort to understand it and its significance for her life. This understanding is greatly informed by her awareness that manic-depressive illness involves a brain disorder, one that produces an instability of mood and thinking processes and is responsive to a medication—lithium—that directly alters the mechanism of the brain.

This understanding is also influenced by her awareness that manic-depressive illness is inherited and is found among persons who are genetically predisposed to it. Still, she insists that treatment involving medications alone is inadequate, and so she strongly advocates psychotherapy as well. One obvious benefit of psychotherapy is that it offers the sufferers opportunity to explore their resistance to compliance with the recommended medical treatment. Other benefits include gaining insight into the ways in which the illness affects one's personal and professional relationships and into how it affects one's sense of oneself as a person of value and worth.

While Jamison does not tell the reader what she and her psychiatrist talked about—and there is no reason to expect that she would or should—my own "curious self" would very much like to know if they discussed her father. If so, was consideration given to the role that his actual illness (not just his genetic makeup) played in her own susceptibility to illness. This is the kind of question that someone with a Freudian or psychoanalytic bias is likely to ask and consider important to ask, as it not only has bearing on her illness but also on her return to a reasonably healthy life.

Experiences with Freudian Psychoanalysts

In the absence of disclosures of what was said and discussed during their psychotherapy sessions, and, more importantly, her own reflections on this question in *The Unquiet Mind,* one can only look for indirect clues in the text itself. For reasons that will be made clear, I think that the best clues are the comments—not included in the preceding summary of the book—that Jamison makes about the Freudian psychoanalysts that she had encountered in her personal and professional life. Two such encounters are presented in the book.

THE DOCTRINAIRE TEST ANALYST

The first occurs in the second chapter of the book, "An Education for Life." She notes that when she began her clinical training as a graduate student in 1971, "psychoanalytic theories still predominated. So for the first two years of treating patients, I was supervised almost entirely by psychoanalysts; the emphasis in treatment was on understanding early experiences and conflicts; dreams and symbols, and their interpretation, formed the core of psychotherapeutic work" (59). When she began her clinical internship at the UCLA Neuropsychiatric Institute, she was introduced to "a more medical approach to psychopathology—one that centered on diagnosis, symptoms, illness, and medical treatment" (59).

Having embraced the medical approach to psychopathology, she has had "many disagreements with psychoanalysts over the years." These included "particularly virulent ones with those analysts who oppose treating severe mood disorders with medications, long after the evidence clearly showed that lithium and the antidepressants are far more effective than psychotherapy alone" (59). On the other hand, she has

> found invaluable the emphasis in my early psychotherapy training on many aspects of psychoanalytic thought. I shed much of the psychoanalytic language as time went by, but the education was an interesting one, and I've never been able to fathom the often unnecessary arbitrary distinctions between "biological" psychiatry, which emphasizes medical causes and treatments of mental illness, and the "dynamic" psychologies, which focus more on early developmental issues, personality structure, conflict and motivation, and unconscious thought. (59–60)

I pointed out in the introduction to this book that mental illness is both a brain disease (an organic abnormality) and a mental illness (disvalued changes in states of being and in social function). Thus I share Jamison's opposition to the polarization of biological psychiatry and dynamic psychologies.

In the next paragraph, though, after noting that "Extremes, however, are always absurd," she relates an incident that presents a psychoanalyst in a very negative light. It involved her training in the administration of various psychological tests. Her first practice subject was her first husband who, as noted earlier, was a talented artist. She administered the Wechsler Adult Intelligence Scale (WAIS), the Rorschach, and the Draw-A-Person test. His Rorschach responses "were of a level of originality that I have not seen since," and his Draw-A-Person drawing, instead of the "revealing self-portrait" she expected, "was a wonderfully elaborated orangutan whose long arms extended along the borders of the page" (60).

Thinking they were marvelous, she took the results to her psychological-testing supervisor. An "entirely humorless and doctrinaire psychoanalyst," she "spent more than an hour interpreting in the most fatuous and speculative manner, the primitive and repressed rage of my husband, his intrapsychic conflicts, his ambivalences, his antisocial nature, and his deeply disturbed personality structure" (60). A man that Kay had never known to lie was being labeled a sociopath, and a man "who was quite singularly straightforward and gentle was interpreted as deeply disturbed, conflicted, and filled with rage. All because he had done something different on a test" (61). The interpretation was "so ridiculous to me that, after having giggled uncontrollably for quite a long while, thus provoking even further wrath—and, worse yet, further interpretations—I half stormed, half laughed my way out of her office and refused to write up the test report. This, too, needless to say, was obsessed over, dissected, and analyzed" (61).

THE MOUSEHEART FACTOR

This is certainly not a very flattering picture of the first of the two psychoanalysts portrayed in *The Unquiet Mind*. The second psychoanalyst appears in the chapter, "Clinical Privileges," in Part 4 of the book. The chapter illustrates how some professional colleagues have responded to her disclosure of her illness in a manner that has been "unkind, condescending, or lacking in even a semblance of empathy" (199). "Not without bitterness," Jamison has come to refer to this "cruelty, intentional or otherwise," from colleagues or friends, as "the Mouseheart factor" (199).

"Mouseheart" is the name she coined for a former colleague who was also, she had thought, a friend. He was a "soft-spoken psychoanalyst" with whom she would get together for morning coffee. Occasionally, they would also go out for lunch and chat about their work and personal lives. After a while, Kay began to feel the real discomfort she would feel whenever "a certain level of friendship or intimacy had been reached in a relationship and I have not mentioned my illness" (200). Not talking about it, "if only to discuss it once, generally consigns a friendship to a certain inevitable level of superficiality" (200). So, with an inward sigh, she decided to go ahead and tell him.

In an oceanfront restaurant in Malibu, she gave him a brief rundown of her manias, depressions, and suicide attempt. Then she fixed her eye on a distant pile of rocks out in the ocean and waited for his response:

> It was a long, cold wait. Finally, I saw tears running down his face, and, although I remember thinking at the time that it was an extreme response—particularly since I had tried to present my manias in as lighthearted a way as possible, and my depressions with some dispassion—I thought it was touching that he felt so strongly about what I had been through. (200)

But then, "wiping away his tears," Mouseheart "told me that he just couldn't believe it. He was, he said, 'deeply disappointed.' He had thought I was so wonderful, so strong: How *could* I have attempted suicide? What had I been thinking? It was such an act of cowardice, so selfish" (200). She realized, to her horror, that he was serious. She was "absolutely transfixed":

> His pain at hearing that I had manic-depressive illness was, it would seem, far worse than mine in actually having it. For a few minutes, I felt like Typhoid Mary. Then I felt betrayed, deeply embarrassed, and utterly exposed. His solicitude, of course, knew no bounds. Had I *really* been psychotic? If so, did I really think, under the circumstances, that I was going to be able to handle the stresses of academic life? (200–201)

She pointed out to him, "through clenched teeth," that she had in fact handled those particular stresses for many years, and, indeed, "if truth be told, I was considerably younger than he was and had, in fact, published considerably more" (201).

She does not now recall much of the rest of the lunch,

> except that it was an ordeal, and that at some point, with sarcasm that managed to pass him by, I told him that he ought not to worry, that manic-depressive illness wasn't contagious (although he could have benefitted from a bit of mania, given his rather dreary, obsessive, and humorless view of the world). He squirmed in his seat and averted his eyes. (201)

The next morning a boxed bouquet of a dozen long-stemmed roses arrived at the clinic for her, and "an abject note of apology was tucked in at the top" (201). She adds, "It was a nice thought, I suppose, but it didn't begin to salve the wound inflicted by what I knew had been a candid response on his part: he was normal, I was not, and—in those most killing of words—he was 'deeply disappointed'" (201).

In both of these accounts, Jamison uses the word "extreme," thus suggesting that the problem with psychoanalysts is that they go to "extremes." She also suggests that both psychoanalysts were "humorless," that they took such a serious view of what was being presented to them that they themselves became ridiculous. In the second of the two episodes, she also suggests that her psychoanalyst friend missed the sarcasm in her comment that he need not worry for manic-depressive illness is not contagious. This is a particularly damning thing to say about a psychoanalyst, as psychoanalysts, at least as popularly viewed, are supposed to be experts in reading other persons' thoughts, the motivations behind the words.

Jamison's Troubles with Psychoanalysis

With one notable exception—her portrayal of a senior colleague dubbed "The Oyster" (133–34)—these are the only unflattering descriptions of colleagues in the book. This prompts me to wonder what it is about psychoanalysis besides its tendency to "go to extremes" that is troubling to her. I also wonder whether the answer to this question might have some bearing on the question with which I began this exercise in curiosity, whether her father's own illness played a direct role in her susceptibility to illness at the time that it occurred?

REFERENCES TO HER FATHER

Psychoanalysis is a conceptual system that places a great deal of emphasis on parent-child relationships and one that has tended, owing to the writings of its founder, Sigmund Freud, to emphasize the role of the father. In this respect, psychoanalysis and *The Unquiet Mind* have a great deal in common. It is not without significance that Part 1 begins with the violent death of a man who could have been Kay's father and that a central theme in the subsequent chapters of Part 1 is her father's mental and emotional collapse.

By the time the second chapter of Part 1, "An Education for Life," concludes, her father has succumbed to manic-depressive illness, has been fired from his position at Rand (no wonder she feared professional reprisals should her own illness come to light!), and her parents have separated, subsequently divorcing. Describing her decision to spend a year at St. Andrews, she says that she was motivated, in part, by a desire to "get away from my father's black, unpredictable moods," as well as "a vague notion that I might better understand my own chaotic feelings and thinking if I returned in some sense to the source" (48). In other words, she would be getting away from him but, in another sense, she would be discovering what they shared in common, what bound father and daughter together. Except for a reference to her father's family history of manic-depressive illness (189), this is the last reference to her father in the text. We do not learn what happens to him. The reader may assume that he died in the interval between his succumbing to mental illness and the writing of the book, but this is not made clear. Instead, he simply disappears.

REFERENCES TO OTHER MEN

Subsequent chapters introduce many other men. The first is a professor who "was himself inclined to quick and profound mood swings" (53). The last is the department chair at Johns Hopkins University. At the time of her hiring, he responded to her worries about her hospital privileges by reaching across the table, placing his hand on hers, and smiling, "Kay, dear, I *know* you have manic-depressive illness." Then he laughed, "If we got rid of all the manic-depressives on the medical school faculty, not only would we have a much smaller faculty, it would be a far more boring one" (209). Regardless of their respective ages, this was a truly fatherly gesture.

PSYCHOANALYSIS AND TRANSFERENCE

It is, of course, something of a popular cliche—which psychoanalysis may be said to have exploited to the full—that as men seek their mothers in the women with whom they become intimately involved, so women seek their fathers in the men with whom *they* become emotionally involved. The psychoanalytic concept that has most direct relevance in this regard is *transference*. Transference suggests that one transfers or displaces emotions relative to one individual onto another. As we saw in chapter 1, Anton Boisen invoked this very concept when he suggested that Alice had been, in effect, his physician. He does not, however, make the more obvious application of the transference concept, that he had transferred feelings toward his mother onto Alice.

The Unquiet Mind exemplifies such transference—its complexities and complications—in a deep and moving way. David Laurie, for example, a tall and handsome man like her father, is also a military man, a representative of a disciplined but romantic tradition with much the same passionate temperament of her father. As she notes, until she met and married Richard Wyatt, she was invariably attracted to men "whose temperament was largely similar to my own" (170)—and to her father's. David's very uniqueness, the fact that he was a psychiatrist with the Royal Army Medical Corps, was also, in its way, another link with her father, for her father was a meteorologist, a man of scientific training who was in the military because of his love of flying.

Moreover, Laurie's role was to treat those military men, who, like her father, were suffering from mental or emotional stress, or who had succumbed to mental illness. While Jamison does not make any direct references to the emotional link between David Laurie and her father, one senses that her grieving for David is also a grieving over her loss of her father that occurred when he sank into his dark and terrible depressions. The Edna St. Vincent Millay sonnet that she read in public tribute to David Laurie years after his death is no less applicable to her father who, in succumbing to mental illness, had also, as it were, become "dead" to her: "I miss him in the weeping of the rain; / I want him at the shrinking of the tide" (Fuller 2000, 267).

Especially noteworthy, then, is her observation that when David died, she experienced a deep, painful grief, but not depression (Jamison 1995, 150). Grief, she notes, "is not without hope." When she returned to visit his grave, she was caught up short by the realization that for the hour she had spent in the graveyard, she "had been thinking, for the first time, about how much David had missed, rather than about what we together would miss" (159).

This suggests that she had begun to let him go and was preparing to move on with her life, a life in which he would live, largely, in the past. Thus, grief was strangely curative. It provided a different way of responding to profound loss than the way she had responded following the emotional loss of her father, the loss that, in my judgment, precipitated her plunge into depression, and prepared the way for the illness that followed in its wake. Grieving the loss of David meant grieving the loss of her father as well, and this also meant gaining personal leverage over her depressions, for depression, as William Styron came to understand, is symptomatic of "incomplete mourning." It also made it possible for her to consider sharing her life with a man who was not like either man, and, most importantly, was not reminiscent of her father. In psychoanalytic language, her father-transference had been "worked through."

The Importance of Empathy

This leads us back to the episodes involving the two psychoanalysts. At the beginning of the chapter that relates the Mouseheart episode, Jamison notes that what has disturbed her the most have been responses to her disclosures of her illness that have been "unkind, condescending, or lacking in even a semblance of empathy" (199). I think that the key word here is "empathy." This word sheds important light on what was so troubling and offensive about these two episodes. By taking a closer look at these episodes in light of the empathy issue, we may be able to gain some important insights into what the mentally ill need—and do not need—from family, friends, and colleagues.

The Test Analyst's Lack of Attention to Kay's Needs

The first of these two episodes focused on the test responses of Jamison's husband, the man to whom she had turned when her father became lost to her. This man appears rather suddenly in the course of her narrative. In the middle of a paragraph about the freedom that graduate school afforded her, she mentions, "I was married, too, by this point" (57). She then proceeds to describe her husband and relate how she met him. What was so infuriating about the first psychoanalyst's assessment of her husband's test results was that Kay had thought that her husband's responses were "marvelous," and she was fully expecting that her psychological-testing supervisor would agree. Moreover, the assessment was presented in a nonempathic manner.

Conceivably some aspects of her husband's personality *did* fit the analyst's interpretation, at least to some degree, but the interpretation offered is not the major issue. More importantly, the analyst seems to have lacked any appreciation for what this interpretation could do to Kay herself, who, at that time, was emotionally dependent on her husband for the stability and steadiness he represented and provided. While Kay's refusal to write up the test report seems to have been the action that the analyst dissected and "obsessed over," the more revealing aspect of the whole incident was that Kay expressed her discomfort by giggling uncontrollably for quite a long while. This slightly manic response enabled her to regain her composure, but it belied a deeply troubled, depressed spirit. Thus, it was not so much the doctrinaire and humorless manner of the psychoanalyst but the fact that she was nonempathic—insensitive to what her interpretation of Kay's husband could do to an already fragile ego—that seems most worthy of censure.

Kohut's Concept of Empathy

About the same time Kay was receiving her psychoanalytically-oriented clinical training, another psychoanalyst, Heinz Kohut, was a rising star in psychoanalytic circles for his promotion of empathy as an essential feature of the psychotherapeutic process. He emphasized that such empathy derives from an awareness that what one is observing in one's patients are conflicts and struggles that one experiences in oneself. In *How Does Analysis Cure* (1984), published posthumously, Kohut says that "the best definition of empathy" is "that it is the capacity to think and feel oneself into the inner life of another person. It is our lifelong ability to experience what another person experiences, though usually, and appropriately, to an attenuated degree" (1984, 82).

This definition, he notes, is "the analogue to my [earlier] terse scientific definition of empathy as 'vicarious introspection'" (82). If introspection means to look into or explore one's own thought and feelings, empathy is a similar act or process with respect to the thoughts and feelings of another. Empathy's "vicarious" nature may mean that the other person is unable to accomplish such an introspective act for herself or himself. Thus, while empathy may evoke the response, "You have read my thoughts and feelings," it may also prompt the other to say, "You know, I think you know my thoughts and feelings even better than I know them myself." Kohut also suggests that we may be the subjects of our own "vicarious introspection." He has in mind here our ability "to step away from ourselves" and perceive our own inner life as if it were that of someone else (220).

Jamison's session with the first psychoanalyst would have gone very differently if the other woman had had the capacity to think and feel her way into Kay's own thoughts and feelings, her own inner life. She may have been aided in this act or expression of "vicarious introspection" if she had recognized in Jamison the same troubled and floundering young woman that she herself had been at Kay's age, the very reason, perhaps, why she, too, had chosen a career in the psychological profession.

Dr. Mouseheart's Sympathy Was Not Empathy

If the first psychoanalyst was nonempathic, what about the second, Dr. Mouseheart? That he shed tears would appear to be compelling evidence of his empathy with her, but empathy and sympathy are two very different emotional responses, and his seems to have been one of sympathy, even of pity. With empathy, one "feels with" the other, experiences to the extent possible what the other experiences. With sympathy, one "feels for" the other, and such "feeling for" may come across, as it does here, as condescension, as looking down on the other from a position of superiority. As the object of sympathy, Jamison felt that she was being cast as some sort of "Typhoid Mary." Her feelings turned to a deep sense of betrayal, embarrassment, and being utterly exposed. This time, however, she did not respond with uncontrollable giggles but with withering sarcasm. In its own way, this was a sign of how far she had come in the intervening years.

To say that Jamison was fully justified in responding as she did may come across as another form of condescension. Some such affirmation, however, is necessary and vital so that my next point is not misunderstood as a critique of her, but rather as an observation about the power of mental illness—and conventional attitudes toward it—to affect interpersonal relationships in a negative way.

As we saw in the case of William Styron, mental illness led to interpersonal misunderstandings and a growing sense of disconnectedness between the sufferer and the persons who loved him. The situation is rather different in Jamison's case. Here, the issue is not that she is disconnected from others but that her illness, which is not, for the most part, perceptible to others, is a topic that needs eventually to be broached if a relationship is not to remain on a superficial level. When this topic is broached, the other person's response will have a decisive effect on the very future of their relationship. Thus, there is a sort of litmus test that enters into the relationship, and some friends pass it while others fail.

From Jamison's account of her psychoanalyst friend, the reader realizes that his response to her self-disclosure was so stunningly inept that a dozen roses and an abject apology could not reverse the damage. We are given to understand that the relationship was over for good. The name, really an epithet, "Mouseheart" not only implies this, but also informs the reader of how far this man had fallen in her personal esteem. The fact that he was a professional colleague, a man with training in the psychological field, makes his response all the more inexcusable.

Yet, one of the major points of Jamison's book is that she herself was extremely slow to realize, despite her own training in this field, that she was suffering from a very serious mental illness. Whether this would be sufficient grounds for her to have reacted to his failure with greater charity, or to have used their friendship to provide him with a much-needed education in manic-depressive illness, is not for anyone else to say. But as I read her account of his initial reaction to her self-disclosure— the tears running down his face—I found myself wondering what was behind the very extremeness of his response. To say that it *was* extreme is to say that it was emotionally "overdetermined." As she points out, it appeared inappropriate to the occasion at hand in light of the fact that she had tried to present her manias "in as light-hearted a way as possible" and her depressions "with some dispassion" (200).

Another Instance of Transference

What were these tears all about? And were the verbal responses that followed in their wake his way of countering the emotions that the tears represented? Were not his reactions and responses highly conflicted ones, suggesting that some sort of *transference* feelings were involved? If, as I have suggested, Jamison was working out the loss of her relationship with her father through her relationships with other men, could it be that her psychoanalyst friend was doing the same as far as his relationship with his mother was concerned? Were his responses to her disclosure "extreme" because it had opened up wounds associated with the very first woman he had loved, the one to whom he owed his very life and being?

In the absence of personal information about him, such questions must remain purely speculative. But when he said to her that he was "deeply disappointed," that her suicide attempt was a selfish act, and that he questioned whether she could handle the stresses of academic life, this may have reflected feelings about his mother and his loss of her, as did, perhaps, his subsequent act of sending a dozen roses and writing an abject letter of apology. It is very possible that he suffered, as many men do, from melancholia, which, as I have suggested in reference to William Styron, is the result of the boy's emotional separation from his mother around the age of three to five (see Capps 1997, 2002).

Empathy from Laurie and Wyatt

Kohut's caution against the "mythologizing" of empathy is especially relevant to Jamison's account of the ways in which David Laurie and Richard Wyatt responded to her disclosure of her mental illness. Even as empathy is not infallible, so it is "not God's gift bestowed only on an elect few. For the average individual, training and learning make the difference, rather than the fact of endowment" (Kohut 1984, 83). Such training and learning were evident in the way in which both David and Richard asked questions and, in doing so, expressed their empathy.

Both men understood that they could not enter into her inner world without guidance from her, as this was a world that they had not personally experienced. Her psychoanalyst friend's error was in his apparent assumption that he knew what it was like to suffer from manic-depressive illness. Significantly, he appears to have asked no questions. In contrast, David "asked me question after question about what I had been through, what had been most terrible, what had frightened me the most, and what he could do to help me when I was ill" (Jamison 1995, 145). Richard responded similarly: "Much as David Laurie had done, he asked me a great deal about what form my illness took and how it had affected my life" (173).

She suggests that the fact that both men were physicians led them to ask "question after question of a medical nature." But instead of finding these questions invasive or objectifying, she experienced them as a reflection of their concern to understand her "inner life." To ask such questions was an aspect of their professional training, but this very fact makes Kohut's point that empathy is a matter of "training and learning," for the way in which they asked these questions was itself reassuring. I think this goes back to what Jamison said earlier about her "curious self" having taken her to places where her emotions would be tested and challenged, and providing her the necessary "distance and structure" to enable her to manage in these very situations.

The curiosity that both David and Richard exhibited was evidence to her that they had a similar capacity to "manage," which, in this case, meant being able to manage the emotional challenges that may present themselves as they shared their lives with hers. Thus, as these two men, through their questions, were demonstrating their capacity to think and feel their way into her inner life, she was engaging in much the same process, and what she found was deeply reassuring. These were men whose own inner lives were trustworthy.

The Healing Springs of Love

Back, then, to Jamison's psychoanalyst friend: Whether she might have been able to respond to this friend less as the insensitive professional colleague that he obviously was and more as a man whose extreme response suggested an emotional pain rooted in his own early childhood is not for anyone else to say. In any case, this is not the central issue. What *is* the issue is the fact that mental illness places a strain or burden on interpersonal relationships, and no one knew this better than Jamison herself. Her relationships with men especially were put to the ultimate test when she revealed to them that she had a serious mental illness. She knew that her relationships with these men would be forever affected, for good or ill, by her disclosure. She knew that each man was weighing in his mind the implications of her disorder for his own future and that his response would reveal to her what conclusions he had drawn.

David Laurie's response—"Rotten luck"—conveyed that he did not hold her responsible. Richard Wyatt's response—"That explains a lot"—conveys that it enabled him to better understand things about her which he had noticed—things, however, that had not been reason for him not to want to be with her and, in fact, may have had the very opposite effect. If, therefore, the situation itself was indicative of the burden that mental illness places on interpersonal relationships, their responses demonstrated that mental illness also affords special and precious opportunities to discover the breadth and depth of human love.

The Nature of Love

If so, this love is not a matter of recognizing that the relationship may present unique challenges that one is willing, even eager, to embrace. If this were what love is all about, it would be indistinguishable from charity. Love flows from empathy; charity, from sympathy. Love is not a benevolent gesture but a desire to know the other as the other desires to be known. It is the capacity to enter into the inner life of the other to such a degree that one makes the other's inner life one's own.

This being the case, Kohut's cautionary note about "mythologizing" empathy applies to love as well. Love is not God's gift bestowed only on an elect few. For the average individual, training and learning make the difference. At the beginning of her chapter, "Love Watching Madness," Jamison tells how she dreaded leaving England after the death of David Laurie because her year in England had "laid to rest most of my incessant wondering about the what-ifs and whys and what-might-have beens" (163). She was afraid that she would lose the gains she had made in this year of rest and restoration, when "life had become worth not losing" (163). She discovered, however, that she "was very wrong in my forebodings," and concludes this chapter with the observation that "if love is not the cure, it certainly can act as a very strong medicine. As John Donne has written, it is not so pure and abstract as one might once have thought and wished, but it does endure and it does grow" (175, referring to Donne, "Love's Growth," 1996, 69). In a word, this is what love teaches us—that we were wrong in our forebodings. Love is the voice—the reality—of reassurance.

NOTES

[1]As Jamison was born in 1946, and I was at St. Elizabeths in the summer of 1961, I imagine the possibility, though not the likelihood, that our paths crossed, however fleetingly. Of much greater historical significance, this was the year that Erving Goffman's *Asylums* (1961) was published, based on his field research at St. Elizabeths. Goffman argued in *Asylums* that the most important factor in forming a mental-hospital patient is not the illness but the institution itself, and he contended that the adjustments the patient makes are similar to those of inmates in other types of "total institutions." "Total institutions" was his term for institutions where "all aspects of life are conducted in the same place and under the same single authority." There "each phase of the member's daily activity is carried on in the immediate company of a large batch of others, all of whom are treated alike and required to do the same thing together." There "all phases of the day's activities are tightly scheduled, with one activity leading at a prearranged time into the next, the whole sequence of activities being imposed from above by a system of explicit formal rulings and a body of officials." There "the various enforced activities are brought together into a single rational plan purportedly designed to fulfill the official aims of the institution" (6). Goffman argued that compliance with this highly regulated system became the basis on which the medical staff evaluated a patient's progress or lack of progress toward the restoration of health.

[2]The fact that Jamison circulated an article on religion and psychosis along with Millay's poem, "Renascence," and that she had previously read William James's *The Varieties of Religious Experience*, suggests that she was very mindful at this time of the link between religious experience and psychotic episodes. While her summary of Millay's poem does not convey this linkage, one need only read the poem to see how deeply related they were in Jamison's mind at the time. The "heightened awareness" of which Jamison speaks is, for Millay, the heightened awareness of God. Toward the end of the poem, Millay declares: "O God, I cried, no dark disguise / Can e'er hereafter hide from me / Thy radiant identity! / Thou canst not move across the grass / But my quick eyes will see Thee pass. / Nor speak, however silently, / But my hushed voice will answer Thee" (Millay 2002, 8). As her *Touched with Fire: Manic-Depressive Illness and the Artistic Temperament* (1993) makes clear, Jamison finds in poets, especially, a powerfully sustaining reference group, one that provides her with a tradition with which she can locate, understand, and appreciate herself, thus countering the power of manic-depressive illness, like any other severely debilitating illness, to produce a sense of self-devaluation. It is noteworthy in this regard that Jamison has more recently received recognition from her beloved University of St. Andrews as honorary professor of English.

[3]Jamison does not identify the poem from which these lines are quoted. It is "Childe Harold's Pilgrimage," and the lines are from Cantos LXXI and LXXII. See George Gordon, Lord Byron, *Byron: Poetical Works* (Oxford: Oxford University Press, 1970), 236–37.

4

STRANGER IN OUR MIDST

JOHN GOVIG

The preceding chapters have focused on accounts written by the person who experienced mental illness. In this and the following chapter, we will be shifting the focus to the perspective of the loved one who chose to write about a family member who experienced mental illness. These accounts are no less painful.

Persons who love a person afflicted with a serious mental illness also suffer, and their suffering is similar in many respects to that of the person who is afflicted. There is the same sense of ill-preparedness, of not knowing what is happening, of having difficulty understanding what *is* happening, and of feeling helpless to do anything about it. Also, as Rose Styron so eloquently puts it in her short essay on her husband's descent into insanity, one feels that whatever connections remain between oneself and the loved one are so very fragile, indeed. Yet, these fragile connections are all that one has to hold onto, for without them, the other would completely slip away. How awful it is to lose a loved one through physical death. Yet, there is a finality about it that enables there to be a cleaner break. With mental illness, the other is in many respects "gone," yet his or her body is still present. This creates the inevitable hopes–the hoping against hope–that the mind will return to its former state and connections will be restored.

In this chapter, we will be exploring another case of schizophrenia. As we saw in the case of Anton Boisen, schizophrenia has devastating effects on the life of the one who suffers from it. Reading between the lines, we could also imagine what the experience must have been like for his mother, for his sister, for his friend Fred Eastman, and also for Alice Batchelder, who, largely against her own will, figured so prominently in the illness and what it meant to him. The memoir that I will present here, Stewart D. Govig's *Souls Are Made of Endurance* (1994), gives voice to those who suffer along with the afflicted one.

The Long-term Perspective

In the preface, Govig indicates that the endnotes to the book contain the titles of resource books and articles on the subject of serious mental illness and the family. He cautions, though, that "Most of them focus on the acute stage," and "seldom is the chronic or long-term situation addressed" (Govig 1994, xi). As if to emphasize how chronic or long-term mental illness and its consequences can be, he notes that the personal anecdotes presented in the book "cover a span of approximately fifteen years" (xi–xii). Fifteen years is a very long time to be engaged with an illness, but the fifteen years in this case is an arbitrary cut-off point. They merely mark the year that Govig decided to write about his experiences with his son's mental illness, for the mental illness that he writes about continues to this day. Indeed, one of the concerns of aging parents in our society today, a concern that Govig specifically mentions, is what will happen to their mentally-ill son or daughter when their parents are no longer able—or even around—to care for them.

Souls Are Made of Endurance: Surviving Mental Illness in the Family is a father's account of his son's mental illness (officially, "affective schizophrenia") and the toll that it took on the family. Because the father wrote it, this book has important connections with Boisen's account of his own struggles with mental illness. Given the early death of Boisen's father, a book similar to *Souls Are Made of Endurance* could not have been written by his father, but had it been, it would have been a great source of encouragement and consolation to Boisen himself.

Another vital connection between the two books is that both authors view the illness as having religious significance. Boisen states in the foreword to *Out of the Depths*, "This is my own case record. It offers it as a case of valid religious experience which was at the same time madness of the most profound unmistakable variety" (1960, 9). Similarly, Govig writes in the preface to *Souls Are Made of Endurance* that he has tried to "downplay the language of popular psychology and give preference to theological thought" (1994, xi), especially in his emphasis on the role of God as one who *sustains* as well as heals and restores. One reason he prefers theological thought to the language of popular psychology is that the latter tends to emphasize "adapting" to the new situation in which the family finds itself, while theological thought, at least, of the kind he presents in the book, focuses on the theme of "endurance."

The Theme of Endurance

Webster's New World College Dictionary (1997, 449) defines *endurance* in two ways, both of which are relevant to Govig's account of his struggles with his son's mental illness and its deep and far-reaching effects:

1. to hold up under (pain, fatigue, etc.); stand; bear, undergo
2. to put up with; tolerate

Thus, one meaning of endurance centers on one's durability, while the other focuses on one's capacity to put up with the pain. While Govig provides much biblical support for the theme of endurance, the book's title is not, however, from the Bible or a theological text. Instead, the title comes from a notebook jotting by the American poet Carl Sandburg. This jotting, never published as a complete poem, reads: "Take up your cross, and go the thorn way./ And if a sponge of vinegar be passed you on a spear, / Take that too. Souls are made of endurance./ God knows" (from a 1902 notebook; no citation given).

I will take up Govig's memoir chapter by chapter, thus following his own effort to come to terms with his son John's illness and to integrate this reality into his own theological understanding of life and its meaning. As we will see, the book is less an account of the mental illness itself and more the story of how the author struggled to understand what was happening to his son, to himself, and to the other members of the family. It consists of three sections with three or four chapters in each: "Finding Out," "Holding On," and "Letting Go." At the time he wrote the book, Govig was a religion professor at Pacific Lutheran University outside Tacoma, Washington. He has since retired from full-time teaching, but he continues to teach courses and to offer workshops on mental illness for clergy and laity groups. John was born in Tacoma and grew up in the Tacoma suburb of Parkland, near the university campus. I will use Stewart Govig's first and last name interchangeably in this chapter, employing "Govig" when referring to his authorial role and "Stewart" when his parental role is central.[1]

Finding Out

Rage in the Rec Room

The first of three chapters of Part 1, titled "Rage in the Rec Room," begins:

> [John's] psychiatrist and I had a long talk about my son's future. For years each of us had tried in different ways to help John turn his life around. Today was different. For the first time the grim word "schizophrenia" entered the conversation. No change for the better was likely, I told myself. I hesitated by the office door. Turning, I asked, "What you see is what you get, is that it? How

long will this go on?" The doctor put his hand on my shoulder. Then I understood that endurance of long-term, challenging mental illness would be a part of our family's history. (1994, 3)

MISHAPS AND BAD LANGUAGE

Stewart acknowledges that during his son's last two years in high school, "he and I had long since lost the capacity for dialogue. I began to slide on the slope of despair; he, in turn, seemed ever more moody and bad-tempered" (4). Possibly he had good reason for this, as "he seemed to have had his share of tough luck" (4). When he was sixteen, he experienced a motorcycle mishap that produced only scrapes and bruises, but this was the prelude for an even more serious accident a few months later. This time he was in the front seat of a friend's car, and a collision sent his head crashing into the windshield. Hospital care and the skill of a plastic surgeon left him with only a nose and eyebrow scar. But were there invisible scars? Stewart now wishes that a brain scan had been performed as it may have revealed brain damage predisposing his son to mental illness.

By this time, "there could be no doubt who the testy and grouchy member of our family circle was" (4), and his irritability soon grew into open rebellion. John scorned family discipline involving coming home at a decent hour. But was this any different from what other parents of adolescents were experiencing? There was no reason, at this point, to suspect mental illness, and every reason to hope that he would "grow out of it."

But something happened when John was seventeen years old. During Stewart's sabbatical year at the University of London, the family had taken a vacation to tour Europe and was in Cordoba, Spain, strolling along one of its medieval streets. John, however, "was on the opposite side of the street, shouting and cursing. To this day, I have no idea what triggered such behavior. He always had a temper, but this was something else, scatological language released in a torrent of fury" (5).

Through much cajoling from home, John managed to graduate from high school, but he had little employment success the following year. The year thereafter he enrolled in a Midwestern college, chosen because it would take him away from home, thus enabling him to make a fresh start, helped in this regard by making new and more wholesome friends. In the fall semester, though, he was suspended for the use of a controlled substance. A short time later he was a passenger in a far more serious automobile accident than the previous one. This time the driver of the car was killed and John was thrown from the car. When aid-givers arrived, they found him in a ditch trying to bury the marijuana that he had in his possession. The surgeon who patched John up informed Stewart that his son was physically intact but then mentioned that "there was something strange," adding, "the language I heard from him when he came out of the anesthesia–awful…I've never heard anything like it. Thought you should know" (5). Was there a link between his semiconscious state on this occasion and the odd behavior in Spain a couple of years earlier? Perhaps, but, at the time, there was no obvious reason to suspect that he was already suffering from a very serious mental illness.

PHYSICAL OUTBURSTS

The college experiment had failed, and he returned home. Now, his bad temper shifted from the verbal to the physical. Once, when he did not get his way, he slammed the thermostat with his fist and kicked in the wall underneath it. On another occasion he yanked the wire out from an extension telephone. When his younger brother Bruce declined a challenge to fight (with no apparent provocation whatsoever), John smashed his fist through a glass window.

Then, however, things reached a new low. The family was finishing breakfast one morning, and Stewart informed John that he could not use the car that day. This step had been taken because John had previously taken the keys and driven off as his father ran out, waving and shouting, to stop him. This declaration from his father infuriated John. He turned over the kitchen table. Juice, milk, and clattering dishes fell onto the other family members' laps with a crash: "He had turned the tables, all right; with an obscene gesture and a string of obscenities, [he] bolted out the front door" (5–6).

At this point in the narrative, Stewart notes that he, like John's maternal and paternal grandfathers and great-grandfathers, is a Lutheran clergyman. He adds:

> We are church people; it is fair to describe us as pietists (no cursing allowed), but hardly as puritans in the popular sense. The tirade in Cordoba and the breakfast incident were so senseless, something unexpected and bizarre. It took years to accept powerlessness in the face of such behavior. (6)

Govig's point here is not only that John did not learn such obscenities at home, but that his use of them violated the family's ethos of civility and decorum. His reference to the fact that there were Lutheran clergymen on both sides of the family for three generations has some bearing, in my view, on John's mental illness. I will return to this later.

A FATHER'S GUILT AND A SON'S PARANOIA

A few months later, the breaking point came. John "burst into another rage at some minor behavior boundary line. This time he slammed the door of the downstairs rec room and turned up the stereo rock music full blast" (6). Moments later, above the sounds of the music, Stewart could hear John's voice, "shouting and babbling [some] fearsome gibberish." He decided that this kind of behavior "doesn't belong in this house" (6). He reached for the phone. Shortly afterward, five sheriff's deputies came to the house and dragged John away.

At the time, Stewart justified this response to the noise in the rec room on the grounds that "we all needed sleep." Moreover, his son's rage "had finally reaped its reward." The longsuffering father had finally reached the end of his patience. (In "Stranger in Our Midst," the video film that focuses on John's illness, Stewart says that, knowing what he now knows, he would not have made the 911 phone call, but would have handled it very differently [Dragseth and Foreman 2002].)

What he did not know at the time was that "such behavior actually signaled madness" (6). Were not John's tantrums and defiance, after all, "sinister portents of a bizarre transformation in the youngster we thought we loved and knew? Had they surfaced *apart from his control?*" (Govig 1994, 6, his italics). But how many parents, in a similar situation, would have considered the possibility, much less the fact, that their son or daughter was mentally ill? As he relives the moment when he reached for the phone, he sees how "a father's guilt and a son's paranoia would haunt the actors in that scene for years" (6):

> Yet, in retrospect, from that episode in the basement we had begun to climb our Mount Moriah and confront not only fear and desperation but also reality. Like Abraham and Isaac, we "walked on together" in grim determination. "Stumbled along" might better have depicted our gait. Years would pass as our journey unfolded, but, in the course of time, we too would reconcile at a place of sacrifice (Genesis 22) (6).

Calling for outside help meant that he "had finally turned away from expecting a solution through prayer" and that he had implicitly acknowledged to himself that "the well-planned assistance of professional counselor friends" had not resulted in progress. Instead, John's angry rebellion, now combined with alcohol abuse, had only accelerated. If Stewart seems to have overreacted to the "rage in the rec room," he doubts that much good would have come from controlling himself. In fact, he believes that his desperate phone call was a behavioral reaction to what he suspected deep inside, that there was more to "the ugliness leading up to that desperate telephone call" than had yet been revealed to him (7).

SEEKING BIBLICAL HELP

In any case, he now felt more in tune with the father in Mark 9:14–29 than with those parents who would be able to continue to manifest long-suffering patience in hopes that their son or daughter would "grow out of it." The father "who had been having trouble with his son" came to Jesus in desperation, having "come to the end of his resources. Had I not also, that night? Even to the point of giving up on a youth in desperate need of help?" (7). On the other hand, he is painfully aware of the difference between bringing one's son to Jesus and arranging for one's son to be booked into jail. He invokes the father's response to Jesus—"I believe; help my unbelief," and shakes his head, ruefully, "A 'family disturbance' jail booking—help *my* unbelief! We had never dreamed of such a thing for one of our own, to say nothing of the 'psycho' ward commitment to come" (7).

How had this family come to the point where one of its members was booked for creating a "family disturbance"? "Had we failed that badly as parents?" (7). After all, they were "praying, Bible-reading people." Had they taken for granted—too easily, perhaps—their ability to achieve a biblical standard for family discipline, expressed, for example, in Ephesians 6:1–4: "Children, obey your parents in the Lord, for this is right...And, fathers, do not provoke your children to anger, but bring them up in the discipline and instruction of the Lord"? And what about 1 Timothy 3:4–5 which charges a church leader to "manage his own household well, keeping his children submissive and respectful in every way—for if someone does not know how to manage his own household, how can he take care of God's church?"

What helped at this time was the fact that he and his wife Alice "were not alone in our bewilderment" (7). They read about other parents who were equally confused during the period of self-doubt and guilt when their son or daughter's mental illness began to come to light. They were especially comforted by the reassurance that most experts on schizophrenia now agree that parents do not cause schizophrenia, that the "explosion" of new research about how the brain works "has taught us that many forms of mental illness are due to abnormalities in brain structure or chemistry. Despite the continuing misinformation placing the blame on dysfunctional and inadequate parenting, this reminder still comes as profound relief" (8). (As the issue of blaming parents or family environment is a continuing theme throughout the book, I will return to this issue later in the chapter.)

THE BURDEN OF ISOLATION

There is also the "burden of isolation" that families experience when a loved one "never seems to respond positively, no matter what" (8). Day-to-day experience of this particular burden has left him "a bit skeptical of quick and decisive intervention strategies." In fact, having lived, now, with a series of "false hopes and fruitless leads," he has had to set aside "any doctrine of progress" (8). Instead, the word that comes to mind is "endurance." This leads him to think of Martin Luther, who "had his share of troubles," especially in later life, suffering from headaches, dizziness, family bereavement, a leg ulcer, and kidney stones. According to some investigators, he was also mentally ill: "His angry, vulgar language–combined with bouts of sixteenth-century 'melancholy'–appear to them as indications of a manic-depressive psychosis" (8). This was the initial diagnosis assigned to John Govig (later revised to schizophrenia). While it was probably small comfort at the time, the fact that John shared with Martin Luther a penchant for "angry, vulgar language" indicated that their son, in this regard at least, was in good company.

Govig was especially interested, however, in how Luther interpreted his illnesses. He focuses on the fact that, for the reformer, these illnesses became a part of his vocational consciousness: "If the Christian life were *without* trials, he insisted, it would not ultimately become a life of faith; *conflict* comes with faith, and trials 'keep faith in motion'" (8, von Loewenich 1976, 134–35). The idea of "faith in motion" led him to the pastoral epistles (James 1:2–4 and 1 Peter 1:6–7) and from there to the conclusion that "faith in motion" means endurance:

> To stand by a person during the onset and treatment of an illness in his or her brain means (once the shock wears off) deciding never to say die. One abandons habits of crisis reaction in view of the long run. One finds oneself adapting, living *through* it but also *in* it. Strangely, one begins to live inside illness: thinking about it and discussing these matters at every opportunity. Some, like me, even write about it to bear witness to its dynamics. (9)

Thus, if his son John was condemned by circumstances beyond his control to "live inside illness," his father would join him there.

A Domestic Chernobyl

In chapter 2, "A Domestic Chernobyl," Govig returns to the "rage in the rec room" incident and reveals that the eventual outcome of his decision to involve the authorities was his son's commitment to the psychiatric ward of St. Luke's Hospital in downtown Tacoma. John remained in the hospital for seventy-two hours. On his return home, a period of several weeks offered grounds for cautious optimism "that our family had at last turned a corner on all this" (13).

HOSPITALIZED

In time, however, John's sullen demeanor and late hours out with unknown friends sparked new worries and fears. Eventually, he moved out of the Govig home and into a house occupied by several other youths that his parents had never met. Before long, he was committed to Fir Lane State Hospital. According to the report of the examining physician, he was "hyperactive, confused and delusional with visions of God talking to him" (14). The report added that he "entertained suicidal thoughts and had been urged by a friend to enter Fir Lane for help...Since fifteen he has used marijuana, angel dust, LSD...and has had bouts of psychotic decompensation" (14).

Govig had suspected drugs were a part of the "mix-ups" at home. He comments that "the full extent of my foreboding was borne out when I came across information disclosing how drug abuse and psychotic disorders may interact and aggravate each other on an escalating cycle" (14). Alcohol and drugs may be used to relieve boredom or counteract feelings of rage or despair, and they may also be used to counteract the psychotic ideation itself. Later in the chapter, Govig cites the case of parents who began to suspect, as he and Alice did, that their son's drug use was "an unconscious attempt at self-medication to prevent these unpredictable outbursts of rage" (18). He might also have added that the drug use was an attempt to counter the very disturbances in his brain—cognitive, perceptual—that were causing his psychotic episodes. The physician's report concluded with a reference to home and family, "Parents are described as devoted, seemingly unable to effect change" (14). Govig adds, ruefully, that the word "seemingly" was superfluous. The diagnosis at this time was "manic-depressive psychosis."

THE TRIGGER TO SUICIDAL THOUGHTS

Apparently, the report did not say what had triggered John's suicidal thoughts. We may guess that he had begun to despair over his future and that such despair may well have been linked to his past. Such links were not only due to the fact that his college attempt had failed, but also to the traumatic experiences he had suffered, especially the automobile accident in which his companion was killed. In *Phantom Illness* (1996) Carla Cantor traces her own mental illness—her hypochondriacal belief that she was afflicted with a fatal disease—to a similar automobile accident when she was seventeen years old. She was the driver and her best friend was killed. Cantor writes:

> Directly afterward, I was numb, and then for many years punitive: I wouldn't allow myself to feel healthy, happy, and strong. I carried the guilt in my body, exorcising it during my early twenties in the rebuking self-starvation of anorexia, and later in a constant certainty of being struck down by illness or death. (1996, 288–89)

If John was reliving an earlier trauma, the trauma that the family was to experience was just beginning. As Govig points out, for the vast majority of families, the first hospitalization traumas are only the beginning of a long and arduous journey. They are forced to recognize the truth of chronicity; their loved one is released and improved, but still showing, once in a while, the symptoms pointing toward crises yet to be faced. They sense, at last, the truth that fluctuating, gravely disabling conditions will be their lot over the years ahead. At this point, however, our family mostly wallowed in ignorance, isolation, and apprehension. (Govig 1994, 15)

ADJUSTED EXPECTATIONS

One of the first signs that family members have begun to realize that "the first hospitalization traumas are only the beginning of a long and arduous journey" is that they begin to readjust their expectations for their afflicted son or daughter. Govig cites the case of Grace and Jim Anthony, parents of a seriously mentally ill son, (15; in Vine 1982, 209–13). Grace commented, "You have to shed dreams in the face of undreamed-of realities" (15). But, for the Govigs, these reflections came later, as the more immediate feelings were guilt and self-blame.

Yet, here again, Grace Anthony's efforts to investigate the family issues in mental illness led her to an idea made famous by Frieda Fromm-Reichman in 1948. This idea, "rejected today," contends "that an essential failure in the maternal response of the 'schizophrenogenic mother' produces schizophrenia" (Govig 1994, 15). Further, Grace read about the "double-bind" theory that Gregory Bateson advanced in 1956: "In this thesis not only the mother's parenting is deficient but also the father's. Somehow the communication between the two of them contains so many mixed messages that as a result the child is overwhelmed in some intolerable double bind" (18). Contending that this theory, too, has been "rejected" by mental illness specialists, Govig turns it on its head and notes the bind in which these theories place the parents: "What parent could ever come to terms with the notion of having *driven one's child insane?*" (15, his italics).

Obviously, these theories afforded no comfort. But Grace Anthony's response to them did:

Like so many others, ourselves included, perhaps such notions contributed to their feeling like casualties of the indifference and suspicion they encountered from certain mental health professionals. When she eventually rejected this cup of remorse, Grace spoke up for scapegoats across the country: "We tried. We were conscientious parents. And we had a child whose needs had been hard to meet. Not only by us but by his schools and teachers and now by other institutions." (16)

A FATHER'S LIBERATION

Govig admits that before "these troubles began at our home," he had "played the bystander role as far as any serious contacts with mental illness are concerned" (16). Having grown up with *Life* magazine photos of asylum horrors, he had never had reason to challenge the causal theories like "the double-bind and faulty maternal care" (16). Therefore, "the liberation" he felt from reading E. Fuller Torrey's *Surviving Schizophrenia: A Family Manual* (1988) was as exciting for him as if an authentic lost letter of Paul had just been verified. He underlined this sentence from Torrey's book: "There is no evidence whatsoever that schizophrenia is caused by how people have been treated either as children or as adults; it is a biological disease of the brain, unrelated to interpersonal events of childhood or adulthood" (16, quoting Torrey 1988, 274).

In addition to reading books that relieved the burden of guilt, Stewart was learning from his exposure to real-life symptoms. Through such learning, which he likens to a sort of internship, he was discovering personal resources that he did not realize he had. On some occasions, he reacted to emergencies as if he had already rehearsed the right response. He noticed one evening that the four newly-prescribed tablet containers were all neatly lined up in a row—and empty. John was already drowsy in the rec room, but this time his father did not panic and call 911. Instead, he informed his son that they were "going downtown," and "dream-like, he heard and obeyed" (17).

The emergency room staff acted immediately, and the relieved father was left to wonder "if the stomach-pump treatment had saved his life." Clearly, he had done the right thing, but one of John's longer hospitalizations followed almost immediately. "Occurrences like this one took their toll on our family and professional lives. Weariness joined anxiety and sadness. Would there ever be a respite from it all? Would we ever see our way through?" (14).[2]

Of Cuckoos Nests and Loony Bins

In chapter 3, "Of Cuckoos Nests and Loony Bins," Govig discusses John's confinement in mental health facilities. He concludes that, on the whole, John's "appearance in general verified the benefits of his newfound refuge and shelter" (29), especially when compared with the jail, which was typically the initial place of confinement due to his continuing habit of driving while intoxicated. He recounts the occasion when John's social worker called and reported that he was "in the tank," awaiting his hearing, but that he was doing okay and that he would call again. A couple of days later, with no intervening call from the social worker, John called from the tank and pleaded, "Dad, that new leather sport coat I got? Sell it for bail money!" Stewart, however, did not comply with his son's request: "Having gotten himself into this mess he would have to see his own way through the consequences. Enough was enough" (24).

OF JAILS AND HOSPITALS

The next communication he received was news of John's hospitalization. The police had found him naked with his head in the toilet and had committed him to the psychiatric ward of the nearest hospital. Several days later, a judge, attorney, several social workers, and medical personnel convened for a formal judicial hearing in the ward to determine whether John could understand his situation. This required evaluating his need for further treatment. His "eyes partly closed, head bobbing slowly, and half stupefied from his medications," John sat at the head of the table as though "presiding over the macabre drama where his fate hung in the balance" (24). His father's presence was acknowledged, but he was utterly superfluous to the proceedings.

Some time later, stabilized, John returned home. At this time, there were no plans for finding work or getting on with college studies, but simply dependence on the efficacy of his medications. Several weeks later, however, Stewart returned from work and was startled to hear his son say that he wanted to return to the state hospital where he had been treated before. When they arrived at the hospital, they were informed that his admission would not be automatic despite the fact that he was a former patient. Eventually he demanded his son's admission, and it was granted.

Months earlier, he could not have imagined that John would have sensed his need to return nor dreamed that he would be grateful for the favor of placing one of his own family members in a mental institution. Visiting his son in the hospital, however, provoked mixed feelings. John was safe and his whereabouts were known. The sinister-sounding telephone calls (drug deals?) had tapered off at home. Daily work routines were restored. Yet the defeat and failure that this new confinement represented inspired thoughts—or were they mere fantasies?—of some new treatment setting that would work wonders, perhaps supplying the magic answer. Meanwhile, however, the ward management by chemistry took priority for, as a first step, John needed to be "stabilized" again (27).

NOT KNOWING WHAT TO EXPECT

Govig admits that he did not know what to expect when he first entered the psychiatric wards of the two hospitals to which John was confined. Yes, he knew of Mary Jane Ward's *The Snake Pit* (1946) and the film based on the novel. He had read a 1948 article in *Life* magazine that compared institutions for the mentally ill to Nazi concentration camps. He had also read *One Flew Over the Cuckoo's Nest* (1963). McMurphy, the hero of Ken Kesey's novel, is placed in a mental ward and suffers the oppression of an institution typified by Big Nurse Ratched and electroshock therapy. Govig knew Kate Millett's *The Loony Bin Trip* (1990), which questions if mental disorder should be treated as an illness at all.

He was also aware of Erving Goffman's *Asylums*, published in 1961, based on field research at St. Elizabeths Hospital in Washington, D. C., the very hospital to which Boisen had avoided being committed because his forestry friends tolerated his deviance and eccentricities. Goffman, Govig notes, concluded that, taken as a whole, the mental institution "became a dehumanizing, demoralizing, and humiliating additional burden on the patient" (Govig 1994, 29). Govig cites Ann Braden Johnson's *Out of Bedlam: The Truth about Deinstitutionalization* (1990) which notes that Goffman blew the mental care system's cover "once and for all." In a footnote Govig also mentions E. Fuller Torrey's view that some persons with more severe symptoms need the "asylum" that only a mental health facility can provide (100–101; Torrey 1988, 242–43).

Aware that "the scapegoating of mental hospitals continues," Govig, a "parent consumer," will not deny the accusations, but he suspects that the issue is much more complicated:

> Such a major unaddressed social problem needs scrutiny from another angle: What is the alternative? How can human dignity in these circumstances be protected and enhanced at the same time? What mistakes of the system need correction first? Could public education relieve the stress and promote a more humane version of the admirable aspects of ancient and medieval hospitality? (29)

In any event, in the lonely family crisis that he and other members had to endure, Stewart was "grateful that at least someone also had acted on John's need for medical care instead of additional jail time…After all, John had not actually been 'sent away' to any cuckoo's nest loony bin; he had gained access to a time-out period when he needed it the most" (30). And John himself had been the one who recognized his need for it.

Holding On

Part 2, "Holding On," begins with chapter 4, "Faith and Frenzy." This chapter focuses on the fact that mental illness is a *disease* and that *illness* involves the process of living in or through the disease.

Faith and Frenzy

Govig indicates that he has long since abandoned words like "insanity," a legal term used to cover the degree of accountability one may or may not have for criminal acts, and "madness," which conjures in his mind visions of insane asylum horrors. The issue of "illness" will be his primary emphasis, as "illness" concerns the form the disease takes in daily life and thus its impact on the family.

SCHIZOPHRENIA AS AN ILLNESS

To appreciate schizophrenia's impact as an illness, one needs to have some idea of what kind of disease it is. Govig begins with the fact that it typically affects "the five senses." Persons suffering from the disease "sometimes hear nonexistent sounds, voices, or music or see nonexistent images. Because these perceptions do not fit reality, they react inappropriately to the world" (34). Like many other diseases, it usually develops gradually, and family or close friends "may not notice the changes in personality as the illness takes hold" (34).

Govig tells several stories that reveal the various ways in which John's illness manifested itself. For example, at a family gathering to celebrate the birthday of his younger sister Ellen, John suddenly jumped up from the table, sped off, and slammed the door behind him. Ellen sighed, "It's another one of those door-slamming parties, I guess." But outside, on the lawn, John puffed furiously on a cigarette. By now, he was utterly distracted from anything inside the house. The family, though, sensed his presence through the wall—"urgent, high-pitched, strange subvocal sounds. At times what seemed like a dog's muffled bark broke through the stormy monologue" (35).

The outburst reminded family members that John suffered from a disease that was being controlled with medications. Alice Govig asked, "Has John taken his meds today?" From all indications, probably not. But who could say for sure? Everyone wanted him to become as independent as possible, and his assuming responsibility for taking his medications was an integral part of such independence. Yet it was tempting to take over control of this aspect of his life because things went so much better when he took his prescribed medications faithfully.

As they listened to the noises emanating from the lawn, wondering what the new neighbors across the street would think, Stewart told himself that this was only a temporary setback and reminded himself that John had "snapped out of it before" (35). Most likely, "he had heard those voices again—too removed for our perception—issuing shattering insults, threats, and commands" (35). As for the furious puffing on a cigarette, solitude with nicotine was "a first line of defense" against the voices. While seemingly unable to remain on a strict regimen of medicine, John at least knew what he needed to do when the voices began to torment him.

On another occasion, father and son were moving along the highway in no special hurry. Traffic was light, the sun was out, and John was doing a good job of driving. Stewart was thinking that John "had stabilized really well." It "was gratifying to see him engaged in a simple pleasure. There were, after all, not too many left after his recent hospitalization" (35).

Then, for no apparent reason, John steered the car over onto the right lane and pulled to a gentle stop on the shoulder of the highway. "Dad, you can drive?"

"But John, why? You're doing fine."

"No, its okay."

By this time he had gotten out of the car and was headed for the passenger side. Stewart surmises that John was hearing voices out on the freeway and that their dire commands gave him only one alternative: pull over and stop. He adds, "More than a dozen years have passed since then, and during them John has never so much as hinted he would want to take the wheel again" (36). If John *was* hearing voices and they were commanding him to pull over (not unlike a threatening state trooper ordering a truly guilty motorist to the side of the road), then perhaps this episode was related in some way to the automobile accidents that had occurred years earlier, especially the one in which his companion was killed. If the voices were accusatory, it may have been a true mark of the progress he had made that he did not, in fact, react in rage and reckless speeding but pulled over and executed "a gentle stop." Yet, as Govig observes, for one who had so few simple pleasures left, it was saddening to think that John would be deprived of this one as well.

On another occasion, also involving freeway driving, the two of them were on a routine errand when, abruptly, John left his father's side to lie down on the van bed.

> Grunts and groans, tossing and turning–through the rearview mirror I saw him tearing at his hair. "If I had a gun, I'd kill myself!" he screamed. Then "Stop!" The truck weighing station came up just at the right time, and when I had pulled over the grimacing youth burst out the side door to commence a rapid, circular, jerky pace. For the first time I saw tears on his face. (36)

Another time Stewart and Alice had decided to visit a state park about an hour's distance. They invited John to join them because he had been so "good" lately–calm although perhaps unusually quiet. Throughout the trip, John had nothing to say, but what matter? As they pulled to a stop to pay the entrance fee, however, the silence broke, and John commanded, "Let me out." Puffing a cigarette, he walked furiously to the edge of the plaza in the direction of the woods.

Realizing that the entrance station ranger was reaching for his walkie-talkie, Stewart intercepted him just in time: "It's okay, he's our son." Puzzled, the ranger laid aside the device and stared. Moments later John appeared as briskly as he had left and climbed into the car as if nothing had happened. The car door closed, and they were on their way again. As before, John was apparently the recipient of powerful voices, issuing their usual insults, threats, and commands. In contrast, Stewart's own alertness and reassuring voice—"It's okay, he's our son"—may not seem like much, and we would not be especially surprised if the ranger had said, "He may be your son, but who are you?" Or "It's your word against his behavior." But he did not do so. The quiet voice of reassurance spoke louder that day than the voices of insult, threat, and command (36).

SEEKING BIBLICAL TRUTHS

As with previous chapters, Govig seeks to bring biblical faith to bear on these episodes. He cites Jeremiah 8:22: "Is there no balm in Gilead? Is there no physician there? Why then has the health of my poor people not been restored?" The implied answer to the first pair of questions is that Gilead has both balm and physicians to apply it. After all, Gilead was famous in Israel for its healing ointments, and many physicians would be there to prescribe them. This makes the failure of health to be restored all the more puzzling and frustrating.

Govig confesses that for a long time he suspected that street drugs and alcohol were keeping John's inner turmoil alive. This was why jobs that began with high hopes ended in dismissal and why a semester at a local college ended with incomplete grades. To counter these habits, they enrolled John in a plan for joining an out-of-state drug rehabilitation program. He paid the price of a radically short haircut and headed south to this modern Gilead. Could it be that the family was past the roughest spots and on the way to restoration? The answer came just a few days later when John reappeared, having hitchhiked his way back. Stewart recalled the comment of a counselor who said that their son was remarkably resourceful when he needed to be. But the ability to hitch-hike home was not part of the rehabilitation plan.

The prophet Jeremiah implicitly promised that a return to the divine Torah would result in the health of the Lord's poor people being restored. Stewart, however, was now prepared to take a step he had been unwilling to take before the failed drug rehabilitation program. In effect, the question was not whether John could be restored but whether he—Stewart—could find balm in Gilead. For this to happen, he realized that he needed to trust in the healing power of Gilead's physicians—hospital personnel, friends, counselors, drug prescriptions—and accept his own "total *powerlessness* to change things for the better" (39). He would let John be responsible for taking his daily medication and "look no further ahead than to that day's reward of peace" (39).

ANTIPSYCHOTIC MEDICATIONS

He concludes this chapter with a brief discussion of antipsychotic medications. He found one book especially helpful in appreciating "the effects of medication as a scientific therapy (even with its trial-and-error efforts) to calm John's emotions and settle his angry behavior" (40). This was Nancy C. Andreason's *The Broken Brain: The Biological Revolution in Psychiatry* (1984). Andreason testified that she is "a religious person" who "believes that religion can often illuminate or help relieve psychotic problems." At the same time, she recognizes that mental illness is "a disease like any other" (citing Andreasen, 11–12). She cites "the large amount of evidence suggesting that mental illness is caused by bio-chemical abnormalities and structural brain abnormalities; weakness of will, bad parenting, and bad marriages are not to blame" (Govig 1994, 40). If this is so, one should take as much advantage of the antipsychotic medicines now available as one would in the case of any other disease. Thus, relief comes from being informed that mental illness is *not* due to bad parenting, family dysfunctionality, and the like, but is a disease of the brain. With this relief comes a new burden, as it were, that of believing in and relying on the efficacy of antipsychotic medicines.

Govig notes that antipsychotic drugs like haloperidol–the most widely prescribed treatment for schizophrenia at the time his book was being written–relieve typical symptoms like delusions and hearing voices in about 70 percent of patients. On the other hand, "they are less helpful in dealing with secondary symptoms like withdrawal, lack of energy and motivation, and an inability to experience pleasure, the symptoms already too familiar in our family" (40). John was suffering from a brain disease, but what his family experienced was the illness itself. In this regard, the hope that medications kindled created new grounds for despair. He concludes this chapter on "Faith and Frenzy" on this note:

> The struggle at our house touched more than simply a "young adult male hearing voices and withdrawing from social contact"; it was embodied in our son and brother. And because I had by this time been thwarted so often, run so many errands, and paid so many bills on his behalf, I also began to share his trials. Mental illness had come to stay at our house. (41)

It is perhaps unnecessary to add that the very fact it was uninvited and unwelcome made its presence all the more irksome.

Give Us This Day Our Daily Meds

In chapter 5, "Give Us This Day Our Daily Meds," Govig returns to one of the themes of his previous chapter, his difficulty in "surrendering faith" in his own "ability to do something about the matter" (42). He invokes the image of "a wilderness experience" (which, as we saw in chapter 1, Anton Boisen also invoked) and cites Karen Lebacqz's identification of the elements of this experience: disruption of normalcy, recurring uncertainty, loss of control, and loss of identity (Lebacqz 1988, 26–31).

LOSS OF CONTROL

Perhaps because he was already well familiar with the first two, Govig focuses in this chapter on the third, the loss of control, noting: "When we lost control of the trails we had to follow within the mental health system, I sensed Sinai in the offing. At this point, seasoned by disruption of normalcy and loss of control, our family continued to navigate through thickets of therapy" (44).

He lists the persons and places that he encountered during the eight-year trek from the time "it all seemed to start back in Cordoba until a psychiatrist gave the enemy its name: affective schizophrenia" (44). The list of people (psychologists, psychiatrists, attorneys, clergypersons, mental health professionals, social workers, teachers, professors, and friends) numbers twenty-eight, give or take. The list of places (colleges, psychiatric wards and hospitals, courtrooms, jails, halfway houses, hospital emergency rooms, homeless shelters, drug rehabilitation centers, church camps and congregations) totals nineteen. What is noteworthy about both lists is that they are comprised of persons and places that, with few exceptions, have the best interests of the wilderness traveler at heart.

Yet, this list is largely a litany of false leads and false hopes, an odd lot mixture of concern and commiseration, ignorance, and indifference. Of all the persons involved, "the psychiatric profession seemed both to hurt and to help the most" (45). Govig cites several examples of rudeness and incompetence on the part of the psychiatrists, mental health professionals, and counselors whom he had consulted. Ironically, the rudeness he learned to tolerate. More difficult to deal with was the bad or questionable advice given in good faith. There was the counselor who told him that his son "has to hit bottom, I know it must not be easy, but back off. He's got to want to *help himself*" and, as parents, they needed to recognize their "enabling role," the fact that "getting him through just one more scrape actually protected him from having to face the outcome of bad choices" (46).

Thinking back on this advice several years later, Govig considers the fact that the assumed sinner in this counseling scenario was, of course, his son. But what about those who took on the role of counselor. Had they not "avoided or denied the likelihood of an illness severe enough to rob a person of reason?" (46). Were they any different from the misguided counselors of Job? And what of his parents? Had they not "surrendered to professional expertise and ignored resources within their own family's religious faith? Looking back, I am inclined to answer yes" (46).

HITTING BOTTOM

At the time, however, the counselor's advice seemed to make sense, and the Govigs "decided on tightened discipline to promote change" (46). (In the video film, "Stranger in Our Midst," Stewart and Alice both refer to this as the "tough love" phase of their wilderness journey.) He describes how this worked:

> If our son *would* not come home at a reasonable hour, he was no longer welcome. We would keep the doors locked at night. Yet in the cold darkness, to keep the door closed before the solitary, unshaven, and disheveled figure standing in the porch light meant anguish difficult to describe. It went against what I think must be one of the deepest instincts of any parent. To have provision and power but refuse it to your own child is a fierce test of endurance. How often Alice and I *almost* opened that front door. (46)

As John continued to come home at unreasonable hours, he slept in the lawn equipment shed a few nights. Then, one evening, he asked a favor: Could he hitch a ride downtown?

> Nearing our destination, he asked to stop for a "treat." Sure: pie and coffee at a dimly lit restaurant counter. Afterward no words were exchanged as he picked up his meager belongings and headed out into the night. On his own, he would have to find a "mission" or church-run shelter. Alcoholics and addicts would be roommates; bright college kids were now a curious thing of the past. (46)

On the way back home, "the splashing of windshield wipers kept time with the flooding waves of my sadness. Even if someone had thought to ask how John was doing, what would I have said" (47). For three weeks, there was no contact with John whatsoever. Then, early one morning Stewart opened the door handle of their aging Volkswagen van, and a movement startled him. The bed was down, and, to his immense relief, John appeared.

"Let's talk about things," he said, and the two of them headed for breakfast. "Bottom had been reached" (47). Fortunately, John was still alive; hitting bottom had not been synonymous with death.

THE WILDERNESS JOURNEY

Moses' band of exiles wandered forty years in the wilderness. For Stewart, the wilderness experience was an eight-year ordeal that seemed like forty. Then he heard the truth with which the book begins, the long conversation with a psychiatrist during which the grim word "schizophrenia" entered the conversation (3). Looking back, he assesses the people he encountered on his wilderness journey:

With the best intentions and good will, most of the other people and places involved also tried to help, but, in the final analysis, they proved as impotent as I was to cure or rehabilitate. Eight years it took to find out—eight years of false hopes, confusion, guilt feelings, and helplessness. (47)

Ironically, but not surprisingly, "learning the eventual truth—finding out— was the key to holding on":

Light began to overcome the dark side of my parenthood dreams, and I discovered life after mental illness. Words like "stability" and "maintenance" became terms of confidence. Contact with other parents in the same situation was water in the desert. Volunteer work at the local mental health center became therapy. (47)

Govig credits "Doctor H" with bringing about a genuine change. Doctor H, a psychiatrist who accepted state medical coupons for a modest fee, said simply, "I think I can help John." And, indeed, he could and did:

Among the several psychiatrists we consulted, he was the one finally to venture John's diagnosis. Gradually, through psycho-therapy and medication, this therapist enabled a stabilization and maintenance period with rare crises. For the first time in years of uncertainty, we found someone to lean on. (47)

An accurate diagnosis, however "grim," was the real beginning of hope, not hope of an eventual cure, but hope based on knowledge and awareness of what they were up against. The enemy who also lurked in the wilderness and seemingly struck at will had a name and was therefore recognizable despite the thick fog that surrounded them. Is this why Jesus asked the Gerasene demoniac to identify his demons (Luke 8:26–39)?

FEELINGS IN THE WILDERNESS

Govig next devises another list for the feelings he experienced during his wilderness experience but now seeks to "break out from." Heading the list is *anger*–anger at John for throwing his life away, anger at street drugs, anger at the stigmatization of mental illness and the vicious stereotyping promoted by films and television, anger at himself for "being duped by so many for so long" (48), and anger at the church for trumpeting justice in distant lands and ignoring Lazarus on its own doorstep.

Next comes *guilt*–guilt for not knowing about his local mental health center, which he could have called the night he summoned the police, guilt for not being a better parent, and guilt for not requesting a CAT scan following the accident when John's head shattered the windshield of the car he was riding in.

Third comes *ignorance,* especially the ignorance of prejudice against the mentally ill based on the false belief that mental breakdowns are a moral cop-out, the sign of a weak character, and that mentally ill persons are dangerous. He counters this image of the mentally ill with the observation of a likeness between them and those who have chosen—or been chosen for—special religious vocations: "Today, silent as Trappist monks, John and his board-and-care housemates sit before a humble meal" (49). Stewart notes their "eerie nobility," which recalls Theodore Roethke's line, "What's madness but nobility of soul at odds with circumstance" on the frontispiece of this book. John had not followed in the footsteps of his great-grandfathers, grandfathers, and father—all clergymen—but his life is now remarkably akin to that of a monastic: unmarried, without an earthly occupation, and having few personal possessions. His life is a witness to the fact that much of ordinary human life is a "chasing after wind" (Ecclesiastes 1:14).

Fourth on Govig's list is *suffering.* This is perhaps the hardest feeling of all from which to break out. He cites Dietrich Bonhoeffer's comment while in prison that there is nothing special or unique about his suffering and that while we like to emphasize our spiritual suffering, this is precisely the suffering of which Christ has relieved us. In effect, Bonhoeffer "reminds us to grasp the divine promise more firmly" (50; Bonhoeffer 1976, 126).

Govig concludes this chapter on the note that time, in its own way, is on his side. He no longer cherishes "romantic visions of miracles, divine or medical," but he holds on to gratitude for the fact that emergency room trips were made in time and for the fact that John "remains one of my closest friends" (50). He accepts the fact that he has lost the child of his dreams, the child who would be happy, would somehow help others along the way, and would enable his father to overcome his own mortality. At first, one resists and delays acknowledgment of the fact that the child of one's dreams has also been a casualty of the wilderness experience, but then acceptance comes, and "eventually we lowered our expectations and managed to abandon a few of the cultural dictates of success. It was then that we caught our first glimpse of the banks of the Jordan" (50).

Exodus to Main Street

In chapter 6, "Exodus to Main Street," Govig focuses on the search for a place where John could live so that normal household routines could resume and John would be safe while being free to follow his own routines. Initially, this involved a social work staff taking charge, "as they do to this day" (51). Later, a more cooperative approach in which John's parents also became involved was devised, working out apartment locales not far from home.

THE PROBLEMS OF DEINSTITUTIONALIZATION

Govig discusses the national program of deinstitutionalization of the mentally ill that followed on the heels of the early success of new antipsychotic drug treatments and notes that the part of the program euphemistically termed "rehabilitation in the community" (30) was never fully implemented. The problem is that the new centers that sprang up were more designed to attract the "worried well" than the "suffering sick." A worried couple having difficulty communicating was more likely to receive help and attention than a person recently released from a mental hospital. Attorneys who concentrated on an individual's autonomy rights, and thus the right not to be involuntarily confined, failed to recognize that "medical treatment often becomes the only avenue for restoring a person's autonomy in the first place" (54). Moreover, they failed "to put comparable efforts into lawsuits seeking to force establishment of community treatment programs" (54).

Govig believes that the criterion for involuntary hospitalization should be changed from "danger to oneself and others" to "unable to care for oneself" (54–55). He tells of having come to the hospital to visit John only to be told that he had been released ten minutes earlier to hitchhike home (55). He also notes that "care facilities" for released mentally ill patients are in industrial areas, in wasted central cities, or out in the countryside. Only once was his son's living arrangement in a "respectable" neighborhood. This, of course, is not surprising. The dream that large mental hospitals–the "warehouses"–would be replaced by "homes" containing mentally ill "families" encountered the same community resistance that would have occurred had there been a similar plan to eliminate federal and state penitentiaries.

MAKING THE TRANSITION

On the other hand, Govig believes that at some point John *did* make the transition from not acting in his own best interests to actually wanting to help himself. He has made the most of the county mental health center's services, which include a protective payee role for supervising the spending of his monthly government supplemental security income check, an adult-care facility for the psychotically disabled which functions as a social center, and social worker services.

In the final analysis, Govig does not want to say that the deinstitutionalization program beginning in the late 1950s was a mistake, but he comments on the "complexities" that he and the family had to work their way through in "our nation's deinstitutionalization climate" (57).

Precisely because the program led to the emergence of a variety of smaller facilities, the Govigs and other parents were spending more money than was spent by earlier generations of families, and, in turn, "the limits of our family resources also became evident" (57). The "investment of time and energy in trying to manage John's symptoms and provide some support took us from activities we neglected elsewhere" (57). One wonders, in fact, how Stewart and Alice would have been able to cope if they or their younger son or daughter had been experiencing their own special difficulties or problems.

Care in Focus

In chapter 7, "Care in Focus," Govig concludes the second part of the book–"Holding On"–with a brief account of John's life in his late twenties. For John, this was a period of wandering.

THE SOLITARY LIFE

Peer group friends disappeared, and he lived a largely solitary life. He would sit for hours in local restaurants, smoking, and having his coffee mug replenished by concerned waitresses. Or he would visit the local public library and listen to tapes (an alternative, perhaps, to the dreaded voices). He continued to drink, and the alcohol threatened his medication regimen, but "at least he managed to stay out of trouble" (59).

He "seemed to understand that if he continued to sustain himself like this he could still count on family for indefinite support as well as for rescue at hospital relapse times" (59). This was the period when, as noted in the chapter, "Faith and Frenzy," the Govigs had decided to leave him in the hands of the Gilead physicians and rely, more or less, on the physicians' healing balm (antipsychotic medications). But it was also a time when the family, despite its qualified faith in the medications he was receiving and his own determination to sustain himself, was heavily involved in his care.

VULNERABILITY FOR FAMILY MEMBERS

What Govig wants to convey in this chapter is that efforts to enhance the independence of the mentally ill person create an atmosphere of vulnerability for family members. Two episodes, seemingly unrelated, illustrate the problem.

The first involved an unexpected meeting of the father and son on the street near John's apartment. Stewart noticed something shining on the outside lower leg of his son's baggy bib overalls. "What is that?" he inquired.

John produced a razor-sharp, two-edged military survival knife and explained, "I need it for protection, Dad."

"But, John, carrying a knife like that must be illegal."

"Oh, no, it isn't," he replied, while Stewart "silently searched for ideas of how I could separate the weapon from its paranoid owner" (60). Later, he learned that the Asian immigrants who lived in John's apartment building were extremely afraid of their neighbor, this solitary man who walked the streets late at night. Did his possession of a knife warrant curtailment of John's independence? Both his parents and his counselors at the county mental health facility decided against this, as they still viewed independence for John as "a necessary step toward recovery and healing" (60).

Then, one Sunday, another event raised questions concerning the very linkage between "independence" and "recovery." Stewart had agreed to teach an adult church school class in a congregation an hour's drive from home. As he had done a few times before, John rode along, remaining in the car during church. They stopped for lunch afterwards. In the cafeteria Stewart "called him—quite mildly, I thought—on rude behavior in the line. He had no answer" (60). They said little on their way home, but this was not unusual, and early in the afternoon Stewart dropped his son off at his apartment.

Later that evening, the doorbell rang. The next moment John burst into the bedroom where Stewart had gone early to bed: "The ludicrous Stetson hat pulled low on his forehead capped an accusing finger; 'You talk through my head,' he snarled. Then, before I could reply, he grabbed my chest with both hands and bounced me up and down, and I felt a fist hit my face" (61).

Their daughter Ellen was the first to reach the bedroom. She pulled John from behind, "John! John!" He pulled back as she cried, "You've hurt Dad!" to which he responded matter-of-factly, "Oh, I *have not*" (61).

Dad *was* hurt, however. Minutes later they were on their way to the hospital emergency room to have his broken nose repaired. He surmised that John's rage "must have resulted from my trivial rebuff at the cafeteria." Then it hit him: John hadn't worn the survival knife to church today. Apparently it was not in his possession when he stormed into the bedroom that evening. But if he could hit his father in the face, was he capable when enraged of knifing him in the chest? Mount Moriah, indeed.

Govig writes, "I knew I was lucky. In just minutes a turning point had been reached. The involuntary hospital commitment criterion, 'a danger to oneself and others,' took life. I finally admitted to myself that our family, John's primary caregivers at that time, needed help" (61).

FOCUSED ATTENTION

They were lucky in another way. As a consequence of this episode, John seemed to get more focused attention from the county mental health center staff. He entered a congregate care facility, a modest house in which eight other men and women resided. He accepted its rules about mealtime attendance and curfew. He began receiving attention to his medical needs. Because a common side effect of one of his medications (probably lithium) was dry mouth resulting in a lack of saliva and devastating tooth decay, therapy allies decided to supervise the removal of his teeth and the obtaining of dentures. "Regulated medication, a proper diet, and psychotherapy including group counseling would work small wonders" (62).

At the time *Souls Are Made of Endurance* was written, John (thirty-four years old) had lived away from home for a full decade. Family-sponsored outings were part of the circle of care, and these included a car ride, a shopping tour, or a home visit, but never overnight. Taking John to his congregate care facility after a visit home continues to be hard, but this is very different from the "tough love" era before he was adequately diagnosed. In fact, as time has gone by, Govig views with wonderment the fact that "in recent years I have moved from feelings of anger, fear, and frustration to sentiments of empathy and compassion" (62).

BECOMING AN ADVOCATE

Furthermore, Stewart has become an advocate for his son and others in similar circumstances. A second episode in this chapter explains how this came about. Stewart had planned a trip to a local mall and invited John to join him. When John entered the car, it was clear that he had not shaved. It also looked (and smelled) as if he had slept in his clothes the past few days. They entered the record shop where Stewart was hoping to find Christmas carol music. Meanwhile, John began to pace a bit. It seemed as if he would need a cigarette to calm his nerves before long. Just then a clerk asked if he could help, and Stewart told him what he was looking for.

Instead of leading the way to the Christmas carol music, the clerk suddenly disappeared. Stewart was puzzled, but, given John's nervousness, he felt it was time to head for the parking lot anyway. As they walked along the various store fronts, John walked ahead, as he often did, seeking the security of the car. Stewart guessed that the Christmas crowds had been too much for him, but the mall exit door was now in view. Stewart paused to put on his hat and coat against the rainy night outside while John waited for him at the door.

Then, suddenly, John called out, "Dad, it looks like we've got trouble here." Stewart turned to see two armed security guards approaching. They demanded identification, and, without thinking, he pulled out his driver's license and university faculty card while John produced his prized city bus pass. The guards said they wanted to ask some questions. Just then, the music store clerk, evidently the store manager, appeared. He claimed that "he" (pointing to John) had been in his office in the back of the store. John vigorously denied the accusation.

Now Stewart became enraged. Picking up his son's use of the word "trouble" just moments before, he told the security guards that he had recently returned from a semester of teaching and travel in the People's Republic of China. Never once did any police officer, soldier, or official ask for his identification in the accusatory way they had done. He asked them, "Do you want trouble?" and then turned to the music store manager. "Search us!" he invited. "Do you want me to call my attorney? Do *you* want trouble?" Moments later, as they walked to the car, John, sober-faced as usual, muttered an ironic, "That was funny, Dad." But Stewart didn't think so:

> Inwardly I excused what I took to be inexperienced and poorly trained security guards. In contrast, the manager had punctured the facade of my personal accommodation to our son's illness and released the winds of resentment at John's outsiderhood. Feelings of frustration surfaced in public. Then I recognized something else: I had become an advocate. By speaking out, I had allied myself with mental health system professionals in confronting public stigma surrounding mental illness. (64)

As they returned to John's congregate care facility, Stewart admitted to himself that his son, owing to his appearance, had probably fit the store manager's profile of a thief. But he also found himself wishing that his son's accuser had been able to understand that in his moment of frightened pacing back at the shop, John would never have had the courage to open the office door, much less to pilfer the room's contents. The irony of the fact that he was in search of Christmas carol music may also have occurred to him, for Christmas honors that other Outsider who said, "Foxes have holes, and birds of the air have nests, but the Son of Man has nowhere to lay his head" (Lk. 9:58), an unsurprising outcome of a life that began in a stable, there being no room in the inn.

Available Living Arrangements

Appropriately, therefore, Govig concludes this chapter with a summary of the types of living arrangements available to sufferers from mental illness. He describes the effect of each on the son or daughter and the parents, and the predictable result. They include jails, streets, private or public hospital, home, and congregate care facilities. Jail and streets result in destruction (son or daughter) and despair (parents). Hospitals offer short-term stability (son or daughter) and respite in hope in medicine (parents). Home offers respite (son or daughter) and burden, disruption, and tension (parents). Congregate care facilities offer long-term stabilization (son or daughter) and support, respite, and teamwork with mental health professionals (parents).

As only the latter is an adequate solution over the long haul, the deinstitutionalization plan of the 1950s was conceptually sound but practically ineffective due to inadequate facilities and public education regarding the facilities that do exist. While he counts their family as being among the fortunate, in that John is now a resident of a congregate care facility, this came after years of floundering, misinformation, and enormous emotional cost.

And what of the future? Might John's realization of long-term stability lead to something more? If earlier dreams of rehabilitation and recovery were hopelessly utopian and misinformed, what about now? Could John ever make it on his own?

Letting Go

In the third section of the book—"Letting Go"—Govig begins the first chapter, "Giving Sorrow Words," with an incident that seems intended to answer these very questions, or, better, to lay them silently to rest:

> Our thirty-four-year-old son has come home for a visit. There he sits, cross-legged on the grass, in the middle of the backyard. At night a cigarette glow betrays the silent vigil in the very same spot. Sometimes he mutters and shouts under his breath but certainly means no harm. It is a rather new thing, this ritual. Like the now familiar Greek fisherman's cap he began wearing two years ago, it adds to the private list of eccentric habits I have witnessed in recent years. What next? I ask myself. Why so exactly in the middle of the yard? Should I laugh or cry? What about the utter absurdity of it all? On a deeper level, is our visitor, this somber guru, actually our John? (69)

Giving Sorrow Words

The question—"Why so exactly in the middle of the yard?"—recalls the observation that Anton Boisen's central theme—his love for Alice Batchelder—was an obsessive idea. Here, we seem to have an instance of compulsive behavior, and this, it appears, is an internal source of stabilization. But Govig is more concerned in this chapter with the question that follows that one: Should I laugh or cry? The issue, in other words, is grief. Not, however, the grief of a parent who has suffered the physical death of a son or daughter, but the death of normal conversation and even physical contact with his son. He can talk with John, but only in simple sentences, and only when Stewart initiates the exchange. Small talk is unwelcome. Hugs are impossible because the medications—or something else—make body boundaries indefinite, and John would rather not touch.

ENDURING GRIEF

This is the sorrow of observing the young man in the middle of the backyard and being unable to erase an earlier picture of a teenager who was full of promise, and by whom and for whom plans for the future abounded. The John who now exists is "quiet and unobtrusive, he does not bother anyone" (71). Still, Stewart admits to a feeling of kinship with the mother, Mona Wasow, who writes the following about her twenty-eight-year-old son: "So unless he commits an outwardly violent act, my son gets listed as a 'success'...That is not how he looks to me. I think he looks like a giant, broken plastic, throwaway toy. And he breaks my heart" (71; Wasow 1989, 71).

But if the grief he feels cannot be "worked through" because it is ongoing, Stewart also feels that he does not have to become its victim. He reintroduces the theme of endurance in the very midst of grief, noting three biblical examples: David's decision to go out and meet his subjects after the death of his son Absalom; Amos's decision not to allow his grief over the people's rejection to become a vision of defeat and doom but of life and renewal; and Paul's transformation of grief into a disposition to hope.

This brings him back to the "guest" who has finished lunch with the family and is about to leave for "home," the house he shares with ten other men, fellow clients of the local mental health center social club:

> It represents an experimental new living arrangement with more independence. The housemates also are under supervised medication procedures. John's polite thank you joins with our promise to keep in touch. Transformed, the posturing out on the lawn becomes a moment of healing. (74–75)

Perhaps, then, the questions with which he concluded the previous section were not entirely in vain. If illness is the way in which a disease manifests itself, is some sort of healing possible—of the illness, not the disease itself—and a realistic thing to hope for?

REALISTIC HOPES

He readily admits that expectations of a completely restored John are no longer entertained. But there are "small wonders," such as the fact that John "has not only accepted community-based treatment but also advanced to more personal independence within it" (75)—a sign of his own endurance. Or the fact that, over the years, his father has become a man who knows what it means to be patient and who is not reluctant to own such patience as a sign of endurance. Or the fact that the two of them together have learned what *joy* is all about:

> Have you ever seen someone, minus false teeth, have a go at a hot piece of pizza? We sat by a modest mall fast-food counter (John's preference) and chuckled together at his eating effort. It

was his thirty-fourth birthday party, and our laughter made me realize how much better things had become. His party was a simple affair, but he was pleased. (76)

Govig concludes this chapter with the story of a mental patient who played the cello in an orchestra. During practice one day the voices "badgered" her

with endless taunts and criticisms, further rattling me by singing the music a half-bar ahead of where we were playing. I couldn't concentrate on playing my cello. The orchestra played on, while I struggled to reestablish my place in the music. It was too much. Uncontrollable tears welled up in my eyes and spilled over. (76; Bachrach 1990, 15)

His earlier portrayal of mental illness as a "thief" seems especially relevant here, as she was robbed of the simple *joy* of playing her part in this common human endeavor. If this is what mental illness does, perhaps the first line of a sonnet by William Wordsworth—"Surprised by joy—impatient as the wind"—especially applies to sufferers of mental illness and their families (Fuller 2000, 107). The joy is always surprising because one has long since relinquished the habit of making arrangements for its appearance.

Reframing

In chapter 9, "Reframing," Govig explores the fact that while the situation in which we find ourselves may be intractable, resistant to our efforts to change it for what we believe to be the better, we can, nevertheless, decide how we will view the situation, the attitude that we will adopt toward it. This is not to engage in "denial," nor is it simply a dogged determination to "look on the bright side." After all, "denial" involves the inability to accept the facts as they are. "Looking on the bright side" is a form of partial myopia, the incapacity to recognize that the bright side could not exist if there were not a dark side against which the bright side stands out in sharp relief and contrast. Instead, "reframing" involves viewing the same set of facts within a different frame of reference, one that enables new meanings to emerge.

PRAYER AS REFRAMING

The "reframing" that he considers in this chapter came after several years of viewing the situation from the perspective of research on mental illness and the therapeutic means and methods currently in use. The reframing was a shift from dependence on this more scientific approach toward "a more disciplined regimen of prayer" (81). To set the context for this reframing, he relates another episode, one that in its basic outlines has by now become rather familiar.

John had called, wanting to go out for coffee. "He sounded really good," Stewart told Alice before driving off to pick him up. The skies were clear, and the temperature was balmy when John appeared at the car door with a pleasant hello. Then Stewart "gently" suggested that he would not need the winter cap and down-filled vest he wore over his sweatshirt. John was not persuaded, so Stewart "let it go as 'his problem'" (79). The drive was pleasant enough—no talk, just radio rock music. Before long they slid into a cafeteria smoking-section booth: "As usual, only necessary words were exchanged, but I had long since accepted the benefit of our mutual presence in the humble enjoyment of food and drink" (79).

But then "it" began: "deep, muttering drags on the cigarette, rubbing the wristwatch face, rocking, and feet-shuffling" (79). Stewart asked, "Are you okay?" No answer, for "by now my companion was entirely occupied with listening to Someone Else" (79). Stewart suggested that they leave, but John said no, that he would just go outside and smoke.

Stewart finished his coffee and dessert and then left the cafeteria. He spotted John thirty yards away. People who were about to enter their cars paused and gaped. Several youths loitering near the cafeteria door fell silent: "Red-faced, with contorted countenance and a white knuckled fist at his side...John was yelping passionately to the Other(s), sort of under his breath, oblivious to everything else" (79). Stewart approached him, and after an interval, during which John continued to stomp around, they climbed into the car "in sweaty, silent despair." They made it back to the house "without even testing the boundary of 'no smoking' in the car" (80).

Should he have tried to explain his son's bizarre behavior to their fellow citizens in the parking lot? Had he lost a golden opportunity to educate the public? Others might think so, but at the time he "had no stomach for it, only a sickening dismay, surprisingly alive after so many years. The unpredictable outburst left me disgusted and angry" (80). All the care and concern of so many had come down to this: an awesome adult rage or tantrum. Of course, John was not to blame any more than his parents were to blame. So perhaps a new "format of meaning" was needed to enable his father to feel less helpless, less victimized himself.

This new "format of meaning" began to appear as he reflected on his son's rage—and his own. Noting that the Greek word *mainomai* (source of the English word "maniac") means to "rage" or "be furious," he recalled the story of the Canaanite woman who pleaded with Jesus to have mercy on her for "my daughter is tormented by a demon" (Matthew 15:22). Familiar utterances from Psalms also struck home, including Psalm 130:1–"Out of the depths I cry to you, O LORD"—the psalm to which Anton Boisen turned in *his* distress. Stewart knew, of course, that these psalms were prayers, not unlike the supplication of the Canaanite woman, but he realized, as if for the first time, that these were "pleas from real people who also groaned in spirit" (80).

Moreover, he began to feel a new kinship with Jesus, as portrayed in Luke, as one who prayed "all night long in a time of crisis; only then did he choose the Twelve" (Luke 6:12–16). He concluded, "So I too could certainly pray for guidance" (81). Because it led to learning–or relearning–the habit of prayer, he suggests that this "reframing"–that this matter of his son's illness and his reactions to it were things he could pray about–might be better viewed as "repentance." To provide the reader with a sense of "the spiritual strength I was seeking" (81), he turns to the "classic biblical story" of Job.

JOB AND REFRAMING

He points out that Job, "bereaved, impoverished, and with his health imperiled," is furious and defiant. He is "unwilling to relinquish his claim that God, not he, is responsible for his plight" (81). Meanwhile, the three visitors tried to console him with "faith notions based on conventional wisdom," including the idea "that suffering is God's own gracious course of education" (81). Their arguments, reflective of "the 'doctrinal theology' perspective," prompt Govig to ask if rigorous theological pursuit results "in distancing *experience* from a passion for answers" (82). Job desperately seeks answers, and he believes that there are such answers, but he also thinks that God, who knows the answers, "*withholds* more than he discloses" (82). How, then, can "anyone deal with a Creator who deliberately withholds crucial knowledge in such a fashion" (82)?

To its credit, the "bible" of the American Psychiatric Association (the *DSM-IV*) does give answers. Govig quotes its definition of a "mental disorder" and notes that it lists nineteen classifications of mental disorders together with scores of subclassifications. These definitions and classifications do not address, however, "the bottom line of suffering" as a "religious reality" (83). He acknowledges that, by taking the longer historical view, the dominant voices of the Bible are able to see the meaning in the suffering that the people endure. But voices like those of Job, which focus on the present, express the *fear* that the suffering makes no ultimate sense, that God is simply arbitrary, that God's ways are far from consistent. Is this true of the sufferings arising from mental disorders?

Two reasons tempt him to agree with Job. One is "the unique sense of meaninglessness ('craziness') in various episodes shared with my son" (83). Another is "the severity of the disabling condition itself, one that seems to strike at the core of John's very being and transform him into another person" (83). Mental illness may therefore be understood as "hinting at the yawning, formless void present at the beginning before God's wind swept over and brought light to original disorder (Genesis

1:1–3)" (83). If John's condition is officially termed a "disorder," then it serves as a terrible witness to the time *before* God began to put things in order. Thus, it reflects the very absence of God in the world.

CHRIST DISABLED

This leads to the final section of the reframing chapter, "Christ Disabled," which, he notes, adds necessary perspective to "the normative vision of the Risen Christ" (84). Reflecting on the meaning of Jesus' healing of Peter's mother in law, Matthew quotes the prophet Isaiah, "He took our infirmities and bore our diseases" (Matthew 8:17). This means that Christ has experienced even more testing and more humiliation than persons like his son "who must contest with those tormenting voices of auditory hallucinations" (84). Because he has such experiences of suffering, Jesus stands "side by side" with people like John Govig. This recognition of the disabled Christ led Govig to an acceptance of "life within limits" and "slowed down [his] pursuit of religious and psychological crutches" (84). As anger began to recede as well, "the strangest reframing of all has taken place: rebirth within the boundaries of God's salvation" (84). Salvation is no longer searched for beyond the boundedness of life and its contingencies and circumstances but within these very contingencies and circumstances. (Theodore Roethke's definition of madness as "nobility of soul at odds with circumstance" is especially relevant here.)

Cheating Winter

In chapter 10, "Cheating Winter," the concluding chapter of the book, Govig focuses explicitly on "learning to hope." He notes that the professionals with whom he has come in contact over the years "have not only urged me to risk more effective treatments in John's case, they have prodded me to take a look at *hope* potential, poised between grief on the one hand and faith on the other" (87). Through the early pages of the book, he has emphasized the *treatment* interventions that have been employed over the years. But now, more than a decade has elapsed since John was accurately diagnosed, and the family is poised for "a different angle of the story, namely, rehabilitation" (87).

REHABILITATION

Professionals on the "rehabilitation" side of things tend to reject the phrase "chronically mentally ill" as it is merely an invitation to pessimistic expectations. Because he considers John's condition to be "mostly a physical, biological brain disease," Govig confesses to having doubts about this. At the same time, he wants to know more about the possibilities for rehabilitation. Thus he cites examples of rehabilitation centers that have emphasized "health induction" rather than "symptom reduction" and have demonstrated "that persons with severe psychotic disabilities have the capacity to recover better health" (88).

On the other hand, those who emphasize rehabilitation note that "false leads" of the past have actually inhibited progress on the rehabilitation path, and they caution against similar mistakes in the future. Govig cites two such "false leads" from their own experience with John. One was the myth that "increasing compliance with drug treatment can singularly affect rehabilitation outcome" (88). Operating on this belief, the Govigs assumed that once on medication John "would come to his senses" and take up normal living again. Eventually, it dawned on them that medications are simply for the control of symptoms and that "kindling within the patient a motivation to take up college again or find employment was another matter" (88).

Another myth concerns the supposition that "a person's diagnostic label provides significant information relevant to his or her rehabilitation outcome" (88–89). While, for the Govigs, the diagnostic label of "affective schizophrenia" brought a needed sense of clarity as to what they were up against, these labels "can steer treatment away from the *person*" (89). Moreover, the *DSM-IV* "fails to connect diagnostic conclusions with adequate bases for long-term treatment planning. Not enough thought is given to the environment the client needs or wishes to live within" (89). The new rehabilitation emphasis thus focuses on the *person* and this person's environmental needs and desires. In other words, we are light years away from the mental institutions of the first half of the twentieth century.

WARY OF NEW LEADS AND HOPES

Having experienced the "false leads" of the more recent past, however, Govig is somewhat wary of these new leads as they may create false hopes. We face the "danger that the more the professionals in the system take responsibility for life choices, the more helpless and dependent clients and their caregiver families become" (89). This may reinforce the stereotypical view of the mentally ill as unable to understand or recognize what they need or what would be beneficial to them.

Moreover, if rehabilitation involves taking seriously the mentally ill person's own environmental needs and desires, this will require a seismic shift in public attitudes about and toward the mentally ill. Govig cites three such attitudes:

1. that persons who are seriously mentally ill are dangerous, unpredictable, and to be feared
2. that what they say is crazy and can be ignored, so it is up to others to decide what is in their best interest
3. that they are more like children than adults

These are prejudices and, like all prejudices, they need to be unmasked. Yet, based on their experiences with John, Govig has to admit that "there is a degree of truth" in each. He concludes the chapter with a pair of anecdotes involving himself and John, the first of which reveals the degree of truth in the "more like children than adults" prejudice, the second of which reveals how "adult" John could be when the occasion required it.

The first episode occurred when John was living in a supervised housing arrangement. Social workers had worked diligently to achieve more independent living for him, had taken him shopping several times, and had provided cooking instructions. It began to look, however, as if he lacked motivation enough to fix himself a decent meal, so when his father came to take him to a favorite buffet-style restaurant, his enjoyment as he piled his plate high with food was evident. As they ate together, there was little talk until John broke the silence with a question, "Have you seen someone slurp Jello?" "No," his father admitted, he never had.

> With a furtive glance about to make sure no one was looking, John lifted a couple of Jello cubes and "slurped" them through his lips. I was awarded with a broad, toothless grin. Childlike behavior for a thirty-something person, I'd say, yet I could not help joining in this simple mirth. In the face of other episodes tempting me to bemoan my parenting fate, the challenge I see now is to cultivate a sense of humor for moments like these. (90)

"For moments like these..." This time there was no sullen reaction to his father's rebuke in the cafeteria that built into a towering rage resulting in a fractured nose. Nor was there the rushed exit from the cafeteria when he began to hear voices that were also, perhaps, stimulated by his father's gentle suggestion that he did not need winter clothing on a balmy day. This was not the adult that, thirty-some years earlier, Stewart would have envisioned when being informed that he was the father of a newborn son. But, while Govig concluded his account of that earlier cafeteria scene with a comment about his son's "inexplicable rage" and acknowledged his own rage at his son's behavior, this time the target of his rage is different: "On the inside, I can't help raging against chronic mental illness" (95). The focus of rage has changed. Yet even chronic mental illness has brought "strange blessings in its wake. For me, the biblical words 'compassion' and 'patience' have become neither unfamiliar nor strange" (95).

The second episode demonstrated John's maturity in a situation where their roles were reversed. Not long after their amusement over John's Jello-slurping skills, the two of them were department store shopping. As was his custom, John stepped out ahead but not so far as to lose track of his father's whereabouts. Suddenly, Stewart tripped and suffered a nasty fall. As he lay on the floor trying to catch his breath, John was the first to reach his side: "Take it easy, Dad." Then, "Where does it hurt?" And finally, "They're coming...you'll be okay." Govig comments, "What better verbal first aid?" (90). This is the "real" John, the one who is himself compassionate and patient, and so very different from the man who entered his father's bedroom, slammed his fist in his face, and denied that he had hurt him. This John emerged at the moment when his father had need of *him*.

THE WAY AHEAD

So where to go from here? Govig makes two suggestions. One way to continue the journey is to "go public." He has tried to do this (and continues to this day) through involvement in the local chapter of the National Alliance for the Mentally Ill (NAMI) and in the World Association for Psychosocial Rehabilitation (WAPR). He continues to encourage churches and their pastors to consider "the situation facing persons with chronic mental illness in our midst" (92–93).

Another way to continue the journey is to "go gentle." Noting that he began the book with an account of his son's rage and recognizing that he has had his own moments of rage, he now finds himself wanting to go beyond mere rage. Referring to Dylan Thomas's well-known poem, he seeks to "go gentle into that good night" in which sanity gives up the ghost, and "instead of lingering by the poet's curse, I shall watch for his hint of blessing" (94–95), as expressed in the line, "Curse, bless, me now with your fierce tears, I pray" (Thomas 2003, 239).

As for the tears, "the biblical field of vision" promises that "the divine endurance will extend to a renewal of the Eden-like peace that reigned before chaos and death invaded our lives," when God "will wipe away every tear from our eyes" (95, paraphrasing Rev. 21:4). Note, he concludes, that "we ourselves cannot wipe away each other's tears; only God can do it. Until then I dream of a day when not the anorexic silent John appears before us but the young man we knew before the stranger took his place" (96).

The Schizophrenic Brain

Stewart Govig's *Souls Are Made of Endurance* is such an honest, faithful, and deeply insightful account of his son's mental illness and of his own struggle to understand it that it seems unnecessary to try to add anything to what he has already said except the quiet "Amen" that I found myself subvocalizing as I completed my first reading of the book. But then I think of his accounts of the times when he and his son would sit together in silence. While he learned to accept this silence, he continues to long for greater conversation between them, including, one senses, conversation about how John himself understands what has happened to him.

Similarly, when an author has written about painful personal experiences and has done so because he believes his recounting of these experiences is not an act of self-indulgence or an expression of self-pity, but may comfort others who read the account, it seems altogether appropriate that a reader, even one who cannot claim to have had the same experience as the author, would add a few reflections of his own in the interest of continuing dialogue.

Cause and Blame

Students in my course on mental illness frequently raise one issue that Govig himself raises. This is the issue of causality, and, implied in this, the matter of blame. The seeming relationship between causality and blame goes back at least as far as Jesus' time, when bystanders asked Jesus, when a man born blind was brought to him, "Who sinned, this man or his parents?" (John 9:2). While Jesus said "Neither," still the question persists.

As we have seen, Govig says that before schizophrenia became a resident in their home, he had no reason to challenge the reasonableness of causal theories that focused on faulty maternal care and the double-binding communication styles in families of schizophrenic children (16). But once it became clear that their son suffered from schizophrenia, he gained "profound relief" to find that these theories had since been discredited and that schizophrenia is now recognized as a brain disease not unlike the diseases that affect other organs of the body. He does not, however, discuss in any detail this newer theory and how it makes better sense of what happened in the case of their son John. Also, by focusing almost exclusively on this particular theory, he does not address the possibility that schizophrenia may have multiple causes.

Govig indicates his own awareness that it may have multiple causes when he says that in view of what he considers "mostly a physical, biological brain disease" (88), he has his doubts about some of the claims being made with regard to rehabilitation. The word "mostly" suggests that other factors may be involved. In the video, "Stranger in Our Midst," in which Stewart, Alice, and John Govig relate their story, one of the clinical experts, Dr. Jarrell Richardson II, a Mayo Clinic consultant in psychiatry, alludes to the discredited monolithic theories of the past. He notes that psychiatrists now operate on the assumption that schizophrenia, like any other illness, needs to be viewed as "genetic, psychological, social, and spiritual" (Dragseth and Foreman 2002). If this assumption is accurate, we may assume that there are various factors involved in why a person becomes schizophrenic, and why the illness manifests itself in the way it does in each individual instance.

Richardson's suggestion that genetics plays a role in schizophrenia is supported by the *DSM-IV*, which indicates that the "first degree biological relatives of individuals with Schizophrenia have a risk for Schizophrenia that is about 10 times greater than that of the general population" (*DSM-IV*, 283). But it goes on to say that "although much evidence suggests the importance of genetic factors in the etiology of Schizophrenia, the existence of a substantial discordance rate in mono-zygotic twins [that is, twins from one fertilized egg] also indicates the importance of environmental factors" (283). Of course, "environmental factors" covers a large terrain, and because it does, it challenges the tendency of earlier theories to focus on a single factor, such as parenting.

An interesting though not necessarily relevant piece of evidence relating to the genetic factor is E. Mark Torrey and Judy Mitchell's notation in *The Invisible Plague* that the highest insanity rates in an 1870 survey of California residents occurred among those who were from Norway and Sweden (4.5 per 1,000), followed by immigrants from Scotland (3.6), France (3.2), and Ireland (3.2) (2002, 251). As the Govigs are of Norwegian descent, does this mean that their son, John, was at higher risk of schizophrenia than his non-Scandinavian friends?

SOCIAL PATTERNS AS CAUSES

Citation of an 1870 survey raises another possible causal factor whose locus is in the mysterious borderland between genetics and environmental factors. This concerns the fact that John was the son of a Lutheran clergyman and that his grandfathers and great-grandfathers were Lutheran clergymen. In *You Can Go Home Again*, Monica McGoldrick, the well-known family therapist, relates fascinating stories about families in which succeeding generations have followed strikingly similar patterns, often without fully realizing that they were doing so. The pattern of accidental deaths, especially among the children and grandchildren of Joseph and Rose Kennedy, is a case in point (1995, 158–61).

If precedents of this nature can be unconsciously adopted by later generations, we are probably justified in wondering if the longstanding pattern of sons (especially older sons?) becoming Lutheran clergy also played a role of a largely subconscious nature in John's incipient psychosis. Was "identity confusion" a factor in his susceptibility to mental illness, particularly that of schizophrenia? (See, on this point, Capps 2003). Was he struggling with the unspoken expectation that he would follow in the footsteps of his father, grandfathers, and great-grandfathers? And, if he chose a different path, that he would suffer the price of guilt for having broken the line of succession? If on one occasion John said his father "talks through his head," could it be that all of these fathers have been "talking through his head," accusing him of having broken the line of succession and failing to become, like them, "a man of God"?[3] If so, his father's observation that he and his housemates lived in Trappist-like simplicity is a word of paternal blessing. Through the circuitous route of mental illness, John *has* become "a man of God."

THE ROLE OF TRAUMA

These comments on possible genetic or genetic/environmental factors are not, however, intended to challenge the basic contention of Govig's book that mental illness is a disease of the brain. It is rather to say that the brain is the organ through which genetics make their influence known and felt.

Before I comment further on brain research findings relating to the "schizophrenic" brain, I would like to consider the role that trauma may play in the incipient stages of psychosis. I have in mind here the automobile accidents in which John was a passenger, but especially the one in which the driver was killed. As we have seen, Stewart expresses regret that no brain scan was performed in the case of the earlier accident, when John's head crashed through the windshield. I, as reader, share this regret. On the other hand, the second accident is also of great interest. In this case, John's own injuries appear to have been relatively minor while the driver was killed. John was found in a ditch attempting to bury the evidence of marijuana. On this occasion, the surgeon commented on the awful language he heard as John was coming out of the anesthesia.

It seems significant, therefore, that several of the psychotic episodes that Govig relates in the course of the book involve John, the passenger, asking to be let out of the car. This is followed by furious stomping around some distance from the car as he becomes the victim of accusatory voices. Is he, then, reliving the trauma of the second accident? Are the delusions in this case an attempt to work through the guilt—the self-accusations and self-blame—that persons typically experience when they survive a situation in which others are killed?[4]

Govig indicates that he has come to prefer the term "brain disease" over "troubled mind," as the former alerts us to the fact that mental illness is organic. On the other hand, the term "troubled mind" may express John's own experience in the early phases of his psychosis, and it may have particular relevance to Dr. Richardson's suggestion that "psychological" and "spiritual" factors are also involved in serious mental illness. If John's subconscious mind was accusing him of being complicit in his companion's death and/or telling him that he had no right to have survived the accident, then it is not surprising that his first hospitalization occurred when another friend became concerned that he was suicidal. Suicide, after all, is one way to silence the accusing voices and pay the ultimate price for one's complicity, real or imagined, in the death of another. If schizophrenia is a brain *disease*, the voices–who they are and what they are saying–reflect the fact that it is also an *illness*.

A BRAIN DISEASE

The issue of trauma, however, also points to the very appropriateness of emphasizing that schizophrenia is a disease of the brain, for the brain is directly affected by environmental factors, especially ones that are as traumatic as this one appeared to be. This brings us back to "brain disease" as the primary cause of John's mental illness. Because this is a very complex subject, Govig was undoubtedly wise in simply affirming his belief that John's illness was "mostly a physical, biological brain disease" and not attempting to go further into the specifics of the disease. Still, it is possible to describe its general parameters. When one does so, the role of environmental factors is further clarified as well.

While today all researchers agree that schizophrenia is a brain disorder, they offer various theories, each with supporting evidence, of how this disorder works, how it comes about, and so forth. I will discuss here the views presented by Gordon Claridge in *The Origins of Mental Illness,* because he emphasizes the way in which the brain processes environmental stimuli and how this is relevant specifically to schizophrenia.

Claridge begins his discussion of schizophrenia by noting that a distinction needs to be drawn "between those primary features of psychological experience that form the psychotic state itself and those aspects which constitute the individual's secondary reaction, or adaptation, to it" (1995, 145). Among the primary experiences, one of the most basic is alteration in simple sensation and perception. The most obvious alteration of this kind is the "hearing of voices," though "changes may occur in other modalities, including disturbances in the visually perceived world" (145).

Thus, Claridge tells of the patient who was sitting and listening to another person. Suddenly, the other person seemed to get smaller and then larger, and then he seemed to get smaller again. Many schizophrenics also report that their sensory apparatus is "flooded" with stimulation, "a phenomenon which, at a higher level of mental functioning, translates into an experience of too many *ideas* coming into the mind at once, leaving the person unable to organize a consecutive train of thought" (146). Occasionally, though, the opposite may happen, "and the person describes having *no* thoughts, as though the mind were an empty vessel" (146).

Given these perceptual or attentional alterations, it is not surprising that language, the vehicle of thought, is often disorganized, that speech is incoherent, and that the ideas expressed seem illogical and tangential to the theme of the conversation. At other times, the structural form of the language is normal, but the content is bizarre. In this case, the ideas or beliefs are logically watertight, but they are based on an initially false premise, "often derived from a misperception of some external event that is wrongly interpreted as personally significant" (146). Thus, "Here we see an example of primary experience giving rise, secondarily, to a disruption of thinking that comes about because the schizophrenic, in this case, is trying to formulate for himself a rational explanation of his peculiar sense data" (146).

EMOTIONS AND SCHIZOPHRENIA

One aspect of schizophrenia, then, is the connection between altered perceptions and the thoughts or ideas that such alteration produces. Another is the role that emotions play in schizophrenia. Sometimes, the emotions displayed by persons suffering from schizophrenia are reactions to the fact that the outside world seems physically distorted. In this case, a common reaction is anxiety. Elation may also occur if the distortion is pleasurable or exciting (as Kay Jamison testifies). Other times, the emotion seems unrelated to perceptual distortions, and the sudden emergence of the emotions is as inexplicable to the person as to the observer. Still, in schizophrenia, the emotional and the cognitive tend to be deeply intertwined and prove almost impossible to disentangle. It is useful, therefore, to view schizophrenia as involving perception, cognition, and emotion, with discordancies occurring among all three (147).

The obvious locus of such discordancies is the brain. Claridge notes that some, perhaps the majority of researchers, have gone straight to "the question of causes." This is usually conceptualized as some discrete underlying abnormality of brain function, either structural or neurological. It has little or no reference point in normal psychology or normal neurophysiology:

> According to this view, the psychological and interpersonal disabilities of schizophrenia can, in effect, be merely regarded as epiphenomena, events which "trail behind" the organic aetiology, certainly of some interest to novelist—even, in the case of their social consequences, of vital therapeutic concern—but of little interest for the medical researcher. (148)

Claridge argues for a different approach, one that focuses on the brain as the central organ of the whole nervous system, but one that takes account of the fact that the brain receives its cues from the eternal environment. Furthermore, the higher functions of the brain are directly affected by the lower ones. In earlier chapters of the book, Claridge discusses other less severe mental disorders—especially the anxiety disorders–in relation to the lower or limbic system of the brain. The limbic system regulates the excitatory and inhibitory responses to external stimuli. Students of the anxiety disorders refer to such responses as the "flight vs. flight" polarity that occurs especially in panic disorder.

The limbic system also plays a role in schizophrenia, in that for some schizophrenics, the "excitation" mechanism is more prominent, as many stimuli are allowed into the nervous system, "giving rise to psychotic symptoms of a more paranoid, emotionally reactive kind" (154). In other cases, the opposite may be true, "the person being psychologically and physiologically shut-off from his surroundings, the signs of psychosis being those of social withdrawal and emotional blunting" (154). Of course, one and the same person may manifest both extremes, with the excitatory process dominant at one time and the inhibitory at another. If, however, the acute phase of schizophrenia tends to reflect the former, the more chronic or long-term tendency is for the "shut-off" or "gating-out" of stimuli to predominate.

Thus, over the course of the illness, there are "alterations in the way the schizophrenic monitors his environment." Specifically, "the excessive narrowing of attention" appears to be "a defensive maneuver against threatening or otherwise intense stimuli" (155). Such "monitoring" may point to a possible physiological mechanism in the brain that, in effect, overcompensates for the excessive stimulation in the acute stages of the psychosis. This means, on the other hand, that

> a crucial feature of the psychotic brain may be a loosening, or relative failure, of its homeostatic regulation, possibly due to a weakening of inhibitory mechanisms, which causes the nervous system to "overshoot'" the acceptable levels of arousal necessary for its normal functioning. (156–57)

SCHIZOPHRENIA AND HIGHER BRAIN LEVELS

Having noted the role of lower-brain functions in schizophrenics, Claridge suggests that viewing schizophrenia solely in terms of "a low-level brain circuit such as the limbic-system is not…entirely satisfactory," for "many of the most striking features of schizophrenia consist of disordered language, distorted thought, delusional belief, a fragmented self-concept and other abnormalities of consciousness that necessarily involve the higher nervous system" (160–61).

These features of schizophrenia have led researchers to study it in relation to the differential functioning of the two cerebral hemispheres, and especially to focus on the fact that "the two halves of the brain contribute two streams of awareness to consciousness" (161). Two questions emerge from this. One is the relation between the differential functioning of the two hemispheres and the limbic systems. The other is the relation between the two hemispheres themselves. The second question has received the greater amount of research attention.

Claridge cites several research studies that challenge the popular assumption that schizophrenia reflects a sort of "split-brain" phenomenon (that is, the two hemispheres operating independently of one another). Instead they suggest that "there is actually *too much* communication between them, a greater flow of information than is desirable, leading to disruption of the brain's ability as a total unit to perform effectively" (166). Thus, if normally, the left hemisphere inhibits the right hemisphere when engaged in a verbal task, such inhibition is weaker or lacking altogether in the brain functioning of the schizophrenic person. The idea that too much communication occurs between the two hemispheres may help to explain the hearing of voices. Because schizophrenics whisper subvocally when they hear voices, it may be that the voices originate in the right hemisphere and represent ideas or thoughts, normally below the level of awareness, which spill over into consciousness and find expression through the left hemisphere's control of speech (168).

On the other hand, another body of research evidence suggests a tendency for interhemispheric inhibition to *increase* in schizophrenia, thus causing "the two halves of the brain to become, to some extent, functionally isolated from one another, each hemisphere taking on a life of its own" (167). This may explain the duality of consciousness that seems to appear in schizophrenia, "a sense not of dual personality as that term is usually employed, but of separating of the stream of ideas, its division into sometimes contradictory elements of thought and impulse, amounting on occasion to a feeling of alien influence" (167). Claridge cites the case of a man who thought of himself as having a normal rational self that deals with the real world and another foreign self that tries to influence his behavior through the voices he hears. He actually located the two parts of his personality on opposite sides of his head.

Claridge suggests that these two apparently conflicting bodies of research can be reconciled by positing an *irregularity* or lack of homeostasis in the schizophrenic brain. The excitatory versus inhibitory processes that interact in the limbic system (the lower brain) also occur in the higher brain processes. Either too much excitation or too much inhibition occurs between the two hemispheres. In general, however, Claridge subscribes to the view that, because there is too much communication between the two hemispheres, they become "relatively less specialized, less distinct in the division of function on which, paradoxically, the unity of the self depends" (170).

ENVIRONMENTAL THEORIES

Much more could be said about the theory that schizophrenia reflects an instability in the way the brain functions, both vertically (higher and lower brain functions) and horizontally (the two hemis-pheres), but enough has been presented here to establish beyond reasonable doubt that schizophrenia is a brain disorder. Does this mean, though, that environmental theories have no relevance whatsoever? Claridge thinks not. He challenges an exclusive emphasis on the "brain" theory of schizophrenia on the grounds that the very characteristics of the nervous system that play a role in all mental disorders—excitation versus inhibition—have personality correlates, and schizophrenia is no excep-tion. Researchers have studied young children judged to be at risk of schizophrenia in later years. They conducted the studies during the period when the corpus collosum (the bundle of fibers that joins the two halves of the brain together) is still developing. Researchers found these children to be somewhat aggressive, antisocial children, and troublesome in their relationships with their peers (185). In a retrospective study, young adults diagnosed as schizophrenics and seen in a psychiatric clinic as children were described as aggressive, but also as worried, moody, restless, and irritable (185). The very fact that preschizophrenic children are typically described by clinics as having both extraverted and intro-verted personality characteristics suggests that they have temperaments comprised of "a disharmony of apparently self-contradictory traits" (187).

In the video, "Stranger in Our Midst," Alice Govig commented on the fact that their son is now "silent and polite" and without a trace of "arrogance," thus implying that at one time he manifested, at least on occasion, opposing personality traits. Also important is the occasion when he claimed that, despite fracturing his father's nose, he had not really hurt him. This may be a reflection of what some clinicians have reported to be a fairly common characteristic of preschizophrenic people, a tendency toward insensitivity to the feelings of others that may, in fact, manifest itself in cruel and inhumane behavior. This was a very different John from the one who stood by his father after his nasty fall, asking where it hurts and assuring him that he would be okay, that help was on the way.

The existence of these "self-contradictory traits," traceable to an instability in the excitatory versus inhibitory processes, is especially likely to have an effect on interpersonal relationships. Relationships involving family members are the most likely to be affected. Specifically, Claridge believes that "because of the arrangement of his nervous system," the preschizophrenic child

> will be at greater risk of misinterpreting nonverbal social signals, because of his tendency to focus on, or attend selectively to their constituent parts rather than consider them in a total context. Put more generally, he might just have more difficulty sorting out meaning in the complicated flow of verbal and nonverbal

interchange that makes up social communication, particularly if this signifies strong emotion, and especially so given the unusual organization of both the expressive and receptive aspects of language in the schizotypal brain. Occurring from childhood onwards this form of interaction with others could exacerbate a pre-existing genetic disposition to produce a cognitive and personality style that is vulnerable to schizophrenic breakdown. (198–99)

Although Claridge goes on to challenge the theory that "social interactions" within the family may cause schizophrenia, he does want to draw attention to the possibility that particular families may, for one reason or another, reflect interpersonal situations with which the preschizophrenic child's "nervous system is ill-equipped to deal" (199). This, however, would make the family milieu a secondary cause at most. Given Claridge's preceding discussion of the self-contradictory traits of the preschizophrenic child that are due to the development of the nervous system itself, it would be appropriate to ask whether any family could possibly provide the "ideal" milieu.

It is interesting to note in this connection that Gregory Bateson, the originator of the "double-bind" theory of schizophrenia, published an edited version of a first-person account by a man named Perceval of his psychosis in 1830–1832, in which it was the "voices" who placed him in a "double-bind." Here is the account:

I was tormented by the commands of what I imagined was the Holy Spirit, to say other things, which as often as I attempted, I was fearfully rebuked for beginning in my own voice and not in a voice given to me. These contradictory commands were the cause, now as before, of the incoherency of my behavior, and these imaginations formed the chief causes of my total derangement. For I was commanded to speak, on pain of dreadful torments, of provoking the wrath of the Holy Spirit, and of incurring the guilt of the grossest ingratitude; and at the same time whenever I attempted to speak, I was harshly and contemptuously rebuked for not using the utterance of a spirit sent to me; and when I again attempted, I still went wrong, and when I pleaded internally that I knew not what I was to do, I was accused of falsehood and deceit; and of being really unwilling to do what I was commanded. I then lost patience, and proceeded to say what I was desired pell-mell, determined to show that it was not fear or want of will that prevented me. But when I did this, I felt as formerly the pain in the nerves of my palate and throat on speaking, which convinced me that I was not only rebelling against God, but against nature; and I relapsed into an agonizing sense of hopelessness and of ingratitude. (Bateson 1961, 32–33).

Notice that Perceval says that these "contradictory commands were the cause, not as before, of the incoherency of my behavior." This "incoherency" reflects an instability in the basic processes of the neurological system (which are responsible, in Claridge's view, for one's temperamental style), those of excitation and inhibition. Because the behavior is not a motor response (flight or fight) but one involving language (whether to speak or not speak), we may assume that the higher brain functions were involved and that he was experiencing too much communication between the two hemispheres of the brain. This account, then, supports the view that schizophrenia is primarily a brain disorder. It is, therefore, somewhat surprising that Bateson would have given primacy to familial communication styles as causative factors in schizophrenia. It makes more sense to reverse the causal sequence and to suggest that the perception of being placed by the persons in one's immediate environment in double-binding conditions has its origins in the brain dysfunction of the preschizophrenic child.[5]

The Stranger in Our Midst

Govig's *Souls Are Made of Endurance* concludes on the note that a "stranger" took the place of the young man they had known before he was afflicted with a severely disabling mental illness. The metaphor of "the stranger in our midst" is the title of the video in which John and his parents appear together with experts on mental illness. I want to conclude this chapter with two brief comments about this stranger motif.

One is prompted by an observation Jay Neugeboren makes about his brother Robert who suffered from schizophrenia. Robert was fifty-two years old at the time Jay wrote his account of his struggles to cope with Robert's illness. On the next-to-last page of his memoir, Jay comments on the "sad truth" that "who he is–his identity as Robert Neugeboren and nobody else, a human being forever in process, forever growing, changing, and evolving–is made up, to this point in time, largely of what most of us have come to call his illness" (Neugeboren 1997, 303). Who, then, would Robert be if he were somehow to be miraculously cured? Since his illness has been central to his life since his teens, what would happen "if he gives that up, as it were" and "does not hold on to his illness and its history as a legitimate, real, and unique part of his ongoing self–what of him, at fifty-two years, will be left?" (303). This, Jay continues, is

> only another way of saying that just as we cannot separate the mysterious ways in which mind and body interact–the ways in which history, memory, and behavior influence the chemistry of

the brain, and the ways in which the chemistry of the brain influences behavior—so we can never separate who Robert is, and how he came to have the life he had, from the life he has, in fact, had, and may yet have. (303)

This does not mean that the Robert his brother Jay knows now is not a "stranger" when viewed from the perspective of Jay's memories of Robert as a child. But over the years, the Robert whose illness is so integral to who he is has become more and more familiar, as one who has his own unique personality, his own identity. As Stewart Govig notes in "Stranger in Our Midst," the years have witnessed an acceptance of "the new person in our midst." Thus, over time, the "stranger" becomes more and more familiar, his behavior less and less alien or foreign. As Govig also says in the video, "That toothless grin is something to see!" Moreover, he has become "our teacher" as he "is satisfied with living." Alice adds, "He is our friend and we are his."[6]

As the film ends, Stewart, Alice, and John walk together away from the camera. Ironically, if the John they had known before his illness were suddenly to reappear, *he* would be the unfamiliar stranger, and *he* would take a long time getting used to. He might even be the object of some resentment, as his parents have become accustomed, over the years, to the John who has been their "teacher" and their "friend."

The second comment is prompted by Julia Kristeva's analysis of Freud's essay, "The 'Uncanny'," in her book *Strangers to Ourselves.* She interprets Freud's essay to be suggesting that what we view as "foreign" or "strange" about others is a reminder of what we have repressed in ourselves, that part of ourselves from which we have become estranged. Thus, "Delicately, analytically, Freud does not speak of foreigners: He teaches us how to detect foreignness in ourselves" (1991, 191). Freud's concern is not merely, then, that of welcoming the foreigner or stranger into our midst—of hospitality—but of acknowledging that the "uncanny strangeness" we see in "them" makes us aware of the "stranger" in ourselves.

One of the central themes of *Souls Are Made of Endurance* is that John's episodes of furious rage found resonance in Stewart's own discovered rage. In fact, in his reflections on the incident in which John rushed out of the cafeteria and had it out with his voices, their rage—father's and son's—is barely distinguishable, and almost impossible to disentangle:

The unpredictable outburst left me disgusted and angry. All the care, treatment, and love of parents, siblings, relatives and friends, health professionals, clerics, counselors, social workers, educators, and other advocates had come down to this: an awesome adult rage or tantrum. (Govig 1994, 80).

But this, it seems, is also where the story begins, as "the rage in the rec room" evoked a similar rage in the bedroom where the father reached for the phone to summon the authorities. Perhaps the vocation of these "strangers in our midst" is to witness to the stranger who lives, unacknowledged and unrecognized, in all of us. Recognition of our own self-alienation is the first step on the arduous journey of making peace with ourselves. In this regard, those who suffer from schizophrenia are truly our teachers.

NOTES

[1] In *Souls Are Made of Endurance*, Govig uses pseudonymous first names for all members of his family, including the son who suffers from mental illness. As he has not felt the need to use this device in his subsequent writings and public presentations, I have taken the liberty of changing the names employed in the book to the actual names.

[2] In *Family Experiences with Mental Illness* (2000), Richard Tessler and Gail Gamache explore the following six questions:

1. what basic needs do family members provide;
2. what troublesome behaviors do family members try to control;
3. how much do family members spend;
4. what are the emotional costs for family members;
5. what are the positive aspects for family members; and
6. how involved are other members of the family household?

In their study of Ohio families in 1989–1992, telephone interviews were conducted with the member of the household who was the primary family caregiver. A major variable was whether the mentally ill person lived at home. A key concern of the researchers was to find out if family members "minded" taking care of the mentally ill person, and who minded the most. In general, the order of "minding" (least to greatest) was child caring for parent, spouse for spouse, parent for child, and sibling for sibling.

[3] Another son and grandson of Norwegian Lutheran pastors with whom I am well acquainted became psychotic in his late twenties. He was a successful aeronautical engineer at the time, and his mental illness led to the termination of his career and the end of his marriage. At a family gathering some thirty years later, he could joke about the fact that he had tried an alternative route to the transcendent (via airplanes that could penetrate the stratosphere), but as a twenty-year old struggling with the fact that continuation of this family legacy depended on him, the only son, this was not a matter that he could joke about. He and his second wife, together with their perfectly normal daughter (whom he calls his "vindication") currently operate a congregate care facility for the mentally ill. In effect, he has become a minister despite the fact that he did not follow in his father's and grandfather's footsteps. He would agree, I believe, with the idea that God works in mysterious ways.

[4] In *A Beautiful Mind*, the biography of the mathematical genius, John Nash, who suffered a schizophrenic breakdown at age thirty, Sylvia Nasar relates an episode in which one of Nash's close friends was tragically killed when Nash was fourteen (1998, 37). Nash and two other boys were making pipe bombs and manufacturing their own gunpowder. The bomb-making came to a horrifying end when one of the other boys, who was alone at the time, was building a pipe bomb that exploded in his lap, severing an artery. He bled to death in the ambulance that came for him. The parents of the other boy sent their son off to boarding school the following fall, an action that seems to have been intended to protect him from Nash's influence. I have written a series of articles about the role that this traumatic experience may have played in Nash's subsequent mental breakdown (Capps 2003, 2004a, 2004b).

[5] In his groundbreaking book, *Childhood and Society* (1963, originally published in 1950), psychoanalyst Erik H. Erikson presents the case of a young girl suffering from

"infantile schizophrenia." He attributed the communication difficulties in the mother-daughter relationship to "a primary deficiency in 'sending power' in the child." In a footnote added in the 1963 revised edition of the book, he explains that he has changed the word "primary" to "clear" because he had been taken to task for seeming to argue for "a strictly constitutional [that is, biological or genetic] etiology of infantile psychosis" (207). His intent, however, was "to counter certain facile interpretations then in vogue which claimed that rejecting mothers could cause such malignancy in their offspring" (207). He views this chapter as an attempt not to isolate "first causes," as such popular interpretations claim to be doing, but "to delineate a new conceptual area encompassing both the struggles of the ego and of social organization" (207). In effect, Erikson's was one of the minority voices in the psychotherapeutic community that abstained from the popular concept of the "schizophrenogenic mother" as the primary causal agent in schizophrenia.

⁶What stimulated this reference to their mutual friendship was a birthday card Alice received from John that said, "To my friend." John Swinton emphasizes the role of friendship in *Resurrecting the Person: Friendship and the Care of People with Mental Health Problems* (2000).

5

WE ARE NOT OUR OWN

▒ JAMES NICHOLS

In this chapter, we will focus on Sue Miller's *The Story of My Father* (2003), another memoir written by a family member of a person suffering from mental illness. Her father's diagnosis was dementia of the Alzheimer's type. As with previous chapters, I will begin with a description of the disease itself. Since Alzheimer's is a particular type of dementia, I will first present dementia and then move to the more specific type of dementia named for the German physician, Alois Alzheimer (1864–1915), who first described it.

Dementia Described

Dementia is a form of mental illness that especially affects persons late in life, with highest prevalence above age 85. According to the *DSM-IV*, it is estimated that 2 to 4 percent of the population over 65 have dementia of the Alzheimer's type, with other types being less common. The prevalence of dementia, especially dementia of the Alzheimer's type and vascular dementia, increases with age, particularly after age 75, with an estimated 70 percent or more of the population over age 85 being afflicted.

The *DSM-IV* notes that, historically, the term dementia implied a progressive or irreversible course. As defined in the *DSM-IV*, however, the term dementia is based on the pattern of cognitive deficits that it manifests and carries no connotation concerning prognosis. Dementias may be progressive, static, or remitting. The reversibility of a dementia depends on the underlying pathology and the availability and timely application of effective treatment. Because the level of disability depends not only on the severity of the individual's cognitive impairments but also on the available social supports, dementia is especially relevant to the underlying theme of this book—that mental illness has an enormous impact not only on the afflicted person but also on loved ones.

The essential feature of dementia is the development of multiple cognitive deficits. These include memory impairment and at least one of the following cognitive disturbances:

1. aphasia (deterioration of language function)
2. apraxis (inability to execute motor activities)
3. agnosia (failure to recognize or identify objects)
4. a disturbance in executive functioning (the ability to think abstractly and to plan, initiate, sequence, monitor, and terminate complex behavior)

Memory Impairment

The cognitive deficits must be sufficiently severe to cause impairment in occupational or social functioning and must represent a decline from a previously higher level of functioning. Memory impairment is required to make the diagnosis of a dementia and is a prominent early symptom. Individuals with dementia become impaired in their ability to learn new material, or they forget previously learned material. While most persons with dementia have both forms of memory impairment, it is sometimes difficult to demonstrate the loss of previously learned material early in the course of the disorder.

One may lose valuables like wallets and keys, forget food cooking on the stove, and become lost in familiar neighborhoods. In advanced stages of dementia, memory impairment is so severe that the person forgets his or her occupation, schooling, birthday, family members, and sometimes even one's own name.

Aphasia

Deterioration of language function (aphasia) may manifest itself in difficulty producing the names of individuals and objects. Speech may become vague and empty, with long circumlocutionary phrases or excessive use of terms of indefinite reference such as "they" or "it." In the advanced stages of dementia, individuals may become mute or have a deteriorated speech pattern characterized by echolalia (echoing what is heard) and palalalia (repeating sounds or words over and over again).

Apraxia

Impaired ability to execute motor activities (apraxia) may also occur despite the fact that motor abilities, sensory function, and comprehension of the required task are still intact. Apraxia may contribute to deficits in cooking, dressing, and writing. Even such simple motor acts as waving goodbye may prove difficult or impossible.

Agnosia

There may also be a failure to recognize or identify objects (agnosia) despite intact sensory functions (vision and touch). Thus, one may have normal visual acuity, yet be unable to identify objects such as chairs and pencils. Eventually, one may be unable to recognize family members or even one's own reflection in the mirror. Similarly, individuals may have normal tactile sensation, yet be unable to identify objects placed in their hands, such as coins or keys, by touch alone.

Disturbance in Executive Functioning

Disturbances in executive functioning are a common manifestation of dementia. Impairment in abstract thinking may be manifested in an individual having difficulty coping with novel tasks and in a person avoiding situations that require the processing of new and complex information. Executive dysfunction is also evident in a reduced ability to shift mental sets, to generate novel verbal or nonverbal information, and to execute serial motor activities (such as counting to ten, reciting the alphabet, and so forth).

The *DSM-IV* emphasizes that the nature and degree of impairment are variable and often depend on the particular social setting of the individual. The same level of cognitive impairment may significantly affect a person's ability to perform a complex job, but not one that is less demanding. Standardized published rating scales that measure physical maintenance (such as personal hygiene), intellectual functioning, and the ability to use implements or tools (such as telephones, washing machines, etc.) can be used to measure the severity of impairment. As noted, a diagnosis of dementia is warranted if there is memory loss and at least one of the other characteristics. Memory loss alone does not warrant the diagnosis.

Associated Features

Associated features of dementia are spatial disorientation, poor judgment and insight, little or no awareness of memory loss or other cognitive abnormalities, and unrealistic assessments of one's abilities. Persons may make plans that are incongruent with their deficits and prognosis (such as traveling alone) and underestimate the risks involved in activities (such as driving a vehicle). Motor disturbances may lead to falls. Also, some individuals with dementia show uninhibited behavior, including making inappropriate jokes, neglecting personal hygiene, exhibiting undue familiarity with strangers, or disregarding conventional rules of social conduct.

The multiple cognitive impairments of dementia are often associated with anxiety, mood, and sleep disturbances. Delusions are common, especially those involving themes of persecution (for example, that misplaced possessions have been stolen). Hallucinations can occur in all sensory modalities, but visual ones are the most common. (This contrasts with schizophrenia where auditory hallucinations are more prevalent.) Delirium is frequently experienced with dementia because the underlying brain disease may increase susceptibility to states of confusion produced by medications or other concurrent general medical conditions. Persons with dementia may be especially vulnerable to physical stress (such as illness or minor surgery) and psychosocial stress (such as going to the hospital or bereavement), and these may exacerbate their intellectual deficits and other associated problems.

Dementia of the Alzheimer's Type

Thus far, we have been considering the general mental disorder known as dementia. Dementia of the Alzheimer's type is an appropriate diagnosis when the course is characterized by gradual onset and continuing cognitive decline. Alzheimer's type tends to be steadily progressive with a loss of three to four points per year on a standard assessment instrument such as the Mini-Mental State Exam. Various patterns of deficits have been observed, but a common one is an insidious onset, with early deficits in recent memory followed by the development of aphasia, apraxia, and agnosia after several years.

Webster's New World College Dictionary defines "insidious" as something "that operates in a slow or not easily apparent manner; thus, more dangerous than it first appears." It also defines "insidious" as "characterized by treachery or slyness, crafty, wily." While the first definition applies formally to Alzheimer's disease, the second seems no less applicable, for this disease is a cunning opponent in the beginning stages, its symptoms being such as to create doubts in the minds of loved ones as to whether it is present or not.

Some persons may show personality changes or increased irritability in the early stages. In the later stages individuals may develop gait and motor dysfunctions, and eventually become mute and bedridden. The average duration of the illness from onset of symptoms to death is eight to ten years. As a type of dementia, it must meet the other criteria: memory loss and one or more additional impairments (aphasia, apraxia, agnosia, disturbance in executive functioning).

As with other types of dementia, it is inappropriate to ascribe Alzheimer's disease to persons whose only cognitive loss is that of memory. (If, however, memory loss is severe, the diagnosis of amnesic disorder is appropriate.) The *DSM-IV* also notes that a person who experiences delirium (a confused state) in which one or more of the characteristics of dementia are present is not necessarily suffering from or on the road to dementia. An indication of the difference is that in delirium the symptoms fluctuate while in dementia they are more stable. Thus, multiple cognitive impairments that are present in an unchanged form for more than three or four months suggest dementia rather than delirium.

The foregoing account of dementia makes clear that it is one of the mental disorders that belong under the heading of "loss of contact with reality." It is therefore similar in this regard to schizophrenia, bipolar or manic-depressive disorder, and major depressive episode. Like schizophrenia, it also has a typical age of onset, as it affects older persons (persons over the age of sixty-five, with prevalence increasing with advancing age).

Sue Miller and Her Father

To gain a sense of its devastating effects on the afflicted individuals and their loved ones, I would now like to turn to Sue Miller's *The Story of My Father* (2003). Sue Miller is the daughter of James Hastings Nichols, a professor at Princeton Theological Seminary until his retirement in 1983. He died in 1991, at the age of seventy-six, due to complications from Alzheimer's disease. While Miller's book includes recollections from earlier periods in their lives, it is largely an account of her father's illness and of her own efforts to come to terms with the fact that he was mentally ill. The book also wrestles with the responsibilities his illness placed upon her as the sibling in closest physical proximity to him in the last years of his life.

At the time she wrote this memoir, Miller was fifty-eight years old, thus two years younger than her mother was when she suffered a sudden heart attack at a dinner party and died on the way to the hospital. Having been asked by the ambulance personnel what medication his wife was taking, James Nichols had driven home to collect the bottle. He was therefore not at her side in the ambulance when she died. As Miller's story unfolds, this, in its own poignant way, was characteristic of his tendency to be disconnected from what was going on around him, a disconnectedness that Miller came to feel was somehow integral to the disease from which he suffered the last several years of his life. Her book is therefore a fitting memoir with which to conclude a book on the "fragile connections" that continue to exist between the mentally afflicted and their loved ones. In the following account, I will focus on the chapters that directly concern his mental illness. I will refer to Miller as "Sue" throughout this chapter to convey the personal tone of her memoir and the fact that it is deeply self-introspective.

I Never Thought I Would Lose My Mind

Following a brief chapter on her father's conscientious objector status in World War II, Miller begins her account of her father's illness in chapter 2 with an event that occurred one morning in June 1986. Having decided to sleep late that morning, she was awakened by her husband. She saw fear in his face as he began speaking to her in a deliberately controlled voice.

The First Incident

What he was saying concerned the police and her father. The police were calling from somewhere in western Massachusetts and apparently had her father in custody. They were on the phone and wanted to speak with her.

She ran downstairs to the phone, and as the voice on the other end of the line spoke, she tried her best to make sense of what he was saying. He said that they had a person in custody whom they had picked up between three and four in the morning in a semirural territory where he had knocked on someone's door, announcing that he was lost. He "claimed" to be her father.

The word "claimed" was both odd and offensive to her—odd that her father's assertion would be open to question, offensive because it seemed that they were doubting his mind. She would have found their word "claim" somewhat more understandable had she known the rest of the story, for he also claimed he had encountered a number of small, strange people in his nocturnal wandering. The caller added that the van he said he had been driving had not turned up despite their search of the area. She asked to speak with him but was not allowed to. Instead, she was to come out, and they would release him to her when she arrived.

As she prepared to make the trip from Boston to western Massachusetts, she and her husband constructed a story that made a kind of sense. Under pressure from his children, who thought he was too isolated since their mother's death six years earlier, her father had arranged to sell his house in Princeton, New Jersey, and to go to live near another daughter in Denver in a new "elderly complex." This was to be a stopgap arrangement until he could gain admission to an ecclesiastical retirement community in California where the waiting list was two or three years long. He had made these arrangements within a year of his wife's death. (She had vigorously opposed this idea because she didn't want to spend her retirement years in the company of ministers and missionaries).

Some of his possessions had been shipped to Denver, others Sue herself had hauled to his summer home in New Hampshire. The last few items were left for him to live with until the closing on his home in New Jersey. He had recently informed Sue on the phone that he was going to rent a small van and take them up to New Hampshire himself. He was planning to spend the summer in New Hampshire and then go to Denver in early fall. Sue and her husband concluded that he had gotten lost in western Massachusetts and "somehow seemed confused enough to warrant a kind of detention, if not arrest" (12).

As she drove, she had trouble imagining that this man, "so modest, so self-effacing as to be almost comical sometimes, so much wishing *not* to trouble anyone" (12–13), could have done what the police claimed he had done. She just could not see him "stumbling around the countryside trying to wake someone, ringing doorbells in the middle of the night. *Bothering People. Not my father*" (13).

When she arrived at the police station, however, she was appalled by his appearance. He looked awful. He was unshaven and clad in his old clothes, worn, wrinkled, and faded. He wore an old canvas hat that was misshapen and stained. He looked like a vagrant. It wasn't, though, so much his clothes that startled her. Rather, "It was the vacancy of his face, the look of nonrecognition—not so much of her as of the world—that made him seem homeless, *lost*, in some profound and permanent sense" (13). Moreover, his responses lacked feeling and depth. He apologized for the inconvenience to her, but casually, as though she'd had to drive a few blocks out of her way for him: "Sorry you had to come get me" (13). That was all.

The police officer gave her his wallet and the few other possessions they had taken from him. They still had not found the van and expressed doubt that there was such a vehicle. When she replied that he had to get from New Jersey to Massachusetts somehow, the officer merely shrugged. After all, he had informed her when she arrived in the station that the people her father had wakened in the night had been frightened of him because he seemed so agitated. The officer also mentioned that her father had been "seeing things." He agreed to call her if and when the van was found. Then she and her father drove off.

Her father was silent in the car, looking diminished and exhausted. When they stopped for breakfast, he ate ravenously, which prompted her to ask him when he had eaten last. He could not remember. She asked him numerous questions while they ate and as they returned to her home in Boston, trying to piece together his itinerary and its timing. It was difficult to figure out, but it became reasonably clear that he had not slept or eaten for twenty-four hours or more. Then he began to volunteer something about the way the stop signs had turned into people in the night. As he talked, there was suddenly more animation in his voice than he had exhibited since she first saw him: "Delight, really—at how they'd spoken to him in the night. Little people" (15).

Attempting to normalize his tale, she inquired, "You mean the tops of the stop signs looked like heads to you?" (15).

He seemed amused, even a bit contemptuous of the flatness of her imagination: "No, they were people. They had bodies—arms and legs."

She was stunned: "And they spoke to you."

He smiled, "Yes."

Unable to bear to hear the answers, she stopped asking questions, realizing that the police had not misrepresented anything. He was exactly the confused, diminished person they had said he was. When he eventually fell asleep, she told herself that lack of sleep and food had created some chemical imbalance that made him hallucinate. As she drove, she looked over at him from time to time, slumped open-mouthed against the car window, his hat riding on the back of his head. She recalls feeling "very distant from him, even angry at him—for his otherness, for what seemed his unconsciousness of the strangeness of what he was going through and what he'd done. I wanted him restored to himself. I wanted my father back. This old geezer made me mad" (15).

Dealing with Dad's Dementia

At home, she fixed him another snack, and made up a bed for him in her son Ben's room, which was located in the basement of the house. He was happy to nap and slept for several hours. Meanwhile, she tried to figure out what to do. She and her husband had planned a two-month trip to France to begin in less than a week. She couldn't possibly let her father return to New Jersey alone to deal with the final clearing out of the house, with his dog, who must be waiting for him with friends or in a kennel, and the van missing somewhere in the countryside.

When her husband came home, she told him some of what seemed to be happening to her father, and they discussed the various options (her father could go to stay with one of her siblings, she could postpone going to France and join her husband later, and so forth). Her husband suggested they see how he was when he woke up and then decide what to do.

Their seventeen-year-old son's bedroom was in a large finished area at the back of the basement. To reach it, one needed to pass through an unfinished part of the basement filled with the accumulated junk of twelve years of living there. Late in the afternoon, she heard odd noises in that part of the basement and called down. After a moment her father appeared in the dim light at the bottom of the stairs, his face smiling. He seemed to see her with pleasure and came up. They had coffee together. She asked questions: How he might have gotten lost, where he thought the van might be. Then he and her husband chatted about events and concerns in their lives. He seemed fine and she began to relax.

But then he said, "You know, the little children in the basement wouldn't say a word when I spoke to them. They wouldn't answer me" (17). He seemed puzzled, perhaps a little hurt, by this.

"What little children do you mean?" she asked.

"Just now, downstairs, Ben and some friends." He looked momentarily confused, then continued, "Or maybe Ben wasn't there. But they wouldn't answer me when I spoke to them. They just moved away."

She reminded him that Ben was seventeen years old and that his friends were big too: "There aren't any little children around anymore."

Just as her husband was also beginning to concur that there weren't any little children in the house, her father said, with a note of triumph in his voice, "There! There goes one."

"Where?" she asked.

He pointed, "There."

She went to where he had pointed and said, "There's no one here, Dad."

He appeared genuinely puzzled, "He must have gone downstairs."

So Sue and her father went downstairs in search of the little children. When their search turned up empty, he agreed with her that there was no one there, and seemed suddenly tired and defeated. They returned upstairs. As they sat in the living room, she said that she didn't think any little children were down there, even earlier, when he first thought he had seen them. After a long pause he said, "So I guess I was seeing things."

She replied, "I think you were," and then noted that he had not slept or eaten in a couple of days and this does things to a person, chemically. They sat in silence for awhile. Finally he smiled ruefully and said, "Doggone, I never thought I'd lose my *mind*" (19).

Miller suggests that there was an unspoken but implicit clause at the beginning of her father's sentence, something like, "I've tried to think of all the ways I might get old, but–." She understood, for the first time, that he had wondered how old age and death would come to him and now, "he was even a little bemused that they should take this unexpected form" (19). He seemed at this moment "to be getting the news about his fate, about how it would be for him." When he took it in, he not only seemed to accept it, but was also somehow interested in it. This, she now feels, was "a moment as characteristic of him as any I can think of in his life, and as brave. Noble, really, I've come to feel" (19).

First Steps with Dementia in the Family

A plan was developed with her sister in Denver. Her father would go there ahead of schedule while Sue would go to New Jersey to take care of the last details in the house, figure out what to do with his car, fetch his dog, and deal with the missing van. Her father, however, would have none of this. He would take a bus home, or fly, and the van would turn up. There was no need for her to trouble herself on his account, as he had been enough of a bother already. When, by arrangement, his daughter in Denver called to invite him to come to Denver right away, his response was the same.

Finally, after Sue and her husband seemed to have exhausted all the arguments for why they could not allow him to go off on his own, she tried one more tactic. She suggested that "if their positions were reversed" and she had shown up at his house, exhausted and seeing things that weren't there, wouldn't he consider it his responsibility, his duty, to be sure that she was all right and certainly not let her go off alone again? A long silence ensued during which he seemed to see his position clearly. She, too, began to realize what it meant: "He understood, and we understood: we were taking the first step into his illness, whatever it was, together. We would be in charge of him now" (24). He looked at her, then looked down: "No," he said quietly, "No, you're right. I wouldn't let you go."

Next day, she and her husband took him to the airport and saw him off to Denver. She went down to New Jersey. When she arrived at his house, the sight was awful to her. He had been living without furniture, a mattress on the floor to sleep on, dog hairs everywhere. She took his dog to his sister's house in Connecticut. The van had turned up and been towed to a nearby garage. Someone at the garage agreed to drive it back to New Jersey for an exorbitant price. The "driver" added insult to injury by making suggestive comments on the phone about her lovely voice, wanting to meet her, and so on. At his mercy, she was "very, very polite to him because I felt I had to be, but it seemed the final, almost laughable irrelevant unpleasantness to get through" (25). Sue and her husband left for France on schedule. A few weeks later, her father, accompanied by her sister, returned to New Hampshire so that he could have his summer, however abbreviated, in his vacation home. Later that fall, her sister called to say that he had been diagnosed with "probable Alzheimer's disease."

A Momentary Dwelling in Introspection and Regret

In chapter 3, after a brief account of how Alois Alzheimer, a German doctor, came to have his name attached to this devastating mental illness, Miller notes that the word "probable" was employed at that time because the only certain diagnosis was by autopsy, after death. Now, she notes, several genes are known to predispose it, so DNA testing would be a possible diagnostic tool. The expenses, however, and the fact that for the patient, already afflicted, it would be useless, means that it is seldom employed.

Sue was the one of her four siblings who saw her father the most after their mother died. She was the oldest daughter and unmarried at the time, so she and her father spent time together, especially at his summer home in New Hampshire. During the six years between their mother's death and the two daughters' insistence that he sell his house in New Jersey, Sue had noticed the little ways in which he was failing. Initially, however, no one else shared her perception. Her brother would say that "He's fine with *me*," leading Sue to "feel accused of imagining things or of responding to Dad in a way that was somehow *responsible* for making him seem vague" (29). Also, when she noticed an occasional oddness, especially in his speech patterns, these oddities came and went, so it was altogether possible that she *was* making something out of nothing.

But then the point came when she knew she had to try to do something about how she felt, as she had seen it once too often, too clearly. His friends and his last living sister had also begun to ask her about it. Given her father's personality and her own, she "moved in slow motion" (29). At first, she tried to talk to him about it, suggesting that he might be suffering from depression, a plausible explanation. She would mention possible medications. But he "was characteristically vague in response," as if to say that it was none of her business. Moreover, she was reluctant to be intrusive. She recalls writing once to his sister that "it seemed wrong to insist to Dad that he needed to have a particular *kind* of old age: as long as he was *all right*, why shouldn't he be sad sometimes, or even scatty, or even not as tidy and fastidious as he once was?" (30).

But *was* he all right? Uncertain herself when his friends asked her, she took the next step of poking into his medicine chest. She made a list of the contents so that she could talk to her own doctor to find out what they were and what they might mean. She discovered an antidepressant among them and relaxed a bit. Apparently, he had gone to his doctor himself, had been diagnosed, and was being treated. But when she checked again, several months later, the bottle was still at the same level, nearly full. Among the possible reasons, the most likely was that he had decided on his own that he did not need them. Given his nonresponsive answers to her questions, she reluctantly called the doctor whose name appeared on the medicine bottle. This doctor, however, was no longer his doctor and had not seen him for several years. He mentioned, however, noticing some memory loss before then. His current doctor *had* seen him within the year, had prescribed some medications, but thought he was in good shape. He didn't know him well enough to comment on memory loss.

Changing His Circumstances

She felt utterly stymied at this point. Unless her father was willing or able to talk to her honestly and openly about his health, there was almost nothing she could do. What she *did* do, finally, and with her sister's support, was to pressure him to change his circumstances. Now, her sister, living ten minutes away from him, found him a new doctor, insisted on thorough medical exams, and got a diagnosis. Sue felt a "guilty relief" in knowing that her perceptions had been accurate all along. What troubled her, however, was that she had not done something earlier: "In my own defense, I'll say that this was born in part of ignorance. I didn't really know much about the disease and the details of its horrible course. And in any case, the relief was mixed, of course, with real sorrow for Dad. But the diagnosis signaled the end to the nameless anxiety that I'd felt had been mine alone for years, and for that, no matter what, I was grateful" (32).

What she herself had been victim of is what the *DSM-IV* calls the "insidious" nature of the disease itself. As noted, Alzheimer's is a form of dementia whose onset is especially insidious, operating in a slow, not easily recognizable manner. Because of this, it seems crafty and wily, creating confusion not only in the mind of the afflicted one but also in the minds of loved ones. These caretakers debate whether something is in fact wrong, or whether they are merely imagining it. Perhaps they are exaggerating the small lapses that everyone experiences from time to time.

Death via Alzheimer's

Sue notes that her father's obituary in 1991, five years after the episode involving the missing van and his hallucinations, indicated that he died of Alzheimer's disease. But, "of course, no one, strictly speaking, dies of Alzheimer's disease. They die of other things, horrible things that happen to them because they *have* Alzheimer's disease" (32). She cites Sherwin B. Nuland's list in *How We Die* (1993) of some of the more immediate causes of death: starvation, because you've forgotten how to eat; pneumonia, because you've forgotten how to walk, how to sit, and your lungs suffer for that; or urinary tract infections and septic decubitus ulcers (or bedsores, which was the cause of death in the case of Dr. Alzheimer's original patient) because you cannot get out of bed (32–33).

Her father's death-by-Alzheimer's occurred when he was living in a continuing care facility forty minutes from Boston. Once he had been diagnosed, he could not go from Denver to the retirement community in California because they had no arrangements there for dealing with Alzheimer's disease. Even with the elaborate support system her sister had set in place in Denver, he had decided that when he got to the place where he could not live alone, he would return back east to live near Sue. She had found Sutton Hill, an especially nice continuing care facility. When a space opened up for him in the fall of 1988, two years after he had gone to live in Denver, it was her sister's turn to experience relief as she sent him back to Massachusetts.

In the three years he lived at Sutton Hill until his death, he moved from being "a fairly functional person to a completely incompetent one" (32). As the family member "in charge" of him as he moved through some of the more humiliating and degrading stages of the disease, Sue struggled with herself "to come up with the helpful response, the loving response, the ethical response." She also "wanted to give him as much of myself as I could" (33).

At the same time, she desired to have her own life. She wanted to be able to work productively (she had already written several novels) and not allow her "sorrow and despair" over her father to color her daily relations with her husband or her contact with her son, who was by then in college. To ready herself for this ordeal, she read a few books on how to approach it and joined a support group of caregivers. But none of the things she read or heard from the group (such as trying not to feel guilty about her negative feelings toward her father, making a special effort to get out often and see friends, and so forth) "seemed to connect with the feelings I had." In fact, she found most of it to be "irrelevant at best, condescending at worst" (34).

The "strains" she felt in her relations with her father were not that he required too much of her time or even—as was the case for some persons in her caregivers group—that he might be draining her financial resources. He received good care at Sutton Hill and really needed very little of her time. He had enough money of his own to manage a long extended illness. Moreover, he wasn't "difficult." If anything, "he wished to be as little trouble as possible. For as long as he could, he acceded to every rule made for him, complied with every restriction—and never complained" (34). In a sense, "the disease oddly intensified—or maybe just laid bare—who he really was. Even when he was deeply gone into it, the phrases of self-effacement rose easily to his lips. 'Oh, don't bother.' 'That's too much trouble.' 'You shouldn't have to do that.' His dying itself was quiet and undemanding—no great drama, not much suffering, I believe. A kind of final self-effacement" (40). (Later, however, Miller will question this view of him as "self-effacing" and search for a better way of expressing "who he really was.")

Sue's Awful Task

What made it hard, even awful, was her sense that her own task was not to let him see how she felt about him. She could not reveal her own awareness that he was ill, would only get worse, and was dying in what was to her the worst way possible. Also, it was not the big decisions but the small ones "that confounded and occasionally dumbfounded" her: Like how to handle the fact that he often thought the phone was some sort of fire alarm or a doorbell and got agitated trying to respond (35).

Those times when he did remember to pick up the phone, it was not unusual for him simply to hold it, having forgotten what to do next. If he successfully got to the next stage and actually lifted it to his ear, he often had it reversed, the earpiece at his mouth. So if she heard silence on the line after the pickup, her eventual strategy was to bellow into her own receiver, instruct him not to hang up but to turn the receiver around, and so forth. Or how direct should she be where his obvious failings were concerned? On an outing, when she needed to visit the restroom, should she lock him in the car, take him with her to the ladies room, or merely tell him to wait, that she would be right back? Feeling that the first option would be demeaning to him, the second too crudely intimate (acceptable if he were a small child), and the third too risky (he might wander off), she instead cut the outing short. This left her feeling guilty for having deprived him of the pleasure of a leisurely walk in the park.

But hardest of all was the experience of watching the person she had known begin to disappear, little by little, before her very eyes. The disintegration of her picture of him was so difficult to bear. For the others in the family who did not see him at the end, who did not witness his slow decline, he may live intact in their memories, much as he was before his illness began to overtake him: "But this isn't true for me. It was in part to exorcise my final haunting images of my father that I wanted to look at, to explain, the way he fragmented and lost himself in his illness; and who he was before it" (40). In writing this account of her father, she hoped to be able to reconstruct her father again for herself, "imagining him whole, putting together the pieces that slowly disintegrated and broke off" (41).

Always Disconnected

This very effort to see him whole again, however, revealed an irony of sorts. The irony lay in the fact that he had always "seemed disconnected" from his own personal history: "He spoke only rarely of his own memories of childhood or youth, and then never at length. And I don't think he *used* his personal memories in coming to understand himself. In that sense, in the sense that one means it in contemporary post-Freudian America, I don't think that he *did* understand himself" (41). She adds, parenthetically, "He knew his Freud, of course. He jokingly said to me once that he was a prime example of what repression could accomplish," meaning, she believes, that there was a causal connection between his inability to recollect or even think about much from his early life and "his energetic, virtually nonstop professional output" (41).

Significantly, "He had no recollection, for example, of his own mother, though he was eight when she died. None. This seems extraordinary to me. Repression indeed" (41). Less surprisingly, he did not recall when, as a thirteen-year-old, he asked his stepmother whether there was any insanity in her family, a suggestion that she vigorously denied. When Sue, having heard the story herself from the woman, her grandmother, asked him about it, he laughed, said he could have asked this but didn't really know (42). As the question would have had no direct genetic importance to him, Sue's own curiosity concerned whether he remembered the impulse to be rather nasty or snide toward his stepmother, whose marriage to his father had occurred when he was ten or eleven.

Also significant in her effort to make him whole again in her memory was her own first memory of him, a memory "not truly of him but of his absence" (43). She was five, and he was in Germany with a group of fellow professors "on a mission to help heal the postwar university system there, decimated by the flight and murder of Jews and resisters" (41). His absence for six months or so followed on the heels of her mother's deep depression only the year before. Although none of her mother's children remembers that episode specifically, her symptoms—"the profound retreat from us into sorrow, the sound of weeping behind a closed door, the sudden tearful recoil from what seemed a harmless remark"—were already part of who she was for them (47). That her father would leave "a depressive woman of twenty-nine with four children under seven to take care of, one of them only a few weeks old, seems strange to me now, almost unimaginable" (47). It was only years later that she thought of "how much he must have *wanted* to go" (48).

In chapter 5, Miller notes that later in her father's life, but before he was obviously ill, she spent long parts of several summers alone with him, and he talked about himself more than he had ever done before. During that time he occasionally expressed regrets to her about the detachment, or distance, that enabled him to roll with whatever punch resulted from his mother's moods, but which was also "the very quality that drove her mad" (69). He thought he had hurt Sue's two brothers by not being more involved with them as children, and he blamed himself for not helping his wife control her drinking and smoking:

> But this was a brief period, really, in his long life—only a momentary dwelling in introspection and regret. Very quickly his dispassion, brought on this time by his disease, came to him again. The dying of his brain took away the possibility of some new way of looking at things which he seemed on the verge of finding. And perhaps, after all, this was a variety of kindness. (69)

Her father's disconnectedness throughout the years that she had known him also prompts Miller to wonder if the disease, in some nascent form, was there all along. She cites an admittedly "highly speculative research project" using writing samples collected early in life from nuns whose histories through old age and death were known and whose lives, because they all lived in the same convent, were presumably controlled after the age of twenty or so for many variables. Those whose writing samples were more elemental—whose thinking, as expressed in the writing, was more reductive—had a very high incidence of later mental impairment or posthumously diagnosed Alzheimer's diseases. In contrast, the writing samples of nuns at twenty-two who were still mentally intact fifty-eight years later reflected "high idea density" and "greater grammatical complexity" (71). One possible implication of this study is that there may be "other markers of the disease earlier than the now-familiar dementia; that there will be aspects of the personality or behaviors we think of now as completely normal that we will come to understand as connected to the illness and symptomatic of it" (72).

After reading this article, Miller spent a few days looking back at her father's "younger self" and wondering whether "some aspects of his personality that seemed so essentially *who he was* might really have been the disease expressing itself. Or, alternatively, whether the disease was so entwined with who he was, even early on, as to be part of him" (72). It might, for example, account for his even temperament, his imperviousness to his children's mayhem and noise, his abstractedness and distractedness (72).

One might then assume that her father's "disconnectedness" from his own early history and his "distractedness" from his wife and children was somehow reflective of the disease in nascent form. That being the case, there was, it appears, a powerful countervailing connectedness that may have played a role in the fact that, unlike most Alzheimer's sufferers, his long-term memory remained intact until his death. This connectedness lay in the fact that both he and his wife could trace their roots through New England families who left England and Scotland for America in the seventeenth and eighteenth centuries, the first of them arriving on the Mayflower.

Moreover, both his own and his wife's fathers and grandfathers had been ministers, and on his side of the family "the line of clergy goes even more deeply back" (63). Like himself, his father, too, had been a church historian. Conceivably, Sue suggests, this longstanding intergenerational history, the fact that he was descended from a long line of clergy, and that he was a church historian were factors in his retention of his long-term memory. Thus he was able to "connect with people from his past—and with me and my brothers and sister—until the end of his life" (39).

Well after he had been diagnosed, he wondered why an old friend felt that she needed to tell him her name when she greeted him, as he didn't need her reminder (79). On the other hand, the very fact that his long-term memory remained intact made his difficulty retaining new information all the more apparent. He had difficulty, for example, with new names. The woman who came to help him get dressed and shaved acquired a variety of women's names and even, on occasion, was simply referred to as "that boy." Her name was Marlene, and he was very fond of her, but there was no way for him to retain this little fact. Why?

[The] part of his brain whose function was to transfer new information into memory, the hippocampus, was being destroyed by Alzheimer's disease. New names, new skills—how to open the door on *my* car, for instance, or how to work the remote controls for a television—these couldn't be retained for more than a few days because they couldn't get past the hippocampus into permanent "storage" in other parts of the brain. (77)

Linguistic Troubles

He also began to have trouble with ordinary nouns, and his speech became increasingly riddled with substitutions. When the region of the brain that is specific to nouns and naming things is damaged, the rhythms of speech are not affected, but one compensates by switching from nouns to pronouns and to generic words and categories. When Sue's brother, his son, and his son's fiancee visited her father, he remembered the visit, but he said that Bob and Marc had been accompanied by "a Chinese man" (77).

When a polite, mentally intact resident at Sutton Hill asked, "Oh, is this your daughter?" he replied, "No, I'm his mother" (78). Still, he could remember his wife by her name and "remember her—not always whether she was dead or alive, but *her*—her being, her essence" (78). Stories about her could still lighten his face and make him laugh. And he almost always recognized Sue. He hesitated once when she arrived, seeming not to know who she was, but he always greeted her warmly and understood their relation to one another, even if he could not always represent it accurately to others.

Visual Failure

The visual pathways in his brain also began to fail. The first thing to go was his ability to read. He could still pick out words, indicating that the problem was not his eyesight, but he could not connect these symbols on the page with the meaning. He believed that the problem *was* his eyes, but a laser treatment to uncloud his cornea (a common occurrence after cataract surgery) did not give back what he imagined it would—"his ability to read and, beyond that, probably, some old sense of himself" (79). He continued to pester Sue to make another appointment with the eye doctor. When she finally acceded to his request, she asked the doctor ahead of time to try to help him understand that new glasses would not help. Her father listened to the doctor's explanation that the problem was organic, not, however, with his eyes, but with the message between his eyes and his brain. For a few days he remembered what the doctor had said, then forgot and began to agitate for another appointment with the eye doctor (79).

Increasingly, too, he "misread" the visual. Shadows became for him not the absence of light but dark objects, and their presence was inexplicably disturbing to him. His own shadow underfoot on a sunny day was often an irritant, a strange black animal dogging his path. He would sometimes kick or swat at it as they walked along. In the later stages of his illness, he stopped seeing food on the left side of his plate. At first, everyone worried about his appetite as he was already becoming very thin, but then an attendant recognized that he always neglected the food on the left side of the plate, so he began to rotate the plate a half circle, and her father would eat everything.

Some apparent "hallucinations" were a misreading of what was there and not a pure invention. The "bull" he saw in the yard outside his window was a misreading of a Victorian iron bench with two curving back pieces like horns and underneath, a pair of floral motifs that looked like eyes. Other times, it was hard to say what was going on. One day, as he and Sue were leaving his room, he gestured at his bathrobe hanging from a hook, and laughed, "Dave Swift. He's been standing there all day." As she looked at the bathrobe, she could see the resemblance to her Uncle Dave, a tall, skinny man, in plaid clothing. But was this a joke, a misreading of visual clues, or a hallucination? Who could say for sure (80)? And what were the impediments that caused him to tiptoe so carefully over something she couldn't see, or that prompted him to get down on the floor and crawl around it? Were they solely due to disturbances in his visual pathways or pure hallucinations? In any case— and perhaps the distinction itself is purely academic—he was typical of Alzheimer's sufferers in the fact that delusional experiences are primarily visual (not primarily auditory as is the case in schizophrenia).

Alzheimer's Delusions

One of his delusions involved his belief that there was an underground railroad at Sutton Hill. When he told Sue's husband about it, her husband laughed, thinking he was making a joke about his wish to escape. But later in the day her father pointed out the spot where he thought the train pulled in. The nurse, Marlene, told Sue that she found him at this spot more than once, and that he had informed her that he was waiting for the train. In a sense, this delusion had a certain logic, for the shops, bank, post office, and grocery store of Sutton Hill were located along what was called Main Street, an indoor walkway with an old-fashioned clock tower at one end: "All had whimsical storefronts. Why not give Main Street a railroad in your imagination too?" (81).

Some of his delusions were painful, such as one he had about Sue's sister being abducted by terrorists. Others, such as the wild lawn and pajama party at which the residents put on a play together, were pleasant. Sometimes he would report hearing a friend lecture or preach or mention having seen his wife. Sue came to feel that these were the residues of dreams, "dreams that seemed no less real to him than the fractured reality he had to live through each day, and so, in his interpretation, became a part of that reality" (81).

Again citing brain studies, she notes that the hallucinations and delusions in Alzheimer's sufferers have their locus in the same part of the brain in which schizophrenics are disturbed—primarily those responsible for receiving visual and auditory signals. But they differ in the fact that schizophrenics—perhaps, in part, because the messages are more likely to be auditory—see themselves at the center of the delusion and as main actors in the drama. In dementia one is more likely to be the observer of events about which one is helpless to do anything (82).

Occasional Violence

As death approached, he was occasionally violent, and one time he was violent with Sue. She was struggling physically with him to bring him inside after a walk because he didn't want to come in. Resistant, "he looked at me with hatred and contempt and I think he didn't know me at all. I hope not, actually. I hope he did think I was someone else" (84).

When she told an old friend of hers about his occasional violence, he said, "Isn't it strange that under that gentle, sweet exterior there should be all that violence?" This comment, in the midst of a conversation in which she was "trying to be pleasant and conversational," produced in her "a real anger, even a contempt, for my friend in his misunderstanding" (84).

To her, he was employing a "Freudian" model "that saw the constraint of the superego eaten away by the disease, and the elemental core, the uncontrolled center, the id, as still remaining, unbuffered. The violent Dad who was secretly always there, emerging now that he'd lost control of himself" (83).

No, she said, "that's not the way it worked. It was his *brain,* not a theoretical construct in his *mind,* that was being destroyed. He was *organically* a different person" (84). If so, however, then honesty demanded that she acknowledge that her belief that "the good stuff" he retained was because of "who he was" was itself a "fiction" she did not want to relinquish. (Later, I will suggest a different way in which someone with Freudian leanings might understand what was happening to him toward the end of his life; this understanding is congruent with her own understanding of "who he was" [169].)

If she resented this seemingly "Freudian" interpretation of her father's violence at the end, her account of the last time she saw him while he was still conscious lends itself to another more favorable and more truly "Freudian" interpretation. This interpretation would suggest that he continued to "know" her as the little girl he had always known her to be, even after she had grown up to be the adult woman who stood before and greeted him now:

When I came into the room, he was standing by his crib bed, gripping its rails with white-knuckled intensity and staring fixedly at something he was seeing on his blanket. He was slightly bent at this point, a gentle Parkinsonian curve to his back. I spoke to him, but he didn't seem to hear me. I went over and touched him, I swung my head just under his face and looked up at him, smiling. "Hi, Dad," I said. He started. "Why, Susie!" he said, calling me by my little girl name. And it seemed that he was actually *seeing* me as a little girl in that moment, his smile was so delighted, his voice so light and glad. (84)

And perhaps there was also something deeply "Freudian" about his request, which he often voiced as she got up to leave, "Say...are you driving? I was wondering if, maybe, you could give me a lift home" (85). Clearly, she had come to be associated with, and perhaps to personify, home, with all its attendant associations and meanings.[1]

Of Course I'm Sure I Was There

In chapter 8, Miller focuses on her father's residence at Sutton Hill. She notes that he was hallucinating from the time he arrived back East to live near her in this continuing care facility in suburban Boston. As this had been only an occasional problem in Denver, she believes the transition to a new, comparatively tiny place (from a two-bedroom apartment to a single room with lavatory) triggered the change. There was also the loss of his books (from a dozen or so bookshelves in Denver to a single one in Boston) and the sudden absence of Sue's sister and her children, who had been a part of his everyday life in Denver.

In retrospect, Sue would have chosen a place for him based on proximity over programs, elegance, and even reputation. It took her forty minutes to drive out to Sutton Hill. This meant that frequent short trips or having him over for a quick meal were largely precluded. Most weeks she saw him only once or twice: "He was, then, really institutionalized, and it was damaging to him. The progression of his disease from this point on was more rapid than it had been before. He changed, and changed again" (119). As he did so, she felt the constant need and pressure to change in relation to his changes.

He never really understood where he was at Sutton Hill. He had to be reminded why he was there over and over, and then he would forget again. When he first arrived, he could still give a kind of lip service to the explanation that he had Alzheimer's disease, but as time went on, Sue would have to remind him that he was at Sutton Hill because they could care for him through the course of the disease. These reminders were in response to his questions about when he would be going "home" or how long he had to stay "in this place" (119).

Changing Reality

Initially, Sue would try to correct him in his delusional life. At the beginning, she had some success in this regard: "No, when you get close you can see it's just a reflection, not someone out there watching you," or "No, that's just a dog barking, not a person calling out" (119–20). When corrected, he would be able to step away from his visions and comment on the oddity of it all. Slowly, however, he was unable to accept her version of things over his own, and conversations in which she corrected him began to create an insurmountable barrier between the two of them. So instead of representing "reality" to him, she began, instead, to enter, as empathically as possible, into his own experiential or inner reality:

> Now when he spoke of animals in the building or visits from my mother, I would commiserate or be pleased for him. And most of the time I managed to feel these things—the appropriate sadness or pleasure to accompany the delusion. I thought of him as *having had* the experience he reported. I thought of them as being part of his reality, a part I needed to accommodate and accept. (120)

In the end, she did accommodate and accept this part of his reality, and so thoroughly "that it began to strike me as odd when others didn't or couldn't. The nursing staff, for instance, was completely unable to make this leap" (120). When he spoke delusionally to them in her presence, they were openly dismissive. They repeated his "mistakes" to her with open contempt. This bothered her, more than a little: "Had they had no training in the way these events seemed to occur to a delusional Alzheimer's patient? I wondered. Could they not flex their imagination a little bit? Their compassion?" (120).

Sometimes, her father's hallucinations were painful. There was his conviction that someone had stolen his books from him and that they were locked somewhere in the basement of the building. He would often ask her to come with him to find them. Initially, she would say that she didn't really think the books were there and that it was her understanding that he and her sister had sorted through them and disposed of most of them. But this "cut no ice" with him, so they would walk around the halls looking for the passageway that would take them to the chamber where the books were kept. They would arrive, to his great confusion, at the activities room, the lounge, someone's office, or the country store. A dead end was evidently the result of a remembered doorway having been plastered over. He would wander around in search of his books when she wasn't there, and this bothered the staff. She decided not to inform them of the purpose of his wanderings because they would only insist that there was no basement and no books, and he would conclude that they were in on a plot to steal his books from him.

Most often, however, the hallucinations that she had chosen to accept as part of his reality were pleasant ones. As noted earlier, her mother came to visit him. So did his parents. He also enjoyed lively visits from friends. And then a pattern or structure began to emerge:

> Sutton Hill became some kind of university, a university in which my father's role was multifarious and changeable. Increasingly, when I'd ask him what he'd been doing, what was new, he'd answer that he'd been preparing a lecture. Or that he had been to a lecture (and he did, in fact, go to some in this well-organized community—on transcendentalism, on art history—which probably reinforced the nature of his fantasies). (121)

Often he would have the sense—common to dream life—that he was either terribly late, or terribly unprepared, "but more and more of the time there was one specific context for this—a scholarly context" (121). One time he reported that he was supposed to lecture on *Hamlet.* He shook his head. Yes, he knew *Hamlet,* but to give a lecture on it? He wasn't sure he could do it, and, in any case, it would be a real chore to prepare. One afternoon, toward the end of one of her visits, he said, "You know, one thing I haven't figured out about this place." "What's that?" "Well, no one ever seems to *graduate* from here." She burst out laughing, so he laughed too, partly at her amusement, as he was unaware that what he had said was enormously funny (123).

The Solitary Life

When a therapist expressed concern that he didn't attend exercises, or musical and craft activities but was always sitting or dozing in his chair, Sue defended his solitariness, pointing out that he had never liked crafts or swing music. She also suggested that she needn't worry about him "because his delusional life was unusually full and satisfying" (122). In retrospect, she wonders if she should have wished for him that he embrace the activities offered to him, for perhaps if he had done these things, he would have made friendships of a sort "and stayed more firmly in touch with all of us too" (122).

In fact, however, she didn't do this. Instead she "welcomed the sense of usefulness and purpose his delusions gave him." If she had to do it over again, she would not have changed her approach: "I would choose to have my father feel happy and competent in some parallel universe, rather than have him build something from popsicle sticks or learn line dancing or reminisce publicly—he who almost never spoke of himself or of his past" (123).

One time, however, his delusions took on a more ominous tone. That morning she arrived after a fire drill during the night. All the residents had been awakened from their sleep and guided or taken outside on the grounds. Her father reported, however, that there had in fact been a fire and that "there were little children killed." Entering imaginatively into his delusions about having to prepare a lecture on *Hamlet* was one thing. This was quite another. Should she pretend a grief she didn't have? Finally she questioned the accuracy of his report.

"Are you sure, Dad?"

"Of course I'm sure. I was there."

"But could it have been a nightmare?"

"It was no nightmare. There were children who died. And everyone around here acts as if they were just…puppies or something" (125).

Sue suggested that the staff was no less upset than he was, but they had to keep the place running. Perhaps they were saving their mourning for later.

His response was sharp, "They are not," and he looked at her "with a gaze as cold and critical as he ever directed at me. Clearly he believed I was as inhumane, as inhuman, as they. And worse, that I was an apologist for them, for their attitude" (125).

Finally, she said she knew how awful it must be for him and that she couldn't begin to tell him how sorry she was that he had to go through this terrible ordeal.

But this did not mollify him. Instead, he replied, indignantly, "I'm not talking about myself. I'm talking about little children."

And when she replied, "I know, Dad, I know, but I was sympathizing with you, with your feelings," he said, "That's hardly the point" (125).

They talked a while longer—or, rather, she talked and he stared coldly at her or at nothing in particular—and she left without taking him for a walk, reading to him, getting the mail, or any of the things they usually did. He was chilly toward her the next few times she visited, though he may not have remembered why, as they never spoke of the fire or the children again. Then, slowly, "his illness closed over the event or his feelings about it," and he forgot her "callousness." Could she have handled this delusion differently? Even now, she doesn't know and finds it impossible to figure out if there is "some lesson I could have learned from all this" (125).

A Wrong Response

Another time, she knew instantly that her response to one of his delusions was wrong. He fell in love with Marlene, a large woman in her thirties with a lovely, softly pretty face. As his private aide, she woke him every morning, dressed him, helped him shave and brush his teeth, did his laundry, took his dry cleaning out, and often took him out for walks. She talked to him easily and sympathetically about her children and his. While she corrected his hallucinations and delusions, she wasn't insistent or unkind about them, and she was protective of him with the nursing staff.

While he never mastered her name with any consistency, he would often speak affectionately of her when Sue came to visit. Over the eighteen or so months that she cared for him, she began to appear in his delusional life. Then, slowly, she became its focus: "He would report to me that he's seen her socially. They went to faculty gatherings together, or lectures, and he was pleased that others in his world liked her, that she was comfortable being among his colleagues with him, in spite of her non-academic background" (126).

When he talked about these events, Sue would say, "how nice" and then carefully mention Marlene's husband and her children. He did not seem uncomfortable with these references, nor did he seem to deny their existence. To her, this was reflective of the fact that to "the Alzheimer's brain it seems there doesn't need to be any adjustment or reconciliation between two conflicting perceived realities" (127).

One summer day, however, when Sue asked him, as she usually did, what was new, he began, "Oh, nothing much." Then, as though just recollecting it, he said, "Say! I got married!" His strong laugh of pleasure followed.

Sue, laughing, offered her congratulations and asked, "Who did you marry?"

He replied, "Oh, you know, Arlette."

"Oh, Marlene."

"Yes."

"I like Marlene."

"Yes, she's a fine person."

The conversation shifted to other topics. Sue thought no more about it, but realized, in retrospect, that she should have. In his mind, this had been a consistent and prolonged delusional episode–the courtship itself had lasted several months–and she should have anticipated, therefore, that he "would take the next logical step after his marriage" (127). About a week later, Marlene phoned, sounding tense and embarrassed. He had suggested to her they go to bed together. She added, "It didn't really *bother* me, you know. He was very nice about it, really. And I sort of brushed it off. I told him I was there just to be his friend, you know, that it wasn't part of the deal." She thought, however, that Sue should know, because she felt she should report the incident to the nursing staff, "You know, in case it happens with someone else." She was apologetic. She didn't like having to report it, and wanted Sue to know that her loyalty was to Mr. Nichols (127–28).

Sue said that *she* was the one who owed Marlene an apology, as she should have told her that she was part of an elaborate delusion and that recently her father had mentioned to her that he was married to Marlene. They both had a good laugh about it. The next day, however, the social service worker called to report the episode to Sue. Sue offered her interpretation based on her awareness of his belief that there had been a proper courtship and a formal wedding, and that sexual relations would be the next step. But the social worker felt that she was making excuses for her father.

Sue had read that some Alzheimer's sufferers go through a stage of inappropriate sexual aggressiveness, and assumed the social worker was also aware of this feature of Alzheimer's, and that she felt they were witnessing this turn in her father's disease. But Sue thinks otherwise: "I think that what happened was born of genuine feeling, not illness. I don't know what the experience of loving Marlene was like for my father—and it's true it was a feeling he might not have had if he hadn't been ill—but I believed then and I still believe that he did love her" (128).

Wandering

As his delusional life thickened and deepened, he lost his freedom to be outside alone. Twice he had stayed away too long on his walks, and the staff had to go out to find him. Another time a nurse had found him outside in the garden in the middle of the night—he had heard a dog barking and thought it needed help. He could take walks with Sue and Marlene, but his patio door was locked, so he couldn't even step outside alone.

During the first year of his residence, Sue signed him up to attend the series of five Friday afternoon symphony concerts that Sutton Hall residents attended together. All bought tickets separately and therefore didn't all sit together, but the staff arranged for another resident to look after him during intermission and at the end of the concert. Once he failed to appear in the lobby at intermission, however. Apparently thinking the concert was over, he wandered outside the Symphony Hall. A search after the concert failed to turn him up. Sutton Hall was notified, and the social worker immediately called the police.

When Sue was notified, her husband went out to search for him while she remained at home in the event the police called. (This was before cell phones). Around nine-thirty, the police called and said they had him in custody. He had wandered into the Roxbury neighborhood and had sat down on someone's doorstep to rest. A passerby spoke to him, recognized that he was confused and delusional, and notified the police. When the police brought him to Sue's home, he seemed oblivious to what had happened. She asked him where he thought he was going when he left the Symphony Hall? "Well, I thought I'd go home, I suppose" (134).

This episode illustrates an effect of Alzheimer's on the mind that Sue considers its most representative feature, that of *wandering*.

> There's a need to get going, an impulse to travel, but it's discon-
> nected utterly from the notion of destination. It is as though

someone had snipped in two the thread that usually connects motivation with activity. Absent also is the sense of pleasurable aimlessness that is part of the *meaning* of wandering for the unafflicted. Purposiveness without purpose, directedness without direction, need without want—these are its hallmarks. (131)

It's as if the *wandering* is a metaphor for the devastation that occurs in the brain itself as its neural pathways become disconnected.

In one sense, his wandering around the city of Boston was merely an extension of his tendency to wander the hallways of Sutton Hill. Since he was the only Alzheimer's sufferer on his floor, other residents would call for him at meal times to walk him down to the day room. Once he wandered upstairs, entered another resident's room, and lay down on her bed. When she returned and found him there, she was both frightened and outraged, feeling that he had done this deliberately, that he had inappropriate sexual intentions toward her (136).

Chapter 8 concludes with an episode in which he imagined there were two Sues, the one with whom he was speaking and the one to whom he wanted to send a message. Eventually, she gave up trying to persuade him that she was the very person he was trying to contact and suggested that he dictate his message and she would see that the other Sue received it. The message, however, became circular: "Dear Sue, I am writing to the one we know as Sue. To be in touch. So that Sue can hear what I need to tell her."

When the Sue sitting in front of him asked what he needed to tell the other Sue, he replied, "That I need to be in touch with Sue." On reflection, she felt that he was getting at some deep reality in his confusion, that over the period of time that he had been at Sutton Hall she had become a different Sue from the one he had known before. She had become "a caretaker Sue," "a cheerful, dismissive Sue," a Sue who, from his perspective, "was grossly insensitive to the shocking and astonishing and sometimes painful things that went on daily in his universe" (137). She realized then that even as he was greatly altered, so was she, "and strangely, in some of the very same ways he was: made bland and callous, *reduced* by Alzheimer's disease" (137).

You Don't Know Who You're Dealing With

Chapter 9 begins with an account of his move to new quarters in Sutton Hall where he would, in theory, receive more concentrated care. Within days, however, "the move that was to have helped him in the course of his disease accelerated it dramatically" (139). He became "radically more demented," and probably the worst element in all this from his perspective was the sudden disappearance of Marlene. She had been looking for a real job and found one just as he was being moved to his new quarters, where the things she had done for him would be part of the daily routine care the institution itself provided. When Sue mentioned Marlene's name one day shortly after the move, he looked stricken. "She cut me dead," he said bitterly. When Sue explained, once again, why Marlene left, he shook his head sadly and replied, "She cut me dead" (140).

Condition Worsening

During the first few weeks in his new quarters, his attention span shrunk dramatically. Occasionally when Sue came to visit, he would be tied down to one of the chairs in his room, having, as staff persons would put it, "gone a little wild" or "gotten upset" (140). He also became violent, first toward the new woman who took him outside for walks, and then with Sue. The other woman decided she would no longer take him outside, that she would confine their walks to the hallways.

Sue, however, continued to take him outside until one day he fought her efforts to get him to return to the building. As they neared the entrance to the ward he turned violently, pulled away, and she pulled him back. In a fury, he charged at her, shoving his body against hers. Her arm bent back, and she stepped away, momentarily shocked by the pain. Then she redoubled her grip: "We stood looking at each other, locked in our strange embrace. Both of us were panting. He said, 'You don't know who you're dealing with,' in a tone of such hatred, such contempt, that I nearly recoiled" (142).

She tried to get him back to his room, but the pain in her shoulder was so great that she and he sat down on a cushioned bench in the day room. They sat silently for a while, side by side. As their breathing slowed, she spoke, telling him that she knew he was angry with her, but that she was concerned for his safety and was acting out of her love for him. He did not answer, nor would he look at her. She said she felt she should go, that they could not have a good visit when they were both so upset. She kissed him and left, letting the nurses know where he was on her way out (142–43).

His violent episodes increased. Once during a particularly prolonged violent episode the staff summoned Sue to come out to Sutton Hill to see if she could calm him down without a struggle so that they could get him tranquilized. Sometimes she could calm him. Certain biblical cadences seemed to work. Singing to him would also have a calming effect, as would holding and stroking him. His fantasies at this time were paranoid. "They" were coming to get him, and he needed to arm himself in preparation. Once he showed her what he would use—his clothes hangers from his closet. "That's all that's left to me," he said bitterly (144).

At the time, Sue did not know that aggressiveness and disruptive behavior are often signs of physical discomfort in an Alzheimer's sufferer.

She now suspects that he was in physical pain during these episodes but had no way of understanding this in the conventional sense, and certainly no way to say, "I hurt." Instead, he incorporated the pain into his delusional life. "They" were hurting him. "They" needed to be fought off. The fact that "they" merely came to restrain him, not alleviate the pain itself, gave his paranoia a certain comprehensibility, even, it seems, a certain kind of truth (145).

The Last Days

In late April Sue decided she "needed to take a break from Dad" and resolved to stay away from Sutton Hill for at least a week unless the nursing staff called her. Her own work had suffered over the past four or five months, and she felt miserable, ineffectual in every part of her life. As no one called from Sutton Hill, she took this as a positive sign. When she returned after a nine-day respite, she waved hello to the nurses and went straight to his room.

She was shocked to see that he was still in bed, still asleep in the restraints they used to keep him from wandering at night. He was unshaven. His color was awful. He looked dead. She returned to the nurses' station, her heart pounding. Why wasn't he up? What's wrong with him? They explained that he had a little bug, a fever, and they had decided to let him sleep. How long had he been sick? Just since yesterday. Had the doctor seen him? No, his doctor was on vacation until tomorrow. But not to worry, it was only a little bug.

Having witnessed her grandmother before her death, Sue was certain that he was dying. She communicated her sense that something was gravely wrong with him to the head nurse, who was apologetic. He had seemed so much better the day before, and the doctor would see him the first thing in the morning. After sitting with him all day, Sue called her brothers and sister that evening, informing them that she felt he was dying. When she told them his doctor had yet to see him, they seemed to question her impressions, much, it seems, as when she first conveyed her feelings, several years earlier, that there was something wrong with him.

The next day the doctor, whom Sue had chosen from a roster of doctors available at Sutton Hill because she was a woman, examined him. She, however, was cold and brusque. She pressed his abdomen, he cried out piteously, leading her to suspect that it was cancerous. He could be hospitalized for tests, leading, most likely, to exploratory surgery. But these would aggravate his Alzheimer's disease, and there would be no assurance of physical recovery. Alternatively, as he wasn't really conscious enough to eat, he would probably die within a few weeks. As he had signed several living wills, the decision itself was not a difficult one. The doctor, whom Sue never saw again, left instructions with the nursing staff that he was to receive morphine so that he would not experience discomfort or pain. Sue called her family members again that evening and this time they believed her, but there was shock in their voices–some of it, she felt, directed at her for the decision that she had made. She "could hear that most of them didn't share the sense I had of a kind of frightened elation for Dad, on his behalf" (151).

Prolonged Grief

He died on the tenth day after she signed the Do Not Resuscitate order, and every one of these days she was with him. And then, the grieving began. It was much longer, however, than she would ever have imagined. In fact, it lasted for several years after she and her husband scattered his ashes according to his wishes at a spot high up on the Androscoggin River in New Hampshire. Through those years she "continued to suffer from what I think of almost as seizures of grief, unexpected and uncontrollable bouts of sorrow and rage, triggered by the memory of my father's helplessness in his illness and my own in response" (155).

She had dreams of him, "dreams in which he was in some situation he couldn't manage, in which he needed my assistance; the dreams in which, in one way or another, I always failed him. I thought of them as *Alzheimer's dreams*" (155). That she would be haunted by him and have difficulty letting him go was not startling to her, but the way she thought of him and of herself in relation to him began "to run on such a well-worn and circular track" that she finally recognized that it was obsessive.

She tried therapy, which *did* help with her anger–at her siblings for not coming to see him while he lay dying and then postponing his memorial service; at the doctor who did not return to see him once after she had signed the Do Not Resuscitate order; at the nurse who withheld his morphine because it wasn't "good" for him; at the Sutton Hill preacher who, in spite of her protests, woke him to semi-consciousness and pain to pray with him; and at herself for anything she had and hadn't done.

The therapy relieved a great deal of the anger but did nothing to staunch the sorrow, "which could still overwhelm me from time to time" (156). That her sorrow could be so overwhelming led to her decision to write an account of his life and, more focally, of his dying. She imagined that this would help someone else in her position, and, of course, she wanted to heal herself. And so she began. It was far more difficult and took much longer to accomplish than she could ever have imagined.

My Father Was Not His Own

The Afterword tells about her efforts to write her story of her father. She begins by noting that she tried three times over the next decade to write it. This was partly because she sensed that a novel about a woman "who bore similarities to my own mother–though she didn't have an eighth of my mother's charms"–would need to come first (157). It was also because she needed to learn how to write in the first person, to say "I" and, in doing so, to own the thoughts, ideas, and feelings that in her novels she could ascribe to others (158). By writing short personal essays on other less difficult subjects than her father's death, she was able to develop a more "assured voice," and the writing itself came with greater ease. But this led to "a more basic confusion," the underlying question about what she was doing, about "what its truest, deepest aim was" (158).

The Purpose in Writing

This question brought her back to when she taught courses on fiction writing. She would use an essay by Flannery O'Connor who quotes this instruction to catechumens by St. Cyril of Jerusalem: "The dragon sits by the side of the road, watching those who pass. Beware lest he devours you. We go to the Father of Souls, but it is necessary to pass by the dragon" (159; O'Connor 1969, 35). She would then explain to students that in writing fiction they needed to construct a *problem* for their characters, ask them to solve it, and watch them in their attempts. Their characters may triumph (slay the dragon), be defeated (devoured by the dragon), or win but lose so much in the process that the victory is barely worth it. Writers may also leave their characters at the moment when they realize there *is* a dragon they will either have to fight or flee.

As she thought about her advice to students, she recognized its relevance to her own effort to write a memoir about her father. For him, the dragon was clear. It was his illness and what he would make of it, how he would deal with it. Much less clear was what her own dragon was, what her character in the story was struggling with, what thing she would vanquish or be vanquished by. This was the *problem,* and up to now she hadn't considered it, much less found a way to solve it.

The memory of having been asked to read Psalm 103 by her sister at her father's memorial service in July–which had been scheduled two full months after his death despite her protests–was on her mind as she began writing the memoir. This psalm stuck in her throat, especially the words, "As for man, his days are as grass: as a flower of the field, so he flourisheth. For the wind passeth over it, and it is gone; and the place thereof shall know it no more" (vss. 15–16, KJV).

Redeeming Her Father

The memoir, she felt, would protest this view of her father: He was *not* as a flower of the field. There was sense–meaning–to be made of his life in terms of a narrative structure, "an explanation of his self" (161). The dragon for her was "the disorder and oblivion that marked his dying and death" (161). This is what she had been struggling with, and this is what she would conquer as she wrote. She would "redeem" him, "snatch him back from the meaninglessness of Alzheimer's disease, from being as the flower in the field when the wind passes over it. *This* was my struggle, I thought. *This* was why I had undertaken the memoir in the first place" (161).

For awhile, this understanding of her task and project worked as the focus of her book. But then, little by little, this formulation of the *problem* began to be replaced by another one prompted by "the unconscious processes of writing" and stimulated by little bits of information that came her way. There was the story that Nancy, who took him for walks each day after he had lost his beloved Marlene, had related to her. Nancy and Sue's father had arrived at the lounge where a group of women had gathered to sing hymns from the hymnals. He entered the room, and, as Nancy related it, "he just threw his head back and sang along with them. Every verse. Every word. *He* didn't need any books" (162).

Then there was the short eulogy given at Princeton Theological Seminary by one of her father's faculty colleagues. It mentioned a framed, cross-stitched sampler that hung on the wall of the dean's office when he was its incumbent. It contained this quotation from John Calvin's *Institutes:*

> We are not our own; let not our reason nor our will, therefore, sway our plans and deeds. We are not our own; let us therefore not set it as our goal to seek what is expedient for us according to the flesh. We are not our own; insofar as we can, let us therefore forget ourselves and all that is ours. Conversely, we are God's: let us therefore live for him and die for him. We are God's: let his wisdom and will therefore rule all our actions. We are God's: let all parts of our life accordingly strive toward him as our only lawful goal. (164–65).

Finally, she remembered the story her father loved to tell about a professor who had gone out for a walk, wheeling his infant daughter in a carriage. He met a colleague and became engaged in a passionate discussion. When he returned home, his wife asked, "But, where's the baby?" At this point, Sue's own father would dramatize blankness, then a dawning horror. The baby! He'd forgotten all about her. Fortunately, the story has a happy ending, for the professor returns to where he left the baby and no harm comes to her.

This story, and her recollection of it now, were important. It was not that her father would have done exactly what the professor in the story was alleged to have done. But she "certainly knew him to be capable of forgetfulness of what to him seemed mundane or unimportant, and this occasionally included obligations he'd undertaken to one of us or to my mother. The anecdote seemed to me to reflect the nightmare of living with someone whose first allegiance is elsewhere, is otherworldly. You are left; you are abandoned. You have no real importance in the great scheme of things" (165).

Claimed Elsewhere

Putting all this together as she worked on the memoir, her initial conclusion was that his Alzheimer's disease "merely exacerbated a lifelong feeling of loss I had about my father. *My father was not his own.* Therefore he wouldn't be anyone else's–and he wasn't" (165). The peculiar emotional potency of Alzheimer's disease was that, in taking her father away, it reminded her that her father "had long since been taken. He'd been gone, claimed elsewhere–by his beliefs, by his convictions, by the way they dovetailed with whom he'd become, growing up with the peculiarly Victorian and religious upbringing he'd had" (165).

She recalls having been terrorized as a young girl by the passage in Matthew (10:37, KJV) in which Jesus speaks of a man's most serious spiritual foes being those in his own household, his intimates ('He that loveth father or mother more than me is not worthy of me')" (165–66). But *she* was that daughter, one to be discarded, "lost with the rest of the believer's worldly life" (166). And so, her father's Alzheimer's disease had come to terrify her once more as her father left her behind once more. It seemed that *this* was her struggle–the dragon that she had to combat–which was "the revisiting of this childhood fear of abandonment" (166).[2]

A Different Story

As she actually did the writing, however, a different story began to emerge. Loss, fear, or terror no longer consumed her. Instead, a sense of pleasure, even excitement, came over her as she researched the disease, remembered her father, and, most of all, became aware of her father's deep involvement in *her* writing life and of the pleasures he took in showing her work off to others. If he had, in fact, been involved in her writing life before his illness and death, was he not present to her in the writing of the memoir itself? Now, she could see the positive side of being with someone who "was not his own." This very sense of himself was the critical resource that was available to him as he lived through the devastation that Alzheimer's disease inflicts on its victims:

> His acceptance of his illness–an illness that would take his intellect, his connection with other people, his ability to speak, to eat, to walk, to reason–seemed to speak of the inner resources he had because he was God's, as he saw it. He thought of this illness without ego, precisely *without* the sense of self and grief for the

loss of self that would afflict me if I found I had Alzheimer's disease. In this way, the way in which I am very much "my own" for better or worse, my father was not. This was the source for him of an almost unfathomable strength as he began his slow decline. And this was part, too, of who he was. (169)

His belief that he was not his own meant that it never occurred to him that he needed "a sense of self," the very "sense of self" that Alzheimer's disease is so intent on destroying, beginning with its assaults on the victim's memory, which is critical to one's having this sense of self.

She discovered, then, that the memoir of her father, one who had been visited by a devastating illness, was "not at all the story of a *self*, narrated by me. No, what I came to see by accumulating my material, by holding it up and looking at it again and again, by revising and revising and revising over the years, was that there was no such narrative to be made of my father's life" (170).

In effect, her original dragon—the disorder and oblivion that marked his dying and death—which she would slay by a heroic effort to create "a narrative structure, an explanation of his self," was no dragon at all. There was nothing to slay, nothing to struggle over, nothing to fight against, for in truth, there was nothing the dragon in his own life—his illness and how he would deal with it—could do to him. His very unselfconsciousness deprived the illness of its customary victim. This very unselfconsciousness is also the reason that "self-effacement," the phrase she earlier used to describe his dying (40), was not the right word for it, for "self-effacement implies an action taken, a willed result," and this was not the case with him (169).

The Burden of Grace

In chapter 4, Sue tells about the time when she, as an ungainly girl of twelve or thirteen, came to her father's study to complain about another statement that Jesus made (also in Matthew's gospel): "For my yoke is easy, and my burden is light" (11:30, KJV). Outraged by this assertion, she wanted her father's confirmation of her outrage. When one thinks of all that is required in the Christian life, all that is insisted upon, all the goodness in intention and behavior, how can anyone seriously think that Jesus' yoke is easy and his burden is light (53)?

Her father replied that he knows what she means. A lot is demanded, and you must demand a lot of yourself if you are to be truly Christian: "But with grace this may sometimes *feel* easy, like a lifting up" (53).

She replied, "But it isn't easy in reality."

He agreed, saying that she had a point. Still, he made one final attempt to mollify the daughter who had interrupted his work: Maybe she should think more about the words *yoke* and *burden*—they're there too, aren't they?–and less about the adjectives. Maybe then the passage wouldn't bother her so much.

As the reader of this memoir, I found myself returning to this discussion between daughter and father. I considered this daughter's conclusion that because her father was not his own he could accept his illness much as he had accepted whatever else happened in his life, for good or ill. I find a certain irony here–and within this irony, an unexpected blessing–in the fact that an effect of Alzheimer's is that the nouns are among the first to go. If this conversation had occurred at Sutton Hill, we can imagine how her father would have struggled over the very words–"yoke," "burden"–to which he drew her attention and that were the basis of his defense of the biblical passage that disturbed her. The very disappearance of these words from his vocabulary would, it seems to me, reflect the place to which his religious faith had brought him–no yoke, no burden, just easy and light. Thus, in an odd sense, his faith and his disease were one.

Ego, Self, and Sense of "I"

I indicated earlier that I would return to the episode in the memoir where Miller refers to the "Freudian" model and contrasts it with the model that emphasizes the brain. My purpose here is not to make an academic point or engage in scholastic nit-picking. I want to offer a psychoanalytic understanding of Alzheimer's disease that is congruent with her own view of who her father was, and, thus, of who he could be– and could not be–for his daughter.

A Freudian Interpretation

The episode that prompted her reference to the Freudian model was her friend's response to her account of her father's occasional violence as death neared: "Isn't it strange," he said, "that under that gentle, sweet exterior there should be all that violence?" This, she suggests, was the Freudian model, "One that saw the constraint of the superego eaten away by the disease, and the elemental core, the uncontrolled center, the id, as still remaining, unbuffered. The violent Dad who was secretly always there, emerging now that he'd lost control of himself" (83).

In one sense, this is not a misrepresentation of the Freudian model, as it suggests that when the "ego" begins to lose its capacity to maintain control over the "id," the id impulses are free to do what they please. As these impulses are, in part, aggressive in nature, they could manifest themselves in violent behavior. As they are also sexual, they could manifest themselves in sexual behavior and thus explain his sexual overtures to Marlene. By his own admission he "repressed" a lot of things, especially experiences in his childhood. Such repression included memories of his mother before her death when he was eight years old.

(Was it her absence that made him receptive to "other-worldly claims"?) This admitted repression would support a "psychoanalytic" proposal that the violence was due to aggressive impulses having been stored up inside of him for a very long time and finally exploding, with a vengeance.

By the same token, however, this "ego-loss" would not result in the constraints of the superego being eaten away, but in the superego's exercising the same tyranny over the hapless ego that the id would inflict. The violence, then, could just as well be the work of a self-punitive superego as of an unbridled id. In fact, because the violence became greater after Marlene, as he put it, "cut me dead," this may have been the superego's way of punishing him for sexual stirrings. This may be true even though both Marlene and Sue knew such stirrings to be utterly harmless and certainly not disrespectful either toward Marlene, a married woman, or toward his own deceased wife. In other words, the superego sees trouble where there isn't any. This is why an ego is needed to restrain the superego every bit as much as it is needed to give the id some guidance and direction.

Psychoanalytic Sense of Self

Of course, this psychoanalytic understanding of the violence is no substitute for the more straightforward explanation that his brain had become dysfunctional. Psychoanalysis, however, provides a story–a mythic account, if you will–that gives meaning to bare organic fact, so that the focus remains "the story of my father" and does not become reduced to "what happens to the brain."

In my view, however, psychoanalytic insights may be brought to bear on Miller's beautiful memoir of her father in a more substantial way. This way focuses on the very issue she addresses in her Afterword–her father's sense of self. Such insights are useful, I believe, for understanding a certain paradox that operates throughout the book and that Alzheimer's disease virtually forces us to reflect upon.

This is the paradox presented in her belief that, on the one hand, her father died "before he lost completely his sense of who he was" (150), and her seemingly contradictory belief that he was, in fact, "without the sense of self" that Alzheimer's disease has the capacity to eradicate and destroy (169). This seeming contradiction is really a paradox, a paradox that can be understood, if not resolved, by invoking some psychoanalytic distinctions. For this, the writings of psychoanalyst Erik H. Erikson are especially useful.[3]

In *Identity: Youth and Crisis,* Erikson introduces a distinction between the ego and the self. He notes that the ego may be consigned a "domain" that it has had ever since it came from neurology into psychiatry and psychology in Freud's earliest days. This is the domain of an inner "agency" safeguarding our coherent existence by screening and synthesizing, in any series of moments, all the impressions, emotions, memories, and impulses which try to enter our thought and demand our action, and which would tear us apart if unsorted and unmanaged by the slowly grown and reliably watchful screening system. (1968, 218)

This "ego," Erikson adds, is "unconscious. We become aware of its work, but never of it" (218). Its "counterplayers" are the id, the superego, and the environment. The

ego's over-all task is, in the simplest terms, to turn passive into active, that is, to screen the impositions of its counterplayers in such a way that they become volitions. This is true on the inner frontier where what is experienced as "id" must become familiar, even tame, and yet maximally enjoyable; where what feels like a crushing burden of conscience must become a bearable, even a "good" conscience. (219)

The ego can become "paralyzed" by these internal counterplayers, but, on the other hand, "id and superego can truly be the ego's allies, as can be seen in sexual abandon and in rightful action" (219).

As for the "environment," Erikson notes that the human environment is primarily social. This means, for Erikson, that the "outerworld of the ego" is made up of the egos of others significant to it:

They are significant because on many levels of crude or subtle communications my whole being perceives in them a hospitality for the way in which my inner world is ordered and includes them, which makes me, in turn, hospitable to the way they order their world and include me—a mutual affirmation, then, which can be depended upon to activate my being as I can be depended upon to activate theirs. (219)

Of course, as there can be mutual *affirmation* between egos, so there can also be *reciprocal negation. Ambivalence* between egos is the counterpart to the *inner conflict* that occurs among the ego and the id and superego.

If the ego is "a slowly grown and reliably watchful screening system," one that synthesizes both inner agencies and interactions with the social (and natural) environment, this system is besieged by Alzheimer's disease. The course of the illness leads to a "paralyzed ego," one that has "become passive," or "inactivated in its defensive and adaptive functions." This paralyzed ego can no longer "screen the impositions of its counterplayers in such a way that they become volitions" (219). This is true both on "the inner frontier" and in the social environment. The various criteria that the *DSM-IV* sets forth for a diagnosis of dementia, but especially "disturbance in executive functioning," articulate this paralysis of the ego.

Erikson's "I"

Erikson emphasizes that the ego is unconscious, that we become aware of its work, but not of it. This being the case, psychoanalytic nomenclature needs a word that takes account of a known feature of human mental life—what we are conscious of *ourselves*. William Styron, for example, related how he watched himself as he went about the rather melodramatic actions in preparation for his self-extinction. Erikson proposes the word "I" for this and suggests that the "I" is "all-conscious," for when we say "I" we know of whom we are speaking.

At the same time, the "I" is aware that it is comprised of various selves that make up our composite Self. These are more or less *pre*-conscious, that is, one or another of them may be brought to full consciousness when the "I" has reason to be especially mindful of it. Erikson provides a whole listing of these various selves (the competent self, the impotent self, etc.) and notes that there are "constant and often shocklike transitions between these selves" (217). Thus, even as the "ego" regulates the interactions between itself and the other internal agencies (id and superego), so the "I" seeks to maintain a certain "coherence" between the various selves that make up our composite Self.

This task is as difficult as the one the ego faces, for the "I" also engages in a continual comparative assessment of the various selves, commending one, remonstrating another, as the occasion befits or requires. If the ego's task is to screen and synthesize, the task of the "I" is to reconcile the various selves. This often means that they need to develop, over time, an empathy toward one another based on the sense that they are friends, not enemies, and lovers, not combatants.

The Eternal Counterplayer

If the ego has its counterplayer in the environment, what about the "I"? Here, Erikson's psychoanalytic discussion takes a decidedly religious turn as he suggests that confirmation of our conviction that we are an "I" can only be vouchsafed to us by "the deity," the "eternal" I. He says that the sense of "I" is "nothing less than the verbal assurance according to which I feel that I am the center of awareness in a universe of experience in which I have a coherent identity" (220). "No quantifiable aspect of this experience can do justice to its subjective halo, for it means nothing less than that I am alive, that I *am* life. The counterplayer of the 'I' therefore can be, strictly speaking, only the deity who has lent this halo to a mortal and is Himself endowed with an eternal numinousness certified by all 'I's who acknowledge this gift" (220).

Erikson cites God's response to Moses' question as to who should he say had called him to go to Egypt and confront the Pharaoh, demanding the release of his people: "I AM THAT I AM" (Ex. 3:14, KJV). Erikson adds:

He then ordered Moses to tell the multitude: "I AM has sent me unto you." And, indeed, only a multitude held together by a common faith shares to that extent a common "I," wherefore "brothers and sisters in God" can appoint each other true "You's" in mutual compassion and joint veneration. (220)

Erikson notes that the Hindu greeting of looking into another's eyes—hands raised close to the face with palms joined—and saying "I recognize the God in you" expresses the heart of the matter. But then, he hastens to add, "so does a lover by her mere glance recognize the numinosity in the face of the beloved, while feeling, in turn, that his very life depends on being so recognized" (221). Thus, ordinary human love between two persons is no less an expression of "a common faith" than one that speaks explicitly of Him who "is endowed with an eternal numinousness certified by all 'I's' who acknowledge this gift" (220). It is this love that Sue Miller expressed toward her father as she searched his face for clues as to what he thought or felt or understood.

Erikson concludes his paragraph on the "I's" eternal counterplayer, though, with the observation that "Those few, however, who have their faces totally turned toward that of the deity, must avoid all love except that of brotherhood: 'unless you are willing to forsake...'" (221). It was precisely her retrospective insight that her father was among "those few" that enabled Sue to understand why ordinary human love had such a hard time of it. His original plan, to live out his final years in an ecclesiastical retirement center in California—to which her mother had said, in effect, "Over my dead body"—reflected this higher allegiance, this avoidance of all love except that of the divine brotherhood.

Losing the Ego and the "I"

I have suggested that what her father had clearly lost in the course of his illness was his "ego," the capacity to "screen and synthesize" the impressions, emotions, memories, and impulses that try to enter one's thought and demand one's action. When this screening and synthesizing system is severely impaired, the ego is paralyzed, reactive instead of active, and confusion reigns.

But what about his sense of "I"? Was it lost as well? Erikson makes two assertions about the "I" that have direct bearing on this question. One is that it takes "a healthy personality for the 'I' to be able to speak out of all these conditions [that is, these various self-expressions] in such a way that at any given moment it can testify to a reasonably coherent Self" (217). The other is that the "I" is "nothing less than the verbal assurance according to which I feel that I am the center of awareness in a universe of experience in which I have a coherent identity, and that I am in possession of my wits and able to say what I see and think" (220). Given these understandings of what it means to have a "sense of 'I'," the conclusion that her father had lost this sense is also unavoidable. The "coherence" of which Erikson speaks was absent, and this meant that his various selves were *decentered,* as it were, and thus floating in and out of consciousness.

Herein lies the paradox: If his various selves were no longer centered around some integrative consciousness—a sense of "I"—one or another of these selves was free to assert itself over against the others. Sue Miller's account of her father's final days gives testimony to this very occurrence. One self did become all the more self-evident as the other selves receded into the background, mere shadows of what they once were.

To clarify this, Erikson's "Epilogue" to *Young Man Luther* (1958) is especially helpful. Here, he notes that, in focusing on Luther, he has necessarily had to deal with "a western religious movement which grew out of and subsequently perpetuated an extreme emphasis on the interplay of initiative and guilt, and an extreme emphasis on the divine Father-Son" (263). Yet, "Even in this scheme, the mother remains a coun-terplayer, however shadowy. Father religions have mother churches" (263). One may say, he continues, "that man, when looking through a glass darkly, finds himself in an inner cosmos in which the outlines of three objects awaken dim nostalgias" (263–64).

One of these objects "is the simple and fervent wish for a hallucinatory sense of unity with a maternal matrix, and a supply of benevolently powerful substances; it is symbolized by the affirmative face of charity, graciously inclined" (264). Perhaps, then. Marlene—with her "lovely, softly pretty face"—awakened a deep nostalgia for his mother, who would likely have been in her thirties, too, when she died. Maybe his very difficulty in getting Marlene's name correct was a reflection of the fact that she was, in a sense, not herself but another.

The second of these "objects" that awaken dim nostalgias is "the paternal voice of guiding conscience, which puts an end to the simple paradise of childhood and provides a sanction for energetic action" (264). This voice "warns of the inevitability of guilty entanglement, and threatens with the lightning of wrath" (264). Finding a way to change "the threatening sound of this voice," typically by means "of partial surrender and manifold self-castration," is "the second imperative demand which enters religious endeavor" (264).

No doubt, his clergyman father's irascible temper—Sue describes him as "a patriarch, remote and exacting and almost childishly quick to anger" (Miller 2003, 65)—made this change more difficult than it needed to be. But, in any case, this second nostalgia may help to explain why her father, as a young man, could leave—*had* to leave—his depressed wife with four young children, one recently born, to go to Germany with other colleagues–the "brotherhood"–to try to save a Nazi-decimated university system.

The Pure Self Is Indestructible

The third nostalgia, however, especially invites our attention here: "Finally, the glass shows the pure self itself, the unborn core of creation, the–as it were, preparental–center where God is pure nothing: *ein lauter Nichts*, in the words of Angelus Silesius [the German mystic]" (Erikson 1958, 264). This "pure self is the self no longer sick with a conflict between right and wrong, not dependent on providers, and not dependent on guides to reason and reality" (264).

In Sue's father's case, this was the self that would emerge victorious over all other selves after it was no longer possible to save "the little children" who first appeared in the basement of Sue's home and then were consumed in the fire at Sutton Hill. (Had not Jesus, also in Matthew's gospel, enjoined his disciples: "Take heed that ye despise not one of these little ones; for I say unto you, that in heaven their angels do always behold the face of my Father which is in heaven" [18:10, KJV].)

At the end, only one self was left. Not much. But this was the self no longer sick with conflict and capable of taking care of itself. Moreover, the very fact that, as Alzheimer's disease progresses, the "object world" becomes so fractured that one may not even recognize oneself in a mirror, gives the ascendancy of this self, for whom God, the "I's" counterplayer, is "pure nothing," a certain blessed inevitability. This, the "pure self," was still intact, and I would suggest that it was this very self that oversaw the writing of the memoirs.

The Caregiver's Imagination

At an early point in her consideration of the purpose for writing the story of her father's mental illness, Sue thought the purpose "would be to help someone else in my position," someone "who found herself taking care of a beloved parent as he disappeared before her eyes, leaving behind a needier and needier husk, a kind of animated shell requiring her attention and care" (Miller 2003, 156). As her Afterword indicates, other understandings of the purpose for writing superseded this purpose. These understandings were more reflective of her effort to solve the problem that her father's illness and death presented her.

The Altered Strategy

This does not mean, though, that the original purpose, however superficial it may have come to be for her, was not also met through the writing and publication of this memoir. In concluding this chapter, I would like to take particular note of the fact that as her father's illness progressed, Sue altered her strategy. She went from correcting his delusions to entering empathically into them, seeking, as she put it, to "feel the things that accompanied his delusions and thinking of him "as *having had* the experience he reported" (120).

Early in her account she tells of having said to her husband that she "was perhaps the worst prepared temperamentally of any of my siblings to be caring for my father as he sank into this terrible illness" (39). Perhaps in one sense this was so. But because she was a novelist by profession, she was, in my judgment, uniquely prepared, by temperament, to care for a father whose last months of life were spent to a large degree in "a parallel universe." Of all the siblings, she, in a unique way, could enter imaginatively into his delusional life. She knew, of course, that his delusions were "fictions," but fictions, after all, have their own kind of truth, a truth that need not be sacrificed or degraded by constant appeals to "reality," to literal truth.

Significantly, though, she was the only one who entered, empathically, into her father's delusional life. Some of his other caretakers were derisive of it; others—like Marlene—corrected him but in a gentle sort of way. All except Sue saw the need to counterpose his inner reality with the external world of actuality. At one point in the memoir, she wonders if this was the right thing for her to do. Should she have shared the therapist's concern that he was not engaging in the group activities that Sutton Hill provided, rather than having countered that his delusional life was serving him well? Would he have "lasted longer, made more friendships of a sort, and stayed more firmly in touch with all of us too" (122)? Perhaps. But whether she was right or wrong, she would "do it again." Why? Because the most important thing was that he would "feel happy and competent in some parallel universe." This appeared preferable to his struggling, even being demeaned, in a world where his incompetencies would stand out and perhaps make him the object of teasing (which, given the state of his mind, might have been interpreted as derision or outright attack).

Support from Freud

Support for her conclusion that she would do it again comes, once more, from psychoanalysis, and this time, from Freud himself. While Freud limited his practice to persons suffering from neuroses and therefore did not treat those who were delusional, he did write a very long essay based on the autobiography of a man who had suffered from delusions and been hospitalized because of them (Freud 1993; originally published in 1911). I mentioned this essay in the chapter on Anton Boisen.

The sufferer was Dr. Daniel Paul Schreber, a highly respected jurist in Dresden. His illness began in the autumn of 1884, and by the end of

1885 he had completely recovered. Freud calls this a case of "dementia paranoides." I will not discuss Freud's analysis of the case, but simply draw attention to his observation that *"The delusion-formation, which we take to be a pathological product, is in reality an attempt at recovery, a process of reconstruction"* (1993, 147, his italics). He acknowledges that "Such a reconstruction after the catastrophe is more or less successful, but never wholly so; in Schreber's words, there has been a 'profound internal change' in the world. But the man has recaptured a relation, and often a very intense one, to the people and things in the world" (147).

The delusions are, then, an attempt to recover the person's relationship with the world—both natural and social—or the "environment," as Erikson puts it. This is a relationship that in the case of dementia in general, and Alzheimer's disease in particular, has been profoundly attenuated by the very fact that the world of persons and objects has lost its accustomed appearance. In effect, then, the delusions are not merely a retreat into a solipsistic world but an attempt to give an account of the catastrophe that the world itself appears to have undergone. Attempts to correct this account fail to consider that the external world itself has changed, and these corrections, whether kindly or contemptuous, "cut no ice" (as Sue puts it) because they assume the world as it ever was. Thus, she was exactly right in her insistence that his delusional life afforded a sense of competence—of meaning-making—that was far more important, socially, than the activities provided by Sutton Hill.

Freud makes another point, however, that has more direct bearing on the past, on her father's "personal history." Freud claims that delusions (like dreams) represent the "return of the repressed" (144). To the extent that the repression has been prolonged and successful—and we have Sue's father's own testimony to the fact that his was both—the "irruption," when it occurs, can be especially powerful and overwhelming. What occurs, in Freud's view, is that the delusion returns to the point of "fixation," the point where the repression originally occurred (144).

As I conclude this chapter, I find myself returning to the death of James Nichols's mother when he was eight years old, to that moment when the world as he had known it became a very different world. This, it seems, was the original catastrophe. His religious faith was "an attempt at recovery, a process of reconstruction," and it served him well—though at the expense of his relations with the persons whose lives were most entwined with his.

Now, in this second catastrophe known as Alzheimer's disease, his delusions broke through the point of fixation, and the coherent Self that his religious faith had legitimated and endorsed began its inevitable disintegration. However, as Erikson suggests at the end of *Young Man Luther*, religion also attests to a "pure self" that exists before birth itself.

Some might interpret this as a basis for saying "you are not your own" for "you are God's." Erikson himself notes that "Luther was psychologically and theologically right when he said in theological terms that the infant *has* faith if his community *means* his baptism" (265).

Others, however, would say that this is to ascribe, retrospectively, to the very "parentalism"–and thus division–that the pure self knows nothing about. This, it seems to me, is what the "oblivion" to which Alzheimer's disease reduces a human person has to teach the rest of us. We need to learn that as far as the pure self is concerned, the source of life is indescribable, unimaginable, and unrecognizable–*ein lauter Nichts*– that is, the very mirror of the aphasia, agnosia, apraxia, and loss of executive functioning that characterizes the one who experiences the full force of dementia. In other words, it is no more–or less–than "I AM THAT I AM."

NOTES

[1] An especially good example of Freud's own interest in the associations and meanings attached to home is his essay, "The 'Uncanny'" (1958; originally published in 1919). In this essay, he explores the fact that the German word *heimlich* (or "homelike") "develops towards an ambivalence, until it finally coincides with its opposite, *unheimlich*" (131). Thus, "home" expresses feelings of familiarity and closeness on the one hand, but separation and estrangement on the other.

[2] As we saw in the chapter on William Styron, it was this very fear that his major depressive episode revealed and enabled him to work through. There are important similarities, therefore, between the two memoirs, as both have to do with loss and mourning.

[3] At the very time (1987–1988) that James Nichols was a resident at Sutton Hill, thus having foregone any hope of living out his last days in California, Erik and Joan Erikson left their home in Tiburon, California, and moved to Cambridge, Massachusetts. Erikson was in his late eighties at the time and in declining physical and mental health. He died in a nursing home in Harwich, Cape Cod, in 1994. Significantly, the Eriksons also had a daughter named Sue, and when she came to visit her father four months prior to his death, "he said 'I know you' but did not appear to be aware that she was his daughter" (Friedman 1999, 472). In assessing Erikson's legacy, his biographer, Lawrence J. Friedman, makes an observation that is relevant to this book, but perhaps especially to this chapter on Miller's memoirs: "Whereas Freud provided Erikson with his first systematic set of ideas and his profession, Erikson just might have preserved some of Freud's intellectual legacy. Almost all Freud's assumptions–from the place of early trauma in human memory to the roles of drives and the organization of intrapsychic life–have come under relentless attack in recent decades. No letup appears in sight. Of course, in some sense, Erikson was also critical of Freud, wanting his psychoanalytic colleagues to excavate less within the inner self along the physicalist lines that Freud had assumed. Through a more decidedly hermeneutic framework, he urged them to map, as broadly as possible (sometimes by drawing upon the patient's personal stories), *how the self connected to social circumstances*. If concern with the mysteries of human interiority is to survive the Freud bashers, it may be through Erikson's more open-ended interpretive perspective. Indeed, one detects a certain resonance with Erikson in efforts by psychoanalytic thinkers of the next generation like Ray Schafer and Donald Spence to determine what makes a personal narrative 'feel true' and convey meaning" (477, my italics).

EPILOGUE

balm: any fragrant ointment or aromatic oil for healing or anointing; anything healing or soothing, especially to the mind or temper.

balmy: having the qualities of balm, soothing, mild, pleasant, etc. (as a balmy day); crazy or foolish.[1]

This book began with Anton Boisen's personal account of his mental illness, which occurred when he was writing his statement of belief while awaiting a call from a church that might want him. In my discussion of Boisen, I cited James E. Dittes's view that Alice Batchelder was an "obsessive idea" for Boisen. I noted that Boisen may have become obsessed with the idea that he and Alice were meant for one another because they shared the same initials. (One can imagine the young forester cutting their shared initials in the trunk of a tree and marveling as he did so at how Providence had brought them together.)

To bring this study of mental illness full circle, I would like to conclude with another minister whose initials were also A. B. No doubt, the need to make this connection reflects a certain obsessiveness of my own, one that led to the insight presented in an earlier book (Capps 2000) that Jesus' ability to heal the demon-possessed was based, in part, on the fact that he did so in the name of "Abba" (an informal word for father). As the local name for the chief of demons was Beelzebul, I pointed out that, alphabetically, A precedes B, so the name Abba has priority and thus power over Beelzebul (191–92). I also noted that "Abba" has a special mystique because it is a palindrome (reversible). But before this leads me to suggest that Anton Boisen ought to have fixed his attentions on a young woman named Betty Allyson, Barbara Andrews, and so forth, I will proceed with the case of Ansel Bourne.

In 1896 William James delivered the Lowell Lectures on Exceptional Mental States at Huntington Hall in the Back Bay area of Boston. James was fifty years old at the time, and the Lowell Lectures, established in 1836, were sixty years old. After recommending another lecturer, James volunteered himself as a possible future lecturer. The purpose of his lectures would be "to bring together the newest insights in the field of suggestive therapeutics with those from psychotherapy, medicine, and psychology" (Taylor 1984, 5). He would deal with subjects relating to mental illness but in such a way as to "shape our thoughts about them toward optimistic and hygenic conclusions" (5). His goal would be to overcome the idea that mental illness or insanity is a taboo subject, one that is inappropriate for a popular public lecture series. His proposal was accepted, and he was invited to give the lectures that very year, beginning in October and concluding in November.

One of the lectures focused on multiple personality disorder, and much of the lecture involved the presentation of cases involving "alternating personality," a form of alienation from oneself that had become more prominent in recent years. Several of the cases that he presented in this lecture involved "fugue" states, or the passage from one state of consciousness into another with complete loss of memory for the previous state. He presented three cases of "fugue" states that involved men who traveled long distances and had no recollection of having left home, of how they got to where they were going, or why they ended up there. He called this "ambulatory automatism," which distinguished it from automatic writing, an automatism that he had discussed in an earlier lecture on automatisms.

The first two of these cases were French patients about whom James had read in the writings of two well-known French psychiatrists, Philippe Tissie and Fulgence Raymond. (Ian Hacking discusses both cases in *Mad Travelers* [1998].) The third case, that of the Reverend Ansel Bourne of Greene, Rhode Island, was a man whom James himself had treated. Born in 1826, Bourne would have been sixty-four years old when James tried to help him. As the Lowell lectures have had to be reconstructed from notes, and James provides a full account of the case in his chapter on "The Consciousness of Self" in the first volume of *The Principles of Psychology* (1950; originally published in 1890), I will use this verbatim account from *The Principles of Psychology*.

The Case of the Reverend Ansel Bourne

"The Rev. Ansel Bourne was brought up in the trade of a carpenter, but as a result of a sudden temporary loss of sight and hearing under very peculiar circumstances, he became converted from Atheism to Christianity just prior to turning thirty, and has since that time for the most part lived the life of an itinerant preacher. He has been subject to headaches and temporary fits of depression of spirits during most of his life, and has had a few fits of unconsciousness lasting an hour or less. Otherwise his health is good and his muscular strength and endurance are excellent. He is of firm and self-reliant disposition...and his character for uprightness is such in the community that no person who knows him will for a moment admit the possibility of his case not being perfectly genuine.

"On January 17, 1887, he drew 551 dollars from a bank in Providence with which to pay for a certain lot of land in Greene, paid certain bills, and got into a Pawtucket horse-car. This is the last incident which he remembers. He did not return home that day, and nothing was heard of him for two months. He was published in the papers as missing, and foul play being suspected, the police sought in vain his whereabouts. On the morning of March 14, however, at Norristown, Pennsylvania, a man calling himself Albert John Brown, who had rented a small shop six weeks previously, stocked it with stationery, confectionary, fruit and small articles, and carried on his quiet trade without seeming to anyone unnatural or eccentric, woke up in a fright and called in the people of the house to tell him where he was. He said that his name was Ansel Bourne, that he was entirely ignorant of Norristown, that he knew nothing of shop-keeping, and that the last thing he remembered—it seemed only yesterday—was drawing the money from the bank, etc., in Providence. He would not believe that two months had elapsed.

"The people of the house thought him insane; and so, at first, did Dr. Louis H. Read, whom they called in to see him. But on telegraphing to Providence, confirmatory messages came, and presently his nephew, Mr. Andrew Harris, arrived upon the scene, made everything straight, and took him home. He was very weak, having lost apparently over twenty pounds of flesh during his escapade, and had such a horror of the idea of the candy store that he refused to set foot in it again.

"The first two weeks of the period remained unaccounted for, as he had no memory, after he had resumed his normal personality, of any part of the time, and no one who knew him seems to have seen him after he left home. The remarkable part of the change is, of course, the peculiar occupation which the so-called Brown indulged in. Mr. Bourne has never in his life had the slightest contact with trade. Brown was described by neighbors as taciturn, orderly in his habits, and in no way queer. He went to Philadelphia several times; replenished his stock; cooked for himself in the back shop, where he also slept; went regularly to church; and once at a prayer-meeting made what was considered by the hearers a good address, in the course of which he related an incident that he had witnessed in his natural state of Bourne.

"This was all that was known of the case until June, 1890, when I induced Mr. Bourne to submit to hypnotism so as to see whether, in the hypnotic trance, his 'Brown' memory would not come back. It did so with surprising readiness; so much so indeed that it proved quite impossible to make him whilst in the hypnosis remember any of the facts of his normal life. He had heard of Ansel Bourne, but 'didn't know as he had ever met the man.' When confronted with Mrs. Bourne he said that he had 'never seen the woman before,' etc. On the other hand, he told of his peregrinations during the fortnight, and gave all sorts of details about the Norristown episode. The whole thing was prosaic enough; and the Brown-personality seems to be nothing but a rather shrunken, dejected, and amnesiac extract of Mr. Bourne himself. He gives no motive for the wandering except that there was 'trouble back there' and he 'wanted rest.' During the trance he looks old, the corners of his mouth are drawn down, his voice is slow and weak, and he sits screening his eyes and trying vainly to remember what lay before and after the two months of the Brown experience. 'I'm all hedged in,' he says: 'I can't get out at either end. I don't know what set me down in that Pawtucket horse-car, and I don't know how I ever left that store, or what became of it.' His eyes are practically normal, and all his sensibilities (save for tardier response) about the same in hypnosis as in waking. I had hoped by suggestion, etc., to run the two personalities into one, and make the memories continuous, but no artifice would avail to accomplish this, and Mr. Bourne's skull today still covers two distinct personal selves" (James 1950, 391–92).

While James was unsuccessful in reconciling the two selves of Ansel Bourne, the Brown-personality's observation that there was "trouble back there" and he "needed rest" may provide the answer as to why the secondary self of A. J. Brown emerged and why it took this particular form. Since Bourne was brought up to be a carpenter and worked in the carpentry trade before he became an itinerant preacher, contemporaries suggested that he had some sort of identification with Jesus (Kenny 1986, 66). His conversion from atheism resulted from the temporary loss of sight and hearing, the very sorts of symptoms with which Jesus' own contemporaries were afflicted, and which he was successful in curing.

Jesus, too, was an itinerant preacher. The crisis that took Bourne eventually to Norristown, however, was precipitated by the fact that he had remarried after his first wife's death in 1881, and his second wife insisted that he remain close to home. He had resumed the carpenter's trade and by 1887 he had money in the bank (66). If, as James indicates, he took money out of the bank to purchase a lot, this would have been another, perhaps decisive step toward settling down for good. His failure to carry through on this plan seems to indicate, therefore, that his unconscious mind was determined to sabotage what his conscious mind was intent on doing. Michael G. Kenny's *The Passion of Ansel Bourne* (1986) is an invaluable resource for gaining some understanding of what was behind this act of sabotage.

Kenny explains how William James came to be interested in the Reverend Ansel Bourne:

The story was heard by a member of the recently formed Society for Psychical Research and, in 1890, was in turn relayed to Professor William James of Harvard College who then had the idea that it might be possible to recover memory of the life of A. J. Brown through hypnosis. On contact, Bourne, who had already been exposed to hypnosis in his earlier days, proved agreeable and was brought to Boston to begin a series of hypnotic sessions that were successful in eliciting some of the contents of his underlife. The subject was sensitive to hypnosis and by this means the Brown persona was again brought into the light and induced to recount his departure from Providence, stops in New York and Philadelphia, and settlement as a shopkeeper in Norristown. But Brown's memory contained facts that were also true of Bourne; he recalled his birthdate but said that he—Brown—had been born in New Hampshire, whereas on the same day Bourne had been born in New York. He also recalled the death of his first wife in 1881 and had a confused, inarticulate, but persistent recollection of "troubles" at home. (1986, 68)

Kenny notes that when James "asked the hypnotically resurrected Brown persona what he had undergone back home," Brown replied: "Passed through great deal of trouble...Losses of friends, losses of property...Trouble way back yonder. All mixed up, confused. Don't like to think of it" (78). In a later session when he was his Bourne personality, he was asked what was troubling him, and he responded, "Something I have been trying to get out for a long time—where I am and where I am going" (78).

Richard Hodgson, who had originally presented the case of Ansel Bourne to the Society for Psychical Research, felt that "a religious factor was also important in Bourne's 1887 transformation" (78). According to Hodgson, when Bourne ceased his itinerant ministry,

he became somewhat troubled, thinking that he was not so active in religious work as he should be. This thought that he was not 'on the path of duty' weighed on his mind, and he seems inclined to think that if he had been in active religious service, and therefore contented with his work, the experiences which he subsequently underwent would never have occurred. (78)

What remained puzzling to Hodgson, however, was "in what way the enigmatic A. J. Brown—who in no essential respect save memory differed in personality from Bourne himself—represented a solution to these difficulties...Hodgson could only conclude that 'taken together, the case is not a little perplexing'" (78–79). If "A. J. Brown" had turned up in Norristown as an itinerant preacher, the case would not have been so perplexing. In that case, A. J. Brown would have been acting on the troubled thoughts of Ansel Brown, who was feeling guilty over the fact that he was no longer engaged in ministry.

Perhaps, however, an important clue toward solving the mystery lies in the fact that although A. J. Brown and Ansel Bourne did not share the same birthplace (A. J. Brown believed himself to have been born in Newton, New Hampshire, while Ansel Bourne was actually born in New York City), they shared the same birthdate. Was A. J. Brown, then, the self that life's circumstances did not allow to develop, the self who was neither the carpenter nor the itinerant preacher, but another self altogether? And was his trip from Providence to Norristown (which included a stop in New York, his birthplace) an attempt to recover this self which had never had a chance to develop? Was this, in other words, an example of Theodore Roethke's declaration that madness is "nobility of soul at odds with circumstance"?

In an earlier essay, "Great Men and Their Environments" (1956b, originally published in 1880), William James had, in fact, noted that what a person becomes in life may turn on some accidental circumstance, so the course that one's life has taken could very easily have been otherwise. His illustration may have particular relevance to the life of Ansel Bourne:

> Whether a young man enters business or the ministry may depend on a decision which has to be made before a certain day. He takes the place offered in the counting-house, and is *committed.* Little by little, the habits, the knowledge, of the other career, which once lay so near, cease to be reckoned even among his possibilities. At first, he may sometimes doubt whether the self he murdered in that decisive hour might not have been the better of the two; but with the years such questions themselves expire, and the old alternative *ego*, once so vivid, fades into something less substantial than a dream. (1956b, 227).

Precisely because Ansel Bourne had no prior experience as a tradesman, his A. J. Brown self may be viewed as "the old alternative ego" that, in the intervening years, had faded "into something less substantial than a dream." If so, he lived this dream for several weeks and, in doing so, proved that he had had the makings of a tradesman. Then, however, the "self" that he had become in his adult life regained the upper hand, and the A. J. Brown self sank again into oblivion. It could only be "resurrected" through the modern technique of hypnosis. Because the two selves represented two very different life trajectories, it is not surprising that James was unable to "run the two personalities into one" (James 1950, 392).

Interestingly enough, the "dream" that Bourne's A. J. Brown self lived out for several weeks included the stocking of the stationery store that he had rented with confectionary delights. James himself refers to it as a "candy store." This seemingly insignificant fact suggests that his unconscious mind may have been attempting to help him escape from the bind that his identification with Jesus had inadvertently gotten him into. As his contemporaries recognized, the fact that he was a carpenter by trade contributed greatly to his decision to become an itinerant preacher. In this, Jesus was his model and exemplar. But, owing in part to his second wife's insistence that he settle down, he had resumed the carpenter's trade, something that Jesus, his model, would never have done. And herein lay the basis for guilt.

Supposing, however, that it had all been a mistake: If he had not become a carpenter, he would not have become an itinerant preacher, and he would not, therefore, be "all mixed up" and "confused." His unconscious mind may therefore be viewed as trying to help him out of his confusion by suggesting a way out of the bind he had gotten himself into: "Do something different with your life." The self that spoke these words may well have been the self that, in Erikson's words, is "no longer sick with a conflict between right and wrong, not dependent on providers, and not dependent on guides to reason and reality" (1958, 264).

What could be more pure and innocent than renting a store and stocking it with confections, thus reawakening his childhood desire for sweets, and expressing a desire to be the adult—the "candy man"—who offers sweets to the youngsters of today. Since, under hypnosis, Bourne lost all memory of his wife and thus of family responsibilities, the Brown self seems to have an affinity with children and seems to be giving expression to the child self that was "murdered" (James's own term) when he became a responsible adult. Instead of listening to the small, impassioned voice of the child in him, however, he reaffirmed the adult, however sickened with the conflict of right and wrong. The degree to which this child self had to be subjected to re-repression is reflected in the "horror" he felt concerning "the idea of the candy store" and in his absolute refusal "to set foot in it again" (James 1950, 391).

My reflections on the Reverend Ansel Bourne's re-repression of his murdered child self led me to write several limericks, which I am rather certain his Bourne self would have considered frivolous but which the A. J. Brown confectioner self may have found amusing and even, perhaps, an expression of empathy for his trials and tribulations. They also support Kay Jamison's view that her capacity for humor (often taking the form of a kind of self-irony) has been an important ally in her struggle against manic-depressive illness. They support Rose Styron's view (clearly shared by her husband in retrospect) that his Paris trip (*his* version of Bourne's Norristown episode) had its hilarious moments. They support Stewart Govig's own pleasure in watching John slurp Jello. And they support Sue Miller's account of her father napping on the bed of a woman resident. Here are the limericks:

And Without the Benefits of Seminary

There was an a-theist named Bourne
Who of God felt bereft and forlorn.
But when he decided
His view was onesided
His mind from that moment was torn.

Confection Buys Affection

There was an ex-cleric named Brown
Who became the toast of the town.
Said he, "It's just dandy
How folks love my candy,
When my sermons made everyone frown."

Bourne Again

When Ansel took cash from the bank
From thenceforth his mind was a blank.
But good doctor Read
Brought him back up to speed,
For which he has Providence to thank.

"I Never Laid Eyes on That Woman!"

When Bourne became Brown in a trance,
He looked at his wife quite askance.
He exclaimed, "On my word,
Of myself I have heard,
But not her, no siree, not a chance!"

Memories of a Sweeter Day

There was a Professor named James
Who possessed the noblest of aims.
He hypnotized Ansel
But couldn't quite cancel
The pleasures that candy proclaims.

The final limerick is, of course, a serious misrepresentation of what James was trying to accomplish in Bourne's behalf. His goal was not to try to "cancel" the A. J. Brown self but to reconcile the two selves that were integral to the man known to Rhode Islanders as the Reverend Ansel Bourne and to Pennsylvanians as the confectioner A. J. Brown. James had reason to believe that these two selves *could* be reconciled because he knew of the case of Mary Reynolds, which he cited in his lecture on multiple personalities just before he discussed the case of Ansel Bourne (Taylor 1984, 77–78). As a young girl, Mary had had an extremely dour and melancholy personality. Then, suddenly, in her late adolescence, she became a very different person, gay, boisterous, and even mischievous.

In discussing her case in the Lowell Lectures, James noted that the two personalities continued to alternate through much of her twenties. Then the gay, boisterous personality gained the upper hand, and the dour and melancholic personality was, to all intents and purposes, extinguished. However, over the next several years, the personality that had been dominant underwent further changes, reflecting a greater sense of social awareness and inner serenity. It was as if the melancholic personality that had been repressed had succeeded, nonetheless, in tempering the gay and boisterous personality and had enabled it to realize greater self-composure and inner confidence. Aware of this and other examples of the unification of what he called the "heterogeneous personality" in *The Varieties of Religious Experience* (1982, 167–70), James hoped that he might be able to achieve similar results with the Reverend Ansel Bourne through hypnosis, thus effecting through brief "suggestive therapy" what Mary Reynolds had taken many years to achieve. But it was not to be. In Bourne's case, there was no quick fix.

The foregoing thoughts are my attempt to explain why James's efforts were unsuccessful. James's own theory of the "murdered self" is key to this explanation. But Freud is relevant here as well, for he would contend that the self one has "murdered" is not destroyed but repressed. It has taken refuge in the unconscious mind, and has now, many years later, reasserted itself—come back from the dead, so to speak—in the form of a delusional state. And however misguided or wrongheaded this delusional state may appear to be, it is trying to be genuinely helpful, to provide the dominant self a way out of its troubles, its sense of "being all hedged in" and unable to "get out at either end."

But then, if Freud is relevant, so, too, is Jesus, for if the dominant self feels that it has fallen away from "the path of duty," and therein lies the source of its troubles, Jesus supports the intentions of the delusional self by offering these quiet words of assurance: "Come to me, all you that are weary and are carrying heavy burdens, and I will give you rest. Take my yoke upon you, and learn from me; for I am gentle and humble in heart, and you will find rest for your souls. *For my yoke is easy, and my burden is light*" (Matthew 11:28–30, my italics). Two weeks in Norristown provided the rest that Ansel Bourne sought, but it was shortlived, and he needed the reassurance that Jesus was one friend he would not lose whatever he chose to do with the rest of his one and only life.

Balm in Gilead

In *Souls Are Made of Endurance*, Stewart Govig notes that Jeremiah's rhetorical questions—"Is there no balm in Gilead? Is there no physician there?"—set the frame for the question that follows: "Why then has the health of my poor people not been restored" (Jeremiah 8:22)? As we come to the end of this exploration into the lives of five persons afflicted with mental illness, this is surely our question, too. As with the Reverend Ansel Bourne, there was no quick fix in the case of the sufferers from mental illness presented in the previous chapters. All were resistant to cure, and the very fact that they were so gave a hypothetical quality to Kay Jamison's question whether she would avail herself of a cure if one were available. These cases, however, point to the fact that there are remedies, such as medications and psychotherapy, hospitalization, and rehabilitation programs. There may even be preventive measures for those who are especially "at-risk" of one or another mental illness due to genetic factors or temperament at birth.

If these are balms that the physicians dispense, I suggest that there are other balms that the afflicted and their loved ones give to one another. One is the healing balm of humor. Rose Styron concludes her essay on her husband's mental illness with the following advice to those who love the afflicted one: "One must be sensitive, nurture the fragile connections, and *humor the sufferer like a baby*" (R. Styron 2001, 137, my italics). I also think of the episode in which Stewart Govig stood up to the security guards at the local mall and said, "Do you want trouble?" As he and John walked to the car, John said, "That was funny, Dad." Stewart could not agree, and there is a part of me that agrees with Stewart. But another part of me wants to agree with John. If *my* son, John, had witnessed me challenging a couple of husky security guards at a local mall and had said afterward, "That was pretty funny, Dad," I would have had to agree, perhaps adding, "It's my tough guy routine. These guys were pushovers, but I wouldn't recommend it with the state highway patrol."

But perhaps the most significant gift of humor in the cases we have reviewed here occurs when James Nichols gestures at his bathrobe, hanging from a hook, and says, "Dave Swift. He's been hanging there all day." He laughed when he said it. And as Sue looked at the bathrobe, hung there like a tall, skinny man in plaid, skinnier than her uncle Dave but not by all that much, she laughed too. The very fact that she could not figure out whether her father had made a mistake or a joke, whether it was a misreading or a hallucination, adds, in my view, to the humor. Yes, there *is* a balm in Gilead, but it is not the one the physicians dispense. It is the one that the afflicted and their loved ones give to one another. You know this balm by the fact that the tears that are being shed are tears of joy and laughter.[2]

If humor is a balm for the mentally afflicted and for those who care for them, love is another. As Kay Jamison notes, "If love is not the cure, it certainly can act as a very strong medicine. Or as John Donne has written, It is not so pure and abstract as one might have thought and wished, but it does endure, and it does grow" (Jamison 1995, 175, referring to Donne, "Love's Growth," 1996, 69).

When he says he had wished love to be pure and abstract, Donne meant that it would not be subject to change. But love is not like this. It is subject, he says, to vicissitude and seasonal fluctuations. Moreover, "this medicine, love" cures all sorrow by adding more sorrow (an analogy to the efforts of doctors of his day to expel a disease by applying a medicine with similar properties).

But Donne's deepest insight into the nature of "this medicine, love" is that it "would sometimes contemplate, sometimes do" (69). In other words, like any other mixture of spirit and matter, love is partly an activity of mind and partly of body. As both, it exemplifies the very connections of mind and body that mental illness threatens and severs.

In some seasons, especially winter, love contemplates; but in other seasons, especially spring, love becomes active:

> Gentle love deeds, as blossoms on a bough,
> From love's awakened root do bud out now.

Their medicinal effect is to expand our very sense of life's connections, enabling us to view our own fragile connections in relation to the whole of all that exists. We can thus see that gentle deeds of love lead inexorably to connections our wintry minds could not have contemplated, for they were hampered and curtailed by visions of life as stable and unchanging:

> If, as in water stirred more circles be
> Produced by one, love such additions take,
> Those like so many spheres, but one heaven make,
> For they are all concentric unto thee,
> And though each spring do add to love new heat,
> As princes do in times of action get
> New taxes, and remit them not in peace,
> No winter shall abate the spring's increase.

Mental illness is one of the vicissitudes of life that threatens the connections—within and between selves—that are essential to human life itself. Love is a balm that salves the frayed connections and creates new connections that were heretofore beyond our capacity to contemplate. It is no accident that the word "religion" is based on the same Latin word–*ligare* (meaning "to bind")–on which the word "ligament" is also based. A ligament is a bond or tie connecting one thing with another, a band of tough tissue connecting bones or holding organs in place.

"Religion" means to "bind back" or to rebind that which has been disconnected. Thus, religion is itself a medicine. No wonder, then, that Paul, in the famous thirteenth chapter of his first letter to the Corinthians, declared love to be the most excellent of all spiritual gifts, greater even than faith and hope. To claim that the medicinal core of religion is the agency of love is hardly a new or novel truth. But we might not have been led to this conclusion had we not focused here on the personal memoirs of the mentally afflicted and their *loved* ones.

NOTES

[1] From *Webster's New World College Dictionary* (1997), 106.

[2] In their article "Laughter in a Psychiatric Ward: Somatic, Emotional, Social, and Clinical Influences on Schizophrenic Patients" (1993), Marc Gelkopf, Shulamith Kreitler, and Mircea Sigal explored the potential therapeutic effects of humor on hospitalized schizophrenic patients. The patients in the experimental ward were shown seventy-two comedic films over the course of several days while the patients in the control ward were shown seventy-two films of different kinds (a few of which were comedies). The effects on the patients were rather modest. There was some evidence of reduced verbal aggression and some reduction of anxiety and depression among patients in the experimental ward. But the greatest effects were on the staff in the experimental ward, as they related to the patients better than before and better than the staff in the control ward. As this book has been concerned to emphasize the role of empathy in maintaining the fragile connections between the afflicted and their loved ones, this study suggests that humor is an aid to empathy.

REFERENCES

Alighieri, Dante. 1993. *The Divine Comedy*. Translated by C. H. Sisson. Oxford: Oxford Univ. Press.

American Psychiatric Association. 1994. *Diagnostic and Statistical Manual of Mental Disorders (DSM-IV)*. Washington, D. C.: American Psychiatric Association.

Andreason, Nancy C. 1984. *The Broken Brain: The Biological Revolution in Psychiatry*. New York: Harper & Row.

Bachrach, Leona L. 1990. Hearing Patients' Words. Address to Association of Mental Health Clergy. New York. May 16, 1990.

Bateson, Gregory, ed. 1961. *Perceval's Narrative: A Patient's Account of His Psychosis, 1830–1832*. Stanford: Stanford Univ. Press.

Blessing, Richard Allen. 1974. *Theodore Roethke's Dynamic Vision*. Bloomington: Indiana Univ. Press.

Boisen, Anton T. 1926. *Lift Up Your Hearts: A Service-book for Use in Hospitals*. Boston; Chicago: The Pilgrim Press.

_____. 1960. *Out of the Depths: An Autobiographical Study of Mental Disorder and Religious Experience*. New York: Harper & Brothers.

Bonhoeffer, Dietrich. 1967. *Letters and Papers from Prison*. Edited by Eberhard Bethge. New York, Macmillan Company.

Brown, George W., and Tirril Harris. 1978. *Social Origins of Depression: A Study of Psychiatric Disorder in Women*. London: Tavistock Publications.

Camus, Albert. 1955. *The Myth of Sisyphus and other Essays*. Translated by Justin O'Brien. New York: Random House

Cantor, Carla. 1996. *Phantom Illness: Recognizing, Understanding, and Overcoming Hypochondria*. Boston: Houghton Mifflin.

Capps, Donald. 1997. *Men, Religion, and Melancholia: James, Otto, Jung, and Erikson*. New Haven: Yale Univ. Press.

_____. 2000. *Jesus, A Psychological Biography*. St. Louis: Chalice Press.

_____. 2002. *Men and Their Religion: Honor, Hope, and Humor*. Harrisburg, Penn.: Trinity Press International.

_____. 2003. John Nash's Predelusional Phase: A Case of Acute Identity Confusion. *Pastoral Psychology* 51: 361–86.

_____. 2004a. John Nash's Delusional Phase: A Case of Paranoid Schizophrenia. *Pastoral Psychology* 52: 193–218.

_____.2004b. John Nash's Postdelusional Period: A Case of Transformed Narcissism. *Pastoral Psychology* 52: 289–313.

Casey, Nell, ed. 2001. *Unholy Ghost: Writers on Depression.* New York: HarperCollins.

Ciarrocchi, Joseph W. 1993. *A Minister's Handbook of Mental Disorders.* Mahwah, N. J.: Paulist Press.

Claridge, Gordon. 1995. *Origins of Mental Illness.* Cambridge, Mass.: ISHK Malor Books.

Collins, Gregory B., and Thomas L. Culbertson. 2003. *Mental Illness and Psychiatric Treatment: A Guide for Pastoral Counselors.* New York: Haworth Pastoral Press.

Dittes, James E. 1990. Boisen as Autobiographer. In *Turning Points in Pastoral Care: The Legacy of Anton Boisen and Seward Hiltner,* ed. Leroy Aden and J. Harold Ellens, 225–29. Grand Rapids, Mich.: Baker Books.

Donne, John. 1996. *The Complete English Poems.* Edited by A. J. Smith. New York: Penguin Books.

Dragseth, Hal, and Larry Foreman. 2002. *Stranger in Our Midst.* St. Paul, Minn.: Seraphim Communications. Videocassette.

Emerson, Ralph Waldo. 1983. *Essays and Lectures.* Edited by Joel Porte. New York: Library of America

Erikson, Erik H. 1958. *Young Man Luther: A Study in Psychoanalysis and History.* New York: Norton.

_____.1963. *Childhood and Society.* Rev. ed. New York: Norton.

_____.1968. *Identity: Youth and Crisis.* New York: Norton.

Fosdick, Henry Emerson. 1943. *On Being a Real Person.* New York: Harper & Brothers

French, Paul, and Anthony P. Morrison. 2004. *Early Detection and Cognitive Therapy for People at High Risk of Developing Psychosis: A Treatment Approach.* West Sussex, Eng.: John Wiley & Sons.

Freud, Sigmund. 1958. The "Uncanny." In *On Creativity and the Unconscious,* ed. Benjamin Nelson, 122–61. New York: Harper & Row.

_____.1960. *Jokes and Their Relation to the Unconscious.* Translated by James Strachey. New York: Norton.

_____.1963. Mourning and Melancholia. In *General Psychological Theory,* ed. Philip Rieff, 164–79. New York: Collier.

_____.1965. *The Interpretation of Dreams.* Edited by James Strachey. New York: Avon.

_____.1989. *Introductory Lectures on Psycho-analysis.* Tranlsated and edited by James Strachey. New York: Norton.

_____.1993. Psychoanalytic Notes upon an Autobiographical Account of a Case of Paranoia (Dementia Paranoides). In *Three Case Histories,* ed. Philip Rieff, 83–160. New York: Simon & Schuster.

Friedman, Lawrence J. 1999. *Identity's Architect: A Biography of Erik H. Erikson.* New York: Schribner.

Fuller, John, ed. 2000. *The Oxford Book of Sonnets.* Oxford: Oxford Univ. Press.

Gelkoph, Marc, Shulamith Kreitler, and Mircea Sigal. 1993. Laughter in the Psychiatric Ward: Somatic, Emotional, Social, and Clinical Influences on Schizophrenic Patients. *The Journal of Nervous and Mental Disease* 181: 283–280.

George, Gordon, Lord Byron. 1970. *Byron: Poetical Works.* Edited by Frederick Page. Oxford: Oxford University Press.

Goffman, Erving. 1961. *Asylums: Essays on the Social Situation of Mental Patients and Other Inmates.* Garden City, N. Y.: Anchor Books.

Govig, Stewart D. 1994. *Souls Are Made of Endurance: Surviving Mental Illness in the Family.* Louisville: Westminster/John Knox Press

_____.1999. *In the Shadow of Our Steeples: Pastoral Presence for Families Coping with Mental Illness.* New York: Haworth Pastoral Press.

Grahame, Kenneth. 1989. *The Wind in the Willows.* New York: Simon & Schuster.

Gray, Jeffrey A. 1982. *The Neuropsychology of Anxiety.* Oxford: Oxford Univ. Press.

Hacking, Ian. 1998. *Mad Travelers: Reflections on the Reality of Transient Mental Illness.* Charlottesville: Univ. Press of Virginia.

Hart, Curtis W. 2001. Notes on the Psychiatric Diagnosis of Anton Boisen. *Journal of Religion and Health* 40: 423–29.

Holzman, P. S. 1978. Cognitive Impairment and Cognitive Stability: Towards a Theory of Thought Disorder. In *Cognitive Defects in the Development of Mental Illness.* Edited by G. Serban. New York: Brunner/Mazel.

Jackson, Stanley W. 1986. *Melancholia and Depression: From Hippocratic Times to Modern Times.* New Haven: Yale Univ. Press.

James, William. 1950. *The Principles of Psychology,* 2 vols. New York: Dover.

_____.1956a. Is Life Worth Living? In *The Will to Believe and Other Essays in Popular Philosophy,* 32–62. New York: Dover.

_____.1956b. Great Men and Their Environment. In *The Will to Believe and Other Essays in Popular Philosophy,* 216–54. New York: Dover.

_____.1982. *The Varieties of Religious Experience.* New York: Penguin.

Jamison, Kay Redfield. 1993. *Touched with Fire: Manic-Depressive Illness and the Artistic Temperament.* New York: Simon & Schuster.

_____.1995. *An Unquiet Mind: A Memoir of Moods and Madness.* New York: Alfred A. Knopf.

_____.1999. *Night Falls Fast: Understanding Suicide.* New York: Random House.

Johnson, Ann Braden. 1990. *Out of Bedlam: The Truth about Deinstitutionalization.* New York: Basic Books.

Kahlbaum, Karl Ludwig. 1973. *Catatonia or Tension Anxiety.* Translated by Y. Levij and T. Pridan. Baltimore: Johns Hopkins University Press, 1973.

Kenny, Michael G. 1986. *The Passion of Ansel Bourne: Multiple Personality in American Culture.* Washington, D. C.: Smithsonian Institution Press.

Kesey, Ken. 1963. *One Flew Over the Cuckoo's Nest.* New York: Penguin.

Kohut, Heinz. 1984. *How Does Analysis Cure?* Edited by Arnold Goldberg. Chicago: Univ. of Chicago Press.

Kristeva, Julia. 1991. *Strangers to Ourselves.* Translated by Leon S. Roudiez. New York: Columbia Univ. Press.

Kushner, Harold I. 1989. *Self-Destruction in the Promised Land: A Psychocultural Biology of American Suicide.* New Brunswick, N.J.: Rutgers Univ. Press.

Lebacqz, Karen. 1988. Imperiled in the Wilderness. *Second Opinion* 2: 26–31.

Leys, Ruth. 2000. Trauma: A Genealogy. Chicago: Univ. of Chicago Press.

McGoldrick, Monica. 1995. *You Can Go Home Again: Reconnecting with Your Family.* New York: Norton.

McGovern, George. 1996. *Terry: My Daughter's Life-and-Death Struggle with Alcoholism.* New York: Villard Press.

Millay, Edna St. Vincent. 2002. *The Selected Poetry of Edna St. Vincent Millay.* Edited by Nancy Milford. New York: Modern Library.

Miller, Sue. 2003. *The Story of My Father.* New York: Alfred A. Knopf.

Millett, Kate. 1990. *The Loony Bin Trip.* New York: Simon & Schuster.

Nasar, Sylvia. 1998. *A Beautiful Mind.* New York: Simon & Schuster.

Neugeboren, Jay. 1997. *Imagining Robert: My Brother, Madness, and Survival.* New York: Henry Holt & Co.

North, Carol, and William M. Clements. 1981. The Psychiatric Diagnosis of Anton Boisen: From Schizophrenia to Bipolar Affective Disorder. *The Journal of Pastoral Care* 35: 264–75.

Nuland, Sherwin B. 1993. *How We Die: Reflections on Life's Final Chapter.* New York: Vintage Books.

O'Connor, Flannery. 1969. *Mystery and Manners.* Edited by Sally and Robert Fitzgerald. New York: Farrar, Straus & Giroux.

Radden, Jennifer, ed. 2000. *The Nature of Melancholy: From Aristotle to Kristeva.* New York: Oxford Univ. Press.

Rizzuto, Ana-Marie. 1979. *The Birth of the Living God.* Chicago: Univ. of Chicago Press.

Roethke, Theodore. 1975. *The Collected Poems.* New York: Doubleday.

Skultans, Vieda. 1975. *Madness and Morals: Ideas on Insanity in the Nineteenth Century.* London: Routledge & Kegan Paul.

Styron, Rose. 2001. *Strands. In Unholy Ghost: Writers on Depression,* ed. Nell Casey, 127–37. New York: HarperCollins.

Styron, William. 1990. *Darkness Visible: A Memoir of Madness*. New York: Random House.

Swinton, John. 2000. *Resurrecting the Person: Friendship and the Care of Persons with Mental Health Problems*. Nashville: Abingdon Press.

Taylor, Eugene. 1984. *William James on Exceptional Mental States: The 1896 Lowell Lectures*. Amherst: Univ. of Massachusetts Press.

Tessler, Richard, and Gail Gamache. 2000. *Family Experiences with Mental Illness*. Westport, Conn.: Auburn House.

Thomas, Dylan. 2003. *The Poems of Dylan Thomas*. Edited by Daniel Jones. New York: New Directions.

Torrey, E. Fuller. 1988. *Surviving Schizophrenia: A Family Manual*. New York: Harper & Row.

Torrey, E. Fuller, and Judy Miller. 2001. *The Invisible Plague: The Rise of Mental Illness from 1750 to the Present*. New Brunswick, N. J.: Rutgers Univ. Press.

Vine, Phyllis S. 1982. *Families in Pain: Children, Siblings, Spouses and Parents of the Mentally Ill Speak Out*. New York: Pantheon Books.

von Loewenich, Walter. 1976. *Luther's Theology of the Cross*. Translated by J. A. Bowman. Minneapolis: Augsburg Publishing House.

Ward, Mary Jane. 1981. *The Snake Pit*. Cutchoque, N. Y.: Buccaneer Books. Originally published 1946.

Wasow, Mona. 1989. The Need for Asylum for the Chronically Mentally Ill. In *The Experiences of Patients and Families: First Person Accounts*. Arlington, Va: National Alliance for the Mentally Ill.

Webster, Christopher D., and Margaret A. Jackson, eds. 1997. *Impulsivity: Theory, Assessment, and Treatment*. New York: Guilford Press.

Webster's New World College Dictionary. 1997. New York: Macmillan.

Wynn, John Charles. 1957. *Pastoral Ministry to Families*. Philadelphia: Westminster Press.

_____.1982. *Family Therapy in Pastoral Ministry*. San Francisco: Harper & Row.